AF652280

Russia, China
and Multilateralism in
Central Asia

Russia, China and Multilateralism in Central Asia

Anita Sengupta

Maulana Abul Kalam Azad Institute of Asian Studies, Kolkata

SHIPRA

All rights reserved. No part of this work may be reproduced, stored in a retrieval system, or transmitted in any form or by any means, electronic, mechanical, photocopying, recording or otherwise, without the prior written permission of the copyright owner and publishers.

Views expressed are those of author and not necessarily of the Institute.

ISBN: 81-7541-235-6

First Published in India in 2005

Russia, China and Multilateralism in Central Asia

© Maulana Abul Kalam Azad Institute of Asian Studies, Kolkata

Published by :
SHIPRA PUBLICATIONS
115-A, Vikas Marg, Shakarpur,
Delhi-110092 (India)
Ph. : 91-11-55277210, 22500954 Fax : 22458662
Email : info@shiprapublications.com
Website : www.shiprapublications.com

Laser Typesetting by:
R.S. Prints,
New Delhi

Printed at:
Chaudhary Offset Process
Delhi-110051

Contents

Preface

As a result of the full-scale attack on Afghanistan, and the perception of this as a "legitimate" threat to the free world after September 11, the global status of Central Asia has been irrevocably altered. Never before has its position been so sensitive and integral to global security strategies. No longer is Central Asia seen as a "traditional land of the Russian Empire", nor used as an energy base for the United States or indeed as a market proliferated by Chinese commerce. In the aftermath of September 11, Central Asia now plays host to a global war against terrorism, the areas of conflict of major powers' interests and the strategic game playing of global geopolitics.

("9-11: The Implications for Central Asia," translated by Zheng Guihong, *China Through the Ages*, October 9, 2002, china.org.cn.)

On September 11, 2001, the twin towers of the World Trade Centre were leveled to the ground and the Pentagon was damaged in the course of terrorist attacks on the United States. The US government announced that it believed that Osama Bin Laden and his transnational organization, *Al Qaeda*, were behind the attacks. Bin Laden and his organization operated primarily out of Afghanistan and were believed to be supported by the ruling Taliban regime in the country. A war against terrorism was launched by the United States in the aftermath of the attack with Afghanistan as the first target. It was predicted that subsequently the war would be extended to the Middle East, Central Asia, South Asia and even South East Asia in order to destroy the international terrorist network.

As a region contiguous to Afghanistan, the implications of this war on Central Asia were projected to be far reaching with a number of changes affecting its future geopolitical status. The first of these changes was projected to be a rise in the status of the geo-political, economic and military importance of Central Asia. The region would no longer be significant merely due to its mineral, oil and gas reserves but also as the focal point of the global war against terrorism. The second of the projected changes would be the rise of significant US strategic and military presence over the area resulting in significant changes in regional security structures. A third change was projected as substantial improvement in regional security through the elimination of its external enemies. All of these projected changes, however, were subject to scrutiny as early as the year following 9/11, thereby calling for critical analysis of the projected transformations, particularly transformations in the security structures of the region.

In the course of any discussion on these projected transformations in the Central Asian security structures the first and most fundamental assumption that one makes is about sufficient commonality in security policy perceptions across Central Asia to call for conceptualizing transition within a common regional security complex. In actuality security perceptions across the states have differed and when one talks of transformations in the Central Asian security structure numerous complexities are ignored and the focus is on certain general trends. Along with this is the reality of an active involvement of external powers within this complex. It is in the background of these that one can then move towards an understanding of the projected systematic changes within the Central Asian security structures.

An understanding of three core issues becomes essential. The first and foremost is an understanding of conflictual or cooperative processes developing within the region. A second is the extent to which the involvement of external powers affects the security of the region. A third is the extent to which evolving security arrangements are capable of responding to threats. While all three remain significant, the interplay between the engagement of external powers in the region and regional dynamics appears as the most crucial. This interplay may work in both cooperative and conflictual ways and four alternative outcomes of this interaction have been suggested.

The first is a situation where the dynamics within the region is mainly conflictual and external powers easily fall in line with regional divisions. Here, if relations between external powers, with an interest in the region, are also characterized by rivalry, then a situation will arise where one or several powers develop relations with individual Central Asian states leading to fragmentation and divisions within the region. The second is when the dynamics within the region leads to cooperation among the states while the external powers are in a state of rivalry. In this situation if the Central Asian states are able to balance a diversified relationship with the regional powers, it could lead to an improvement in regional security. A third would be if the external powers were prepared to cooperate in a situation where strong conflictual dynamics exists in the region, the powers may still be able to influence the security situation leading to a resolution of conflicts. A fourth would be when regional dynamics is cooperative and external powers cooperate towards the formation of a new multilateral security framework. Which or a combination of which of these will emerge, remain debated in the literature on the region.

The last decade witnessed a broadening of the notion of security from states to societies leading to an increasing differentiation of security arrangements. It has been proposed that this transformation can be conceptualized as security governance, characterized by a fragmentation of initiatives among a diverse group of actors. The end of the Cold War had witnessed the dissolution of the bipolar security arrangement where the Atlantic Alliance pitted itself against the Warsaw Pact. But more significantly it witnessed the emergence of new bilateral and multilateral security arrangements and the subsequent emergence of regional and sub regional institutions with common and competing interests in international security. In fact, the complexities of the new structure were such that it was assumed that it could not be defined merely by the concept of multipolarity.

The new structures that emerged had numerous centres, but these were no longer states, but regional and sub-regional institutions through which an increasing range of activities could be carried out. The membership of and the relations among them were varied and overlapping, as were their functions and obligations. These new institutions were created to address specific security needs of particular regions. Most of these were based on values of peace and collaboration, non-expansive behaviour and the wish to reduce the cost of security. Many of these dealt with localized or non-traditional threats to security and were more fluid and flexible than security regimes or communities. They often emerged from unique interests and resources of a set of actors in solving a particular regional security problem. While this was accepted as a general norm, the events following September 11 was seen as a watershed that would transform security structures in the entire region neighbouring Afghanistan. Since a large part of this region comprised the Central Asian states, it was predicted that the regional security structures of the region would be irreversibly transformed.

In the aftermath of 9/11, it was predicted that the global security environment would be transformed, as "regional and state" security would become increasingly dependent on global organizations. This change would herald what was identified as the *post-post Cold War* scenario where global security would be the guiding norm. This was projected as a significant marker of the emerging international order. Of course, since the end of the Cold War certain fundamental changes had already transformed security and political relations over much of the world. The end of the Cold War witnessed the dissolution of the bipolar security arrangement where the Atlantic Alliance pitted itself against the Warsaw Pact. But more significantly it witnessed the emergence of new bilateral and multilateral security arrangements and the subsequent emergence of regional and sub-regional institutions with common and competing interests, in international security. The membership of and the relations among them were varied and overlapping, as were their functions and obligations. The post-post Cold War scenario was assumed to be one that would herald the submergence of these regional multilateral arrangements within global ones.

The analysis of this security structure, which complemented traditional models of alliances and security regimes, was seen to reflect the significant fact that while the state retained its central role the cooperation and resources of non-state actors and international organizations would become increasingly crucial. The post-post Cold War scenario would further reduce the significance of the older structures and result in realignments where the very basis of a multilateral security structure would be undermined. The undermining of multilateral security structures would mean a transition back to the bilateral in terms of security arrangements. Once this was accepted as the emerging scenario, the conceptualizing of a new theoretical framework for analyzing evolving security structures became evident.

In the Central Asian case the assumption was that the NATO sponsored Partnership for Peace (PfP) would emerge as the most significant security organization in the region as the transition from regional to global security became the guiding norm. This assumption was, however, not a recent one. As early as 1997, Zbigniew Brzezinski had talked about a "new cooperative trans-Eurasian security system" and the NATO had expanded its presence in the region since the mid 1990's. As part of this emerging significance of global security arrangements, it was also argued that in the post 9/11 era Sino-Russian arrangements for regional security would no longer play any significant role in the efforts to deal with terrorism in the region. The absence of the Shanghai Cooperation Organization (SCO) in the war against terrorism was taken as the perfect example. Any rearrangement of the security structures would therefore move towards the bilateral rather than the multilateral.

What actually happened was a somewhat different scenario. Rather than bilateralism or multilateralism, the Central Asian states opted for what was termed as a *multivector* policy where choices were kept open for both bilateral and multilateral agreements on particular issues according to specific security perceptions. Options for bilateral agreements were kept open with all the major powers, Russia, China and the United States. On the other hand, attempts by regional powers to reinforce multilateralism since 9/11 has been seen to be on the increase.

In the period following September 11 certain strategic realignments, that had already taken shape over the last few years, came into sharper focus. The Central Asian states were already members of the Partnership for Peace (PfP) initiative and the NATO presence in the region was a reality when the US asked for strategic cooperation. The watershed that Russo-US relations apparently underwent, with the Russian acquiescence to the presence of US troops in Central Asia, has also been subsequently reexamined. In the course of this it has been noted that most of the Central Asian states did not actually request Russian permission, before offering their basing rights to the United States.

It is not surprising, therefore, that within a year statements from Moscow began to sharply criticize the US presence in the region and alternative Russian bases emerged, often within miles of the US base, under a revitalized Collective Security Agreement of the Commonwealth of Independent States (CIS). The influx of American troops into the region and the subsequent establishment of American bases was also taken as the signal that the Russian and Chinese position in the region had been irreversibly altered. Within a year these positions had once again changed with Russia focusing on the Collective Security Agreements of the CIS as a means to forging collective security and the emergence of a revitalized SCO.

These cleavages came sharply into focus and culminated in the course of the US intervention in Iraq when Russia moved away from its position of collaboration with the US and supported the Franco-German line. The transatlantic divide over Iraq clearly illustrated that while the US was in fact at "war" against terrorism the Euro-Asian powers were engaged in a "struggle", not against any one state per se but rather against international terrorism as a stateless phenomenon. The intervention against Iraq, also inaugurated a revolutionary notion of pre-emptive strikes, that was a challenge to existing international norms, and was subsequently put forward by Russia as a proposed move in the post Beslan situation. In fact the US intervention in Iraq possibly marks a more significant watershed in terms of strategic alignments and also the juncture at which the re-emergence of multiple poles became evident once again. It was also in the course of debates surrounding the viability of military intervention in Iraq that the divergence between the western allies came into sharp focus, a fact that brings into question the whole concept of a common strategic alliance.

An understanding of these global developments and their impact on the Central Asian region remains incomplete without a close reading of the Central Asian security paradigm, of how the region itself perceives of its "national" and "regional" security. Underlying these national priorities are a set of assumptions about the security of the state and how shifting alliances with other states can best preserve this. This rather realistic understanding of the situation, of course, is not without its problems. Not the least of which is that states often do not act as unitary and rational actors. In actual situations state decisions are often determined by an interplay of domestic and international factors and influenced by partisan interests.

How then does one evaluate the post September 11 changes in Central Asia? Was the "global status" of the region actually irreversibly altered or was this a myth that was generated in haste? Did the post 9/11 era herald a transformation of security arrangements where existing multilateral arrangements with Russia and China were bypassed in favour of bilateral agreements? And more significantly, to what extent have the positions of Russia and China, as significant partners in security arrangements, changed in the region vis a vis the United States?

The following chapters will attempt to answer some of these issues. The principle contention in the chapters that follow is, that contrary to the opinion that there is today a revival of the great game in the region, co-operation and multilateralism seem to be the watchwords of diplomacy for Eurasian powers. This brings into question the continuing interpretation of the history of the region in terms of an intense rivalry for control over the so-called "heartland of the world". In fact, no major geopolitical conflict now divides the powers of the Eurasian heartland and there is a new rapprochement over the region. While, on the one hand, this calls for a reinterpretation of the viability of the great game theories, on the other, it calls for a new look at the emerging multilateralism in the region. In the light of this contention, an attempt will be made to examine Russian and Chinese interactions over the region and the effect of the US presence on this interaction.

One way to look into the Russian and Chinese position in the region and the effect of the US presence would be to simply examine Russo-Sino-US interactions over the region. A more useful way is to examine as to what compels this interaction and here an examination of domestic compulsions become crucial. In the post September 11 era, it became acceptable to assume that the dynamics of international politics would be the guiding norm in the determination of the direction of relations between states. This study moves away from this position to focus on the extent to which the dynamics of domestic processes and paradigm shifts in them continue to affect foreign policy thinking.

Particularly significant here is the ideational basis on which the policy is made. As Jack Snyder suggests: "the key to the explanation of why the state behaves the way it does lies in the way its decision makers define their situation". This basis determined within the domestic political structures of the state, significantly influences foreign policy orientation. This study seeks to demonstrate this by examining how concepts of "national" identity, nationalism, globalism, multilateralism, and sovereignty influence transnational choices of linkages through an analysis of the Russian and Chinese relationship with the Central Asian region and the role that the presence of the United States in the region plays in determining this relationship. The primary concern of the study will be to highlight how the states relate to realities outside their region and visualize their linkages to various events and developments within these countries in terms of their own domestic compulsions.

The extent to which ideas and debates within the domestic context influences foreign policy choices has been comprehensively debated in various international relations theory approaches that have advanced varied explanations. The realist approach builds its explanation on a struggle for power and security by states within an anarchic international system but tends to ignore processes, by which state interests are shaped, the content of these new interests and the role of ideas and debate in the process. International systemic approaches, on the other hand, argue that foreign policy outcomes result solely from changing external constraints and not from domestic changes. Since states and not individuals are seen as most important in world politics, individuals and ideas are seen as unimportant. The major problem here lies in the identification of the state as a unitary actor. In contrast to these macro-theories, micro-theories of decision making identify how within the broad framework of foreign policy making individual decisions play a part. The assumption here is that while international factors do play a role in shaping the states' interests, the real challenge is to understand as to how they are perceived.

Political bargaining approaches note that a perceptive way of examining the domestic content of foreign policy making would be to emphasize that while ideas and perceptions are important these have to be examined in terms of the political processes in which they are selected. It is not enough to simply identify foreign policy ideas but to know whether a consensus developed through a process of political bargaining. Institutionist arguments note, on the other hand, that it is significant to keep in mind that ideas can affect or constrain policy when they become embedded in institutions. Administrative agencies, laws, norms and operating procedures mediate between ideas and policy outputs. When ideas become institutionalized, their impact can be greatly prolonged, thus making the significant point that new concepts and beliefs do not operate within a vacuum.

A major problem with most of these approaches is that they are exclusively concentrated at either the individual, domestic or international levels of analysis and they fail to capture the full array of factors that affects a complex process. Integrative approaches have attempted to bridge this gap by stressing on the interaction between the individual, domestic and international levels. Interesting examples include Robert Putnam's two-level game approach where political leaders are seen to be attempting to achieve their goals at both the domestic and international arenas, simultaneously.

Rather than building on any one of these approaches this study will seek to adopt insights from various approaches to come to an understanding of Russian and Chinese policy in the Central Asian region. The role of ideas, the mechanisms by which these ideas affect policy options and the development of a consensus are examined in the background of "national" interests and an international environment compelled by a global "war against terrorism".

The conflict between the "Eurasianist" and the "Atlanticist" viewpoint in Russian politics today determines a significant part of the dialogue between the Central Asian states and Russia. Current political and academic discussions in Russia regarding Central Asian issues reveal a wide variety of views, some of them of extreme polarity. It has been argued that the intensity and the divergence of these discussions and views are reflective of the fact that Russian-Central Asian relations goes beyond the realm of practical policies and acquires a philosophical or even an existential dimension. At stake is not just a set of geopolitical, economic or military strategic issues, but its very "civilizational" quintessence and a debate as to whether Russia is a European or Eurasian power.

At a juncture in history when Russia is once again engaged in fashioning a state and society, the Eurasian debate is projected as having resurfaced as an ideology to hold her together and provide a direction for the future. In fact, it is argued that to an extent it is this duality that determines all other issues with relation to the Central Asian states, that are today identified as significant, like the question of ethnic Russians in these states and their status as new minorities, dual citizenship, economic union and security of the "soft underbelly" of the state. However, while the rhetorical significance of this need not be reduced it is necessary to examine the significance of these issues in some detail.

While this duality is today couched in a rhetoric about the significance of Eurasianism as an ideology for the Russian state, in actuality it now involves a choice about the recognition of the extent of the Russian sphere of interest in the post Soviet space and debates around the exclusivity of such interests. This is a debate that has become crucial, in Moscow as well as within the newly independent states themselves, as they seek their place in the post Soviet world. Russian politicians and intellectuals have remained divided on the issue of national self-identification and the future of Russia. How should Russia perceive of itself as a nation? Has Russia been guided by its own unique laws of historical development or is Russia a nation that shares patterns of social life with other countries? And is Russia an exclusively European country, or should it adopt a dual heritage that recognizes the validity of the Eurasian ideology? And consequently, how should relations between Moscow and its regions develop in the future?

Chinese policy towards Central Asia is largely determined by two factors. The first is the effect of the emergence of the new states on the regions in China bordering the newly independent states. The second is the broader issue of the Chinese emphasis on multilateralism accompanied by opposition to extension of American influence in her immediate neighbourhood. In China, the new geopolitical landscape in Central Asia has been viewed as a mixed blessing. Three out of the five Central Asian Republics of the former Soviet Union now border China and China's common border with Russia has been significantly reduced, particularly in the Northwest. While, on the one hand, the newly independent Central Asian states were seen as significant markets for Chinese goods, on the other, they were viewed as potentially destabilizing factors for China's Xinjiang Uighur Autonomous Region, which in turn was viewed as threatening to China's national security and territorial integrity.

The new Chinese policy towards Central Asia, defined as "political stability through economic cooperation and development" therefore reflects the dilemma of an extensive common border that provides enormous opportunities for trade but also represents all the problems of the possibility of import of transborder nationalism. Since the Central Asian Republics are now independent states, with different and sometimes divergent foreign policies, flexible policies are now required to meet regional challenges. The challenge before China is to develop a coherent foreign policy in the region.

For China, the reemergence of the concept of "Turkestan" is said to have assumed significance in terms of development of its relationship with the Central Asian region as both Chinese economic and strategic interests in the region are based on the supposed fact that the populations in eastern Turkestan, i.e, Xinjiang and western Turkestan, i.e the Central Asian Republics share a common Turkic identity. While on the one hand the reemergence of this Turkic identity could revive linkages with kin groups across the borders and promote separatism, on the other the projection of these linkages could increase the significance of Xinjiang as point of contact for increased economic and trade linkages. This stems partly from the fact that organizations and movements that today seek greater autonomy, in the inner Asian regions, once again define themselves as a movement for Eastern Turkestan.

However, while Central Asia remains significant in China's national security strategy and in the economic development of China's underdeveloped northwest, it continues to be peripheral to Chinese foreign policy. A major policy consideration here is recognition of Russian interests in this region, which neither China nor the Central Asian Republics themselves can ignore. This pragmatic recognition is reflected in a number of other areas. In recent years Russia and China have cooperated and supported each other in international and regional matters.

As multi-national states both Russia and China are concerned about ethnic separatism. For Russia, Central Asia has become a critical southern perimeter and significant as the home to large numbers of ethnic Russians. For China, Central Asia is now an unpredictable zone from where Turkic nationalism could radiate to its own western frontiers. Russia and China now see the eastward expansion of the NATO and separatism within their borders as more of a threat than any that they could pose to each other. A reflection of this concern is an emphasis on multilateralism, as opposed to an emerging unipolar direction in terms of strategic alignments, which defines both Russian and Chinese policy. It posits itself in the form of organizations like the SCO. Sino-Russian rapprochement has meant that numerous border disputes between the two have now been reduced. Also

Russia exports what China requires, military hardware and energy resources while China provides investment and manufacturing products at competitive prices.

For the United States, the Central Asian region traditionally represented an alternative source of energy. Energy security has been a priority with the Bush administration ever since his assumption of office. In his second week in office, the President established the National Energy Policy Development Group directing it to develop a national energy policy. In May 2001, the group presented its assessment of the "energy crisis" in the United States along with a long list of recommendations to avert the crisis and to enhance the nation's energy security. The thrust of the report was that the US was too dependent on one source of energy, oil, and on too few regions, particularly the Middle East to provide it. The September 11 attacks and the political developments in their aftermath heightened US's sense of energy insecurity. Accordingly, the Bush administration became even more concerned about the need to enhance the predictability and reliability of oil supplies.

It was noted that diversification was the first principle of energy security. This could be done either by substituting oil with other energy sources or by exploring and developing energy sources outside the Middle East. Thus, it was suggested that the United States should encourage oil imports from other friendly producers, such as Russia to replace the oil from the Middle East. The Bush administration focused on Moscow for two reasons. The first was the sharp increase in Russian oil production and export since the late 1990's. Russia now has sufficient crude supplies to contribute to American and global energy security. Second, President Vladimir Putin made a significant strategic choice early on to ally his country with the United State and Europe in return for economic incentives. Central Asian and Caspian reserves played a very significant role in the changes that Russo-US relations underwent.

However, the future of Russo-US relations will not be dependent solely on the politics of oil. Russian response to the US will depend on the extent to which it considers that its own interests in the Caucasus and Central Asia will be preserved. A number of issues remain unresolved. There is of course appreciation of the fact that Russian financial resources are insufficient to develop the hydrocarbon resources of the region. But, also of the fact that the stability, that is so crucial for the development of these resources, can only be maintained with Russian assistance.

The dynamics of Russo-Sino-US interaction, in the post 9/11 context, therefore requires reexamination. Before the terrorist attacks, China saw its strategic situation as improving gradually. Relations with Russia were deepening and tensions between Washington and Beijing were receding. Beijing wanted to expand her role in Central Asia and limit the US position in the region. However, the events following September 11 and America's response to it expanded American regional presence in the region. This increased Chinese fears of encirclement, for a number of reasons. Despite the recently signed Sino-Russian Friendship Treaty and professed unity in opposing hegemony, Moscow offered broad-based support for America's military campaign. Similarly, the Central Asian states began to move towards offering support to the US. As a conclusion to the campaign, a pro-American government emerged in Afghanistan, potentially limiting Chinese influence.

Within China, it has been noted that the Chinese leadership is divided into two groups each with distinct views of the United States. The first group, that represents a majority, doubts that long term accommodation with the United States is possible because it believes that the United States will not tolerate China as a world power even in Asia and it is highly suspicious of the US military strategy in East Asia and its alliances, particularly with Japan. A second group, which is a small but a highly influential one, hopes to reach an accommodation with

Washington by 2010 and believes that in the long run US forces in Asia will provide stability and will be important for dealing with the dangers from countries holding weapons of mass destruction and supporting terrorism. This faction has also been the leading voice for integrating China with multilateral organizations such as the World Trade Organization.

At present the more moderate group seems to be ascendant. Since the September 11 attacks China has cooperated closely with the US in its war against terrorism. China has also pledged US $ 4150 million for the reconstruction of post war Afghanistan and may provide troops for UN peacekeeping force in Afghanistan after US troops are withdrawn. All of this is a far cry from the tensions over a US spy plane that collided with a Chinese fighter jet near Hainan Island or the near rupture in relations when US warplanes bombed the Chinese embassy in Belgrade during the NATO led war against Serbia.

Chinese strategy, with respect to the American presence in the Central Asian region, will depend on the growth of China's own capabilities as also the larger contours of Sino-US relations. Examinations of China's strategic culture seem to point to the fact that China has historically exhibited a relatively consistent and hard *realpolitik* that has persisted across different structural contexts. This strategy stresses on absolute flexibility and conscious sensitivity to changing relative capabilities. In situations where the equilibrium is favourable offensive coercive strategies are adopted. In situations where the equilibrium is less favourable accommodative strategies are adopted till the balance turns favourable. This is clearly evident in Chinese policy vis a vis Russia and the US in the Central Asian region.

In Chinese strategic writings Russo-Sino-US interaction, traditionally viewed as a triangular relationship, is now visualized in somewhat less competitive terms as representing a situation of compromise. In a situation where Russia, China and the United States increasingly expand the convergence of their national interests, the gain of one side would not necessarily mean the loss of the other two sides. Rather, they would be mutually related and at the same time mutually independent. This new relationship will also focus on non-confrontation. For instance, out of their respective national strategic interests, while maintaining friendly relations with each other, neither China nor Russia wants to confront the US. The US also endeavours to maintain cooperative relations with both China and Russia even if there are differences, and attempts to prevent contestation from escalating into confrontation. Secondly, the new relationship has the feature of coexistence of cooperation and competition. Each of the three countries has their specific strategic intentions and goals and adjustment of the relations among one another is still underway. But all of them are attempting to seek the convergence of their national interests, i.e, to maintain and promote regional and world peace and development. However, there is recognition that the relationship is also asymmetrical and that the comprehensive strength of the US in world politics is greater.

It is this realization that has led to the search for new partnerships. One such proposed alliance is a strategic partnership between Russia-China and India. This proposed partnership was not just aimed against the eastward expansion of Western alliances but also as a means of counterbalancing the influence of neighbouring countries in the region. Whether this relationship will emerge as significant remains to be seen. However, as a counterbalance to the unilateralist trend emerging from the US, Russia and China have advocated global multilateralism and have emphasized the necessity of strengthening the role of the United Nations. They have also sought multilateral solutions to conflicts in their immediate neighbourhood. They share similar views with regard to opposing unilateralist actions by a US led NATO extending beyond Europe into Central Asia and South Asia. The extent to which such common concerns can lead to the development of multilateral co-operation in particular regions remains to be seen, particularly in the light of fact that multilateralism is often variously defined by them and commitment to multilateral options have varied, particularly in cases which are identified as significant in terms of national interest.

The debate on a new strategic environment therefore hinges on a large number of local, regional and international issues. While the contours of this new environment are still to take shape certain factors need to be taken into account in the course of examining this. The first is how far this strategic environment is "new" in terms of involving a radical reorientation of the security arrangements in the region. The second is the Central Asian position on this new environment. A third is the extent to which this affects the security environment in the South Asian region.

It is with a view to addressing some of these issues that this study has been attempted. The study begins with an examination of Russian and Chinese positions in Central Asia and then goes on to examine the Russo-Sino-US interaction on the region, in some detail. As an extension of this it examines the positions of transnational organizations of the region. It concludes with an examination of the South Asian and particularly the Indian position in the shaping of an alternative multilateral strategic dialogue. In such a situation a number of issues assume significance. The first and foremost is the question of the viability of multilateralism in the region and the extent to which the states themselves are willing to be part of multilateral process. A second issue is the attitude of Russia and China towards multilateralism in general and about the status of their role in multilateral processes in the Central Asian region, in particular. A third is a debate on the role that India, as part of Russia-China-India axis, can play in the multilateral process in Central Asia.

This study was undertaken as a project for the Maulana Abul Kalam Azad Institute of Asian Studies, Kolkata. The author remains indebted to the Institute, its Director Professor Mahavir Singh, and the Chairman, Executive Council, Professor Devendra

Kaushik, for the support extended during the period that the study was conducted.

A number of scholars shared ideas and resources and expertise with the author. The author is particularly grateful to Professor Tatiana Shaumian, Professor Tatiana Zagorodnikova, Dr Euginia Vanina, Professor Aziz Niyazi, Professor Shanken Nadirov, Dr Andrei Grozin, Professor Meruert Abuseitova, Professor Gulbakhram M Molotova, Dr Dosym A Satpayev, Zhanar Sagimbayeva, Dr Leila Muzaporova, Dr Askar Shomanov, Zukhra Akisheva, Anar A Khamzaeva, Aditi Bhaduri, Professor Purobi Roy and Professor Ranabir Samaddar. Parts of the study had been presented in seminars and the comments and suggestions emerging from the discussions have been particularly useful.

This book is for Rajarshi and Nayantara.

Chapter 1

Russia in Central Asia

The Ongoing Debate

A significant part of the writings on the emerging relations between Russia and Central Asia stress that a new reassertion of Russian influence in the region is on the cards. In his state of the nation speech, in May 2003, Russian President Vladimir Putin emphasized boosting cooperation with the former Soviet states, as his top foreign policy priority.[1] Concurrently, there is disillusionment in the Central Asian region with the US aid package. While these positions require more critical examination, what is particularly significant is the fact that Russia's relations with the Central Asian states seems to have come full circle. From a position of separation in the immediate aftermath of the breakup of the Soviet Union, to attempts at reintegration in the face of increasing western influence over the second half of the last decade, to what is projected as a willingness to allow western military presence and finally attempts at reassertion in the wake of the *post-post Cold War* scenario.

It is in keeping with this reassertion that towards the end of 2002 it was reported that Russian military units were returning to Kyrgyzstan, after having left in mid 1999, in the name of fighting terrorism and maintaining *regional stability*.[2] Russian military jets began landing at Kant airport, about 20 kilometers from the capital, Bishkek. The Kyrgyz Defence Minister Esen Topoev pointed out that the Russian air base was being set up in accordance with the Collective Security Treaty of the Commonwealth of Independent States. Some 25 kilometers from Kant, 3,000 troops from the US and other Western nations are deployed at Kyrgyzstan's Manas airport. Both the forces ostensibly have the same aim, to fight terrorism and Islamic extremism and provide stability in the region. Yet, this return is today being interpreted as a strong sign that a "new" rivalry is developing between Moscow and Washington in Central Asia.

It would be interesting to begin defining the nature of this "stability" and how it reflects on the emerging relationship between Russia and Central Asia. In fact, today there is consensus on the fact that "stability" is likely to be the key word in the determination of Russian policy towards Central Asia. At the same time it is significant to keep in mind that the term has numerous, and sometimes conflicting, connotations. Stability is primarily defined as an absence of major regional conflicts that may pose a threat to the Russian hinterland, its borders and interests. It is also looked upon through a socio-economic prism to imply the relative effectiveness of local economies and the capability of Central Asian regimes to resolve complicated social issues. Central Asian stability may also be understood in terms of the evolution of ethnic and religious relations that involve Russian minorities. Ecological and demographic situations in Central Asia are progressively becoming crucial in evaluating the region's stability and prospects for development. Finally, there are a number of problems that have their bearing on the stability of the region, including trafficking of narcotics, illegal trade in arms, the spread of separatist groups and extremist forces. A wide polarity of opinion exists on the appropriate mechanisms and the extent of Russian involvement to maintain stability in the region. Here, the interests of various institutions, political groups and economic structures contradict each other.

Current political and academic discussions in Russia regarding Central Asian issues reveal a wide variety of views, some of them of extreme polarity. It has been argued that the intensity and the divergence of these discussions and views are reflective of the fact that Russian-Central Asian relations go beyond the realm of practical policies and acquires a philosophical or even an existential dimension. At stake is not just a set of geopolitical, economic or military strategic issues, but its very "civilizational" quintessence and a debate as to whether Russia is a European or Eurasian power.[3] From a more realistic perspective others have argued that the formulation and execution of the "near abroad" policy has been largely influenced by the interests of various groups within Russia. For instance, as in Tsarist Turkestan, which was governed by the Ministry of War, rather than the Ministry of Interior, in the recent past, the Russian military has been crucial in determining the framework and character of Russian presence in Tajikistan and the most vocal group opposing US military presence in the region as a whole. Consequently, over the years Russia's proclaimed goals and principles have been modified towards reassertion of Russian control in the post Soviet space. Tajikistan has been exemplified as the testing ground for Moscow's drive towards "reintegration" of the former Soviet Republics into a new confederation.[4] On the other hand critiques of the policy have noted that during the entire post Soviet period, relations with Central Asia have developed in spurts without the emergence of any coherent policy.[5]

While each of these positions is partially correct, what principally characterizes Russian policy towards the Central Asian region is a duality. On the one hand there is the recognition of a difference between the two regions. A difference that has been projected in Slavic/Turkic terms and recognized by Tsarist, Soviet and post Soviet Russia. Therefore, the nature of Tsarist Russian administrative policies, with regard to Turkestan, the numerous experiments of the immediate post Tsarist period that continued in the 20's and 30's and finally the events following the demise of the former Soviet Union, when these republics were denied a role, in what was essentially conceived as a Slavic union. On the other hand, there always remained a pragmatic recognition of the significance of these regions for Russian national interests. The "drive down south" to the warm water ports, significant for Tsarist Russia, called for Russian involvement in the "heartlands" Asia. Similarly, the recognition of Central Asian borders as the "soft underbelly" of the CIS, calls for Russian involvement in Tajik affairs. In fact, the very coinage of the Russian term "near abroad" rather than "newly independent states" or "post Soviet states" to define these states is significant. It signaled a difference of policy that was to mark relations in the future.

While this duality today is couched in a rhetoric about the significance of Eurasianism as an ideology for the Russian state, in actuality it now involves a choice about the recognition of the extent of the Russian sphere of interest in the post Soviet space and debates around the exclusivity of such interests. This is a debate that has become crucial in Moscow as well as within the newly independent states themselves, as they seek their place in the post Soviet world. Russian politicians and intellectuals have remained divided on the issue of national self-identification and the future of Russia. How should Russia perceive itself as a nation? Has Russia been guided by its own unique laws of historical development or is Russia a nation that shares patterns of social life with other countries? And is Russia an exclusively European country, or should it adopt a dual heritage that recognizes the validity of the Eurasian ideology? And consequently, how should relations between Moscow and its regions develop in the future?

The domestic debate over foreign policy is therefore inextricably tied to the issue of how Russian citizens defined themselves, their territory and their relationship with the outside world. Which ideas would be chosen to define Russia's identity influenced how the former Soviet states were perceived and thus the development of Russia's foreign policy towards the near abroad. Here there were many perspectives, for instance, one way of defining "who the Russians are" was in terms of language, so that Russia would include all "Russian speakers" in the former Soviet states. A second way was to define Russia ethnically, so that it would be composed only of those with ethnic Russian origins. A third way was to define it as a Slavic entity, thus including all peoples of Slavic origin. A fourth possibility was to give Russia a broader "Union" identity. Another key distinction in the position on identity concerned Russia's 1991 borders.

Generally those who argued that Russia should be a civic state were in agreement that the 1991 borders of the Russian Federation should be kept intact. In contrast those who defined Russia in terms of language interpreted Russia as including the Russian Federation but also the areas of the former Soviet Union inhabited by Russian speakers.[6] All of these, in their turn, influenced the way the former Soviet states were defined.

One would have to begin an examination of these debates by taking note of the fact that a plurality of visions exists on these issues within the Russian state, a plurality that is of significant divergence. Apart from the Eurasianists and the Atlanticists, there are, within Russia neo-imperialist groups, who have demanded the reintegration of the old Russian and Soviet empires, with Vladimir Zhirinovsky as the most prominent exponent of the view. Others have held that Russia should declare the territory of the former Soviet Union to be its exclusive sphere of interest. On the other end of the spectrum are politically active segments of the Russian population, with strong isolationist sentiments who called for the rejection of the "great power" complex. Andranik Migranyan, for instance, has argued that Russia should now abandon its attempt to integrate Central Asia in a single linguistic and cultural space, but should instead concentrate on making the region a neutral buffer zone.[7]

In the post Soviet era three foreign policy orientations and specific policy proposals have been identified, though by 1993 it is noted that, pragmatic nationalist ideas were becoming dominant and the rhetoric of Russian foreign policy was moving towards a centrist direction.[8] These provided several options concerning how to define Russia and shape its future development in terms of national identity, geography, mission, self-perception and economic and political direction. As these options, ideas and underlying preferences coalesced they helped to structure debates about foreign policy. The ideas underlying the orientations provided the background that helped frame foreign policy issues and support policy proposals.

However, these varying policy orientations have faced criticism as lacking a definite purpose. Irina D Zviagelskaya remarks :

> The Central Asian policy of the Russian Federation is to all appearances distinguished by the absence of clear-cut ideas about the purposes Russia is pursuing in this area of the world and the means necessary to achieve them. It would seem that the question, "What do we need Central Asia for?" so frequently asked in Russia after the disintegration of the USSR, has still not found a precise answer, despite developments that have taken place in the Russian approach to the region after 1991. Such uncertainty is to a certain extent traditional for a significant part of the Russian public opinion.[9]

Zviagelskaya goes on to quote Fyodor Dostoyevsky to prove that this ambiguity is not of recent origin. Dostoyevsky remarking on the Russian society's perception of the place of Central Asia in Russian politics had remarked :

> And in general all our Russian Asia, including Siberia, still exists for Russia as some kind of appendage, in which our European Russia seemingly does not even want to be interested....There were even very bitter voices: "Oh, this Asia of ours! We cannot make an orderly arrangement for ourselves even in Europe, but now they thrust Asia on us as well. This Asia is of no use to us at all, we'd better leave it to somebody else!" Sometimes our wiseacres express these judgments even now, out of their great wisdom, no doubt.[10]

In the 1990's such ideas were echoed by Atlanticists, though their position has now been substantially weakened, with the recognition of the significance of the region.

Prior to an examination of Russian policy in the region, it is necessary to emphasize that the projection of a unified bloc of Central Asian states, with common domestic compulsions and similar foreign policy orientation, is as problematic as an unified

Russian policy towards the states. It would be correct to deal with issues that concern each of the states separately. For instance the large Russian minority in Kazakhstan ensures that it remains the most significant issue in Russo-Kazakh relations. As a consequence, prospects of a common Eurasian home is much more acceptable to President Nursultan Nazarbaev and the granting of dual citizenship more significant for Russia in the Kazakh case. On the other hand security issues are more important, vis a vis Tajikistan, given its long borders with states in conflict and the fact that it is recognized as the southern border of the CIS. Of course, there does remain some issues of concern that cut across state borders. However, for the sake of convenience this chapter reduces these individual differences and deals with the imperatives that govern Russian policies towards the region, as a whole.

While this chapter recognizes the significance of a number of diverse factors that play a part in the formulation of Russian policy towards Central Asia, it begins with an examination of the debates over Eurasianism that is seen as the ideological basis of the relationship and then goes on to examine other factors that are important in the determination of the policies. The last section examines the changes that the post September 11 scenario is seen to have brought about in the relation. The chapter argues that the current Russian position in the region should not simply be visualized as an attempt at reintegration of the "heartland" but rather as part of a larger policy that favours multilateralism as a governing principle of international relations. This argument is continued in Chapter 3 that examines Russo-Sino-US interactions over the Central Asian region in some detail.

The "heartland" and its "rim": Eurasianism as an ideology

The English tremble over India, but need we tremble over Tashkent?

Russia would remain Russia even without Central Asia...

M.N. Katkov, *Moskovskiye Vedomosti*, 1879.

What for? What future/ What is the need of the future seizure of Asia? What's our business there? This is necessary because Russia is not only in Europe but also in Asia; because the Russian is not only a European, but also a Asiatic. Not only that in our coming destiny, perhaps it is precisely Asia that represents our main way out....

In Europe we are hanger-ons and slaves, whereas to Asia we shall go as masters. In Europe we are Asiatics, whereas in Asia, we, too, are Europeans. Our civilizing mission in Asia will bribe our spirit and drive us thither. It is only necessary that the movement should start. Build two rail roads: begin with the one to Siberia and then to Central Asia and at once you will see the consequences...

Feodor M. Dostoevsky, 1881.

As the above-cited passages indicate the debate about Russia's relations with the Asian "heartlands" began in the 19th century. In the last decade of the last century these debates were revived at a juncture when the need for formulating a policy towards the newly independent states arose. The demise of the Soviet Union and Russia's new sovereignty led to soul searching reminiscent of the one in the 19th century generating a discussion about Russia's place in world history and politics. The debate was reopened in March-April 1992, in connection with Russia's new foreign policy concept by Sergei Stankevich, the then political counselor to President Boris Yeltsin and Andrei Kozyrev, the then Russian foreign minister. The two presented what came to be known as the "Eurasian" and the "Atlanticist" approaches to Russian foreign policy. This discussion, however, was not limited to just Russian foreign policy at the end of the 20th century. It continued the debate started by Slavophiles and Westerners about Russia's future choices regarding what came to be termed its "near abroad".

It should be emphasized, at the onset that Russia was not defined exclusively as a European country by either the

Eurasianists or the Atlanticists. Like the Eurasianists, the Atlanticists spoke of Russia as a Eurasian power. They also did not differ significantly regarding Russia's role vis a vis the post Soviet space. However, the Atlanticists were especially emphatic in their rejection of the idea that Russia could develop democracy at home while using strong-arm tactics abroad. On the other hand, for all their advocacy of Russia's special role among the newly independent states, the Eurasianists admitted that this special role had yet to be earned and Russia would have to prove its new character to its former satellites. Though, they did emphasize the fact that Russia could perform exceptional functions both for Europe and for Asia, including Central Asia, as an intermediary in economic, political, military and other affairs.[11]

The Eurasian debate is principally concerned with the place of Asia in the Russian mind and about the position that the Asian space, as the larger portion of the dual Eurasian continent, has occupied in Russian/Soviet geopolitical thinking. At the turn of the millennium, the problem of the civilizational identity of Russia assumed particular importance. Some Russians claimed that Russia was a European country, a few thought that it belongs to Asia, the majority are in favour of its finding a third way of its own. Many saw its present situation of civilizational ambiguity as responsible for a serious imbalance in the general principles of Russian thinking. The "civilizational" approach is dominant in Russian thinking today. National security concerns are formulated in civilizational terms and other paradigms are considered deficient.[12]

This "civilizational" debate, however, is not without its problems. For one, it reduces differences within "Russianness" when recent events within the Russian Federation has demonstrated its significance. Critiques note that Russia has none of the qualities that pertain to a normal civilization. It lacks a system of common values and symbols, which can unite its citizens, irrespective of confessional, class or ethnic identity, and it has no unifying great idea or great tradition. Those who believe that there exists a self sufficient and self sustained Russian civilization, on the other hand, note that, despite this, Russia has somehow proved able to solve all its problems and contradictions, to provide socio-political stability, to organize vast territories populated by different peoples of European and Asian origin into some kind of unity and to withstand aggression from without. In general they argue that Russia has its own civilizational code and the Russian civilization, like all others, is programmed for immortality.[13] The problem of civilizational identity has become a central issue of political debates today and "civilizational factors" influence priorities in the formulation of national interests and foreign policy.

From the late seventeenth century to 1917, Russia was perceived as part of Europe. This pro western orientation met with opposition from the Slavophiles who based their view on Orthodoxy and glorified Slavic values. However, Russia's Asian legacy also cannot be ignored as it affects both domestic and foreign policy. An examination of the genealogy of Russia's "Europeanness" versus "Asianness", shows in the construction of Russian nationalism, Asia played the role of the "other". This in its turn, had a major role in the construction of the cultural stereotype of Central Asia in the Russian mind. It was Russia's claim towards forming a part of Europe and to being Europe's shield against the onslaughts of Asia that constituted her credentials for admission into the Concert of European powers. During a long period of her history, Russia's intellectual life had been directed westward. However, while the content of the classical Russian culture was Western in origin, it has been pointed out, that its manifestations were often Oriental in intensity.[14] While for the most part, even anti-western trends in Russian thinking viewed Russia as belonging to Europe, not to Asia, there remained a group, which hoped that the "Turanian" elements shaping Russian culture would produce something "spiritually distinct" from Europe. It was also disappointment in the European proletariat and the European middle class that directed the hopes of Russian revolutionaries like Alexander Herzen to the East.

Herzen blessed the Mongol yoke for preserving such Russian peculiarities as the rural *mir* commune. In fact, it was argued, folk Russia had never fully followed St Petersburg into westernization and its peasant rebels had cooperated with Turkic and Mongol nomads, time and again as was witnessed during the Pugachev Rising of 1773.[15]

This was a line of argument that was followed by the Eurasianists who argued that Eurasia, the territory of the former Soviet Union and the Russian Empire, is unique. It has evolved as a civilization over the past 700 years since the Mongol conquest of Russia in the 13th century and it combines within itself Orthodox Christianity, Buddhism and Islam. The doctrine was proclaimed, immediately after the Russian Revolution in 1917, by a group of distinguished émigré scholars led by N.S. Trubetskoi.[16] Its polemical purpose was to argue that Russia had, by denial of its obvious fate, involved itself in Europe and European politics to the point of its own extinction. The significance of the doctrine lay not in its having shown the importance of the Mongols and the steppes to the early and modern Russian history, but in having presented them as constituting Russia and the Russian Empire. However, nationalist Russian interpretations of history treat the "Mongol yoke" as an unmitigated disaster. The Mongols hover on the periphery of history as barbaric, nomadic and pagan whose power was eventually broken by the great Muscovite Tsars. It was a combination of these two visions that shaped Russian attitudes towards Asia.

While this debate was carried on with great intensity, by Russian intellectuals themselves, it was Sir Halford Mackinder who focused attention on the implications of the development of a Russia dominated "heartland" in Eurasia and its impact on the other Great Powers. In a way, this had begun the debate on the Russia's extraordinary position as a European and an Asian power. It is necessary, therefore, to briefly examine Mackinder's position on the "heartland" and its "rim" in order to gain a correct understanding of the debate. Mackinder's heartland concept was formulated in the course of a lecture given in January 1904, at the Royal Geographical Society, entitled "The Geographical Pivot of History". Here, he made a bold statement regarding the superiority of land power to sea power. Mackinder also revised the Eurocentric vision of history in favour of the geographer's vision where the pivotal role of Europe would be eclipsed by the ascendancy of the new "geographical pivot of history" namely the "heartland of Euro Asia". The main geostrategic advantage of this imaginary centre of a true world empire, that would be invulnerable to the direct application of sea power, he called the World Island. Thus, in Mackinder's prophetic vision the fate of the future Empire of the World would depend on the control of this central core, the "heartland". However, it has to be recognized at the outset that Mackinder had envisioned this invulnerability in a pre missile technology age.

Mackinder's genius consisted of his ability to reduce the complexity of world affairs to a single problem of who would ultimately control the "heartland". Mackinder had envisaged that the strategic control over the heartland would belong either to Russia exclusively or to Russo-German combination. In 1919 Mackinder expanded his heartland thesis by shifting his centre of gravity radically westward to Europe, locating the "Pivot Area" in the contested zone, lying between the German and the Russian spheres of expansion. He believed that this area would be critical to political developments worldwide. In his book *Democratic Ideals and Reality*, he stipulated the dictum, "Who rules Eastern Europe commands the Heartland; who rules the Heartland commands the World Island; who rules the World Island, commands the World.[17]

With the disintegration of the Soviet Union, Eurasian ideas became acceptable to a majority of Russians. The key word in the new Eurasian discourse was geopolitics. Geopolitics is everywhere. There is a Geopolitical Committee in the State Duma, political leaders philosophize about the geographical space and the foreign policy of all states is interpreted in geopolitical terms. Official documents, however, are cautious about using the Eurasianist terminology, though it is not completely avoided. In the National Security Concept, approved by special Presidential decree in December 1997, Russia is called a "European-Asian" power and its "unique strategic location on the Eurasian continent" is stressed as a determining factor of its internal and foreign policy.[18]

While at first sight this dual position appears as an advantage to Russia, it also introduces an insurmountable ambivalence into Russian policy making. This was clearly visible in the former President Mr Mikhail Gorbachev's efforts to claim that Russia was an integral part of the "common European home" while announcing that it was also a member of the booming "Pacific rim".[19] The term Eurasia is, in fact, a testimony to this ambivalence. This duality poses a problem to Russia for two principal reasons. It is undeniable that physical geography has placed severe limitations on the amount of communications between Russia and heartlands. But this pales into insignificance in comparison to the central difficulty, namely the fact that the so-called Eurasian "heartland" is predominantly non-Russian. Today, Eurasianists will also have to take note of the fact that the Central Asian states have their own "ethnocracy" and that to a large extent Russia is unprepared to fully assume its former role for a number of reasons mostly internal to it. Eurasian projects, have, in general, been rejected by the newly independent states.

At a juncture in history, when Russia is once again engaged in fashioning a state and society, the Eurasian debate is projected as having resurfaced as an ideology to hold her together and provide a direction for the future. In fact, it is argued that to an extent it is this duality that determines all other issues with relation to the Central Asian states, that are today identified as significant, like the question of ethnic Russians in these states and their status as new minorities, dual citizenship, economic union and security of the "soft underbelly" of the state. However, while the rhetorical significance of this need not be reduced, it is necessary to examine the significance of these issues, in some detail.

The "Post" Soviet and Russian policy in Central Asia

In order to assess Russian policy towards the Central Asian region, it is necessary to briefly examine the last decade of the 20th century, the years immediately after the demise of the former Soviet Union.[20] This examination is important, as it clearly indicates the duality of position with regard to Russian policies that this chapter argues.

Towards the latter half of the 1980's, the regional balance of power in the then Soviet Union began to acquire important political meaning in the fight for succession, within the hierarchy. Here it is important to remember that at this stage, Mikhail Gorbachev could rely on almost total support of a "monolithic block" of Central Asian deputies in the then Supreme Soviet of the USSR, in his fight against internal opposition that, since 1989, was being identified with Boris Yeltsin. The Central Asian republics were staunch supporters of Gorbachev's 9+1 proposal for ensuring the survival of the USSR. When this plan was abruptly brought to an end with the Minsk Agreement, which excluded there republics, the Central Asian republics reacted by attempting to create the "Turkestan Confederation". Open confrontation between the Slavic and the Turkic republics of the former Soviet Union could only be averted by the efforts at conciliation by leaders like Nursultan Nazarbaev who helped to negotiate the Central Asian membership in the CIS, in Almaty in December 1991.[21] However, the early years of the decade were marked by steps by the new Russian state that demonstrated her independent status and her separateness from the former Central Asian republics.

However, this position changed with the emergence of a coalition which spoke in favour of restoring Russian-Central Asian "special relations". It included influential industrial groups who were dependent on Central Asian raw materials and semi finished products and on Central Asian markets for their finished products. Some communist factions were also to be found in this coalition who stood for preserving ties with Central Asia as a means for restoring the Soviet legacy. There were also groups of Russian nationalists who considered Russian-Central Asian relations as a prerequisite for "Eurasian unity". They were joined by parts of the Russian military-industrial complex that perceived the disintegration of the Soviet strategic space as a threat to Russian security interests. Support for this "reintegrationist" approach came from the Russian National Security Council as also the Russian Supreme Soviet and the ministries like the Ministry of Defence, Interior and Counter-intelligence.

The bitter internal conflicts in Russia, in October 1993 and the ensuing move towards Presidential rule, ushered in a new stage in policies. It was evident that under the pressure of nationalists like Vladimir Zhirinovsky and in view of the failure of the pro-western policies, there was a change in rhetoric, if not in perceptions. A noteworthy trend began with the emphasis that Russia could not "leave" the Central Asian region thereby putting its "soft southern underbelly" in jeopardy. However, after a certain warming of relations in the wake of the Tashkent summit, the "Belovezhskaia Pusha" syndrome once again recurred in 1993, with the announcement of the formation of an economic union between Russia, Ukrain and Belorussia, in the wake of the participation of the Central Asian states in the OEC.

In the meantime, the Central Asian states themselves began to realize that intra-regional integration was a necessity. On the one hand it was dictated by the desire to launch and make the most of the mechanism of common political and economic interests and to smooth the difficulties of the transition period. On the other hand the states of the region could expect to create some kind of counterbalance to Russian policy and to avoid pressure on them from Russia. The Central Asian Union, comprising Kazakhstan, Kyrgyzstan and Uzbekistan was created in 1994.

As Russian perspective on its relations with the West changed, so did its approach to third party involvement in Central Asian politics and economics. It was suddenly recognized that by "abandoning" Central Asia and reducing its presence in the region, Russia left vacuums that had begun to be filled up by others, particularly western countries, including Turkey as a NATO member, as well as China, Iran, Saudi Arabia and Pakistan. Turkey was recognized as a particularly alarming case because of its cultural proximity to the republics and its political backing from the West. Examples of this concern abounded. In May 1993, a quasi official article, by the Ministry for Foreign Economic Relations, was published in the *Nezavisimaya Gazeta* that lashed out against the decision adopted by the five Central Asian states to create the Central Asian Regional Council, that was intended to exclude the Russian Federation. It was asserted that this intraregional integration was hostile to Russian interests and that it undermined the previous agreements on a single CIS military-strategic space. It was also claimed that these integratory attempts were being orchestrated by Turkey and other Western powers.[22] Similarly, when in the summer of 1993, the majority of the Central Asian states supported the Turkish idea for the creation of a custom and tariff union, the then First Deputy Prime Minister of Russia, A. Shokhin, declared that Central Asian regimes had to make the choice between integration with Turkey or with Russia, Ukraine and Belarus. Central Asia could not be involved in both the communities.

Concurrently, Russia became more perceptive about what could be considered as "positive" tendencies and moves in the Central Asian states. As ideas about the Eurasian school of thought began to take root in the official Russian thinking compatible ideas began to be felt in the Central Asian context, specially in Kazakhstan. It was under such conditions that the proposals on creation of a "confederate union" between Kazakhstan and Russia were put forward at a Congress of the Socialist Party of Kazakhstan, that took place on March 14, 1992. At a later stage some other Kazakh political groups, notably the Peoples' Congress Party, headed by O. Suleimenov, supported the idea of a Russia-Kazakhstan Confederation, although other such groupings of nationalist orientation rejected the idea, fearful of the eventual degradation of such a confederation into a federation and the reestablishment of total Russian control over Kazakh independence and sovereignty.[23]

In the winter of 1995, Moscow took a number of steps for the reintegration of the post Soviet space, in the wake of the crisis in Chechnya and the threat of NATO expansion towards the east. It included the signing of a customs and free trade agreement with Belarus and Kazakhstan and the call for an active reintegration policy. In short, while through most of 1992 the Yeltsin government showed little or no interest in Central Asia due to political as well as economic reasons, during the next phase (much of 1993) Russia began to assume a major role in the CIS and decided it best to include the Central Asian Republics within the CIS.[24] This was reflected in the "Concept of the Foreign Policy of the Russian Federation" which was adopted at the end of 1992.

The policy included:

> deepening political, economic and military cooperation within the newly independent states within the framework of the CIS as well as on bilateral basis;
>
> broadening and strengthening the CIS infrastructure;
>
> conclusion of agreements on protection of rights of Russia citizens with each of the newly independent states;
>
> conclusion of agreements on protection of rights of Russian citizens with each of the newly independent states;
>
> collective protection of the CIS borders, and
>
> formation of the CIS peacekeeping forces. [25]

However, under the then Foreign Minister Andrei Kozyrev's guidance it was decided that a separate ministry to deal with these newly independent states would not be formed. Since Russia had entered the CIS on the principle of full equality with the other independent states, the creation of separate ministries may suggest that they were being treated as less sovereign than other foreign countries. As a result management of relations with the states was assigned to different directorates of the Foreign Ministry.[26] In the two years with Yeltsin and Kozyrev in charge, Russia is noted to have moved towards "regathering" into the CIS the lands of the Russians. Reintegration could mean a *federation*, a *confederation* or a *union of the CIS countries* with the Russian Federation.

Significant international and domestic changes necessitated a more assertive policy in Asia and the setting up of methods to achieve them. An attempt was made to work out a new policy doctrine for Asia, whose main principles were (1) that no contradictions with any country in the region were irreconcilable and that Russia should work consistently towards stable and balanced relations with all of them (2) that the development of economic relations with the regional countries was a main priority and (3) that the response to challenges to regional security should be made on a collective coordinated basis. Elaborating on the last principle Kozyrev spoke in favour of creating a collective or cooperative security system, a "security community" open for every regional country to join.[27] His proposals, however, failed to evoke any favourable response.

A course towards reintegration was made into law by a decree of September 1995 and received further impetus with the departure of Kozyrev and the appointment of Yevgeni Primakov. Primakov advocated, not only economic but also political and military reintegration of the former Soviet republics. With Primakov's appointment, the CIS headquarters was moved to Moscow. Also the Foreign Affairs Ministry was given a coordinating role in the implementation of Russian foreign policy. A new concept of

Russian foreign policy and national security in international affairs was formulated by Primakov which included three basic principles (1)multipolarity as a governing principle of international relations and active opposition to attempts to establish a unipolar world order (2) constructive partnership with all countries instead of permanent coalitions (3) integration on a voluntary basis within the CIS.[28] From 1991 to 1996, the narrowing of stated views, towards a geopolitical emphasis upon traditional ties and close relations with the near abroad and the endorsement of the use of military force to protect Russian interests, led to a broad consensus over foreign policy principles which were outlined in the new Foreign Policy Concept and Military Doctrine. The formal adoption of these principles represented a conceptual shift in the foreign policy thinking.[29]

The endorsement of Vladimir Putin by Russian voters is said to have marked a new dynamic and active phase in the relationship between Russia and Central Asia. It has been noted that Putin's past experience is likely to guide his policies, particularly, his "near abroad" ones. Putin's focus on Central Asia is being pointed as relatively new in the post Kozyrev period. While under Primakov, a Eurasianist stand did enter post Soviet Russian policy in the mid 1990's, it was the NATO intervention into the Balkans and its encroachment into the former Soviet bloc that turned Russia's focus to Central Asia. In the Russian assessment of 1999, Moscow viewed Central Asia as the key component of Moscow's economic future. President Putin spent the weekend of May 19-21, 2000, in Ashqabad where he reached an agreement in principle to increase gas purchase from Turkmenistan. Beyond natural gas talks, Russia and Turkmenistan established an intergovernmental commission for general economic cooperation and agreed to enhance bilateral relations. Russia also agreed to take over Kazakhstani energy operations from the Belgian company Tractebel. Moscow has also increased its concerns about militancy in the Central Asian region with President Putin indicating that the recent fighting in the Central Asian region would be a priority topic at the Yalta CIS summit.[30]

The significance of this activism may be noted in the fact that with the election of Putin, as the President of the Russian Federation, there was an increase in US diplomatic activity in the region. Washington sent a number of high officials including CIA Chief, George Tennet, FBI Director, Louise Freeh and Secretary of State, Madeline Albright to the region. Though this attention has been welcomed by the Central Asian Presidents, this has also meant that they now have to walk a tightrope maintaining political and economic partnership with Russia as well as close ties with the US. Here, actions and policies have been ambivalent. For example, Kazakh moves towards decreasing dependence on Russian transportation lines had been noted in the beginning of the construction of the Baku-Ceyhan line. But this pipeline can only be viable if Kazakhstan pledges 20 million tones of oil a year to the project. Recently, however, it has been noted that Kazakh officials seem to be backing away from such a commitment, either under Russian pressure or because the projections about the volume of oil and gas had been misleading. Similarly the Kyrgyz President Akaev pledged to make Russian the official state language, demonstrating what is being perceived as evidence of the re-expansion of the Russian sphere of interests in the region.[31] Here, a dilemma is faced by most of the states that are caught in a predicament about finding a balance between their need for Western economic aid and security guarantees from Russia.

Critical Issues in The "New" Heartlands

In any examination of Russian policy towards Central Asia, it is necessary to take into account a number of factors. First, there are genuine Russian interests in the region, which some Russian leaders have called the "soft underbelly" of Russia and also Russians who wish to incorporate the area into the Russian Federation. Secondly, there are a number of problems facing the Central Asian states that make them vulnerable to Russian efforts to reassert control. Third, in addition to Central Asian vulnerabilities, there are also a number of Russian weaknesses that hamper Moscow's efforts to extend its influence into Central Asia.[32]

In a more general sense, Russian policy towards Central Asia developed along three intertwined lines: political, military and economic. Political exchanges have dealt with most general issues of bilateral and multilateral affairs; the future of the CIS, problems of borders, and local conflicts, the status of minorities and foreign nationals. Dialogues within the political ambit have borne a fairly formal character and as a rule have been called upon to minimize or conceal differences. Whereas economic interaction is the most considered and in many respects the most vitally important area for the interests of Russia and its Central Asian counterparts, military relations is an even more involved area. Under current conditions it includes military and political cooperation, addressing the resolution of issues related to the presence of Russian troops, installations and property as well as the conduct of joint peace keeping operations.

Russia's military relations with its Central Asian neighbours is regulated, in the most general sense, by the Treaty on Collective Security, signed in Tashkent on May 15 1992. The Treaty sets out the obligation of the non-use of force or the threat of force in the relations between its members. The members also have to resolve their differences by peaceful means, abstain from entering into blocks hostile to each other, conduct consultations on security matters and coordinate their defence policies. For that purpose the Council on Collective Security was created. However, like most other treaties and agreements made within the ambit of the CIS it has failed to be implemented. Another crucial Russian concern, after the dissolution of the USSR, was preserving for itself former Soviet property left in the territories of the newly independent states. Negotiations on installations like the Baikanur launching facility and bases for Russian troops as well as the presence of these troops in the Central Asian states, were concluded to establish general framework and payments for the use of appropriate installations. The financial burden created for Russia was substantial.

The area of peace keeping proved to be more productive in terms of military-political and military-operational cooperation between Russia and Central Asia. Early attempts at regulating joint Russian and Central Asian activities in conflict management, including peace keeping, date back to March 1992, when a CIS decision was adopted on creating military observer groups and collective peacekeeping forces, which were originally conceived as non combative. The growing intensity of the conflicts however, demonstrated the insufficiency of such forces and events in Tajikistan were most significant.

The Tajik conflict demonstrates various policy options that were explored by Russia and the strategy that was finally evolved. Zviagelskaya notes that the choices open to Russia, in the early stages of the conflict, were just two; to withdraw its troops and border guards, completely ignoring what was going on or to intervene on the side of the pro-government forces.[33] The first action was regarded as highly speculative. Although the Russian government tried to avoid intervention, it could not close its eyes to the interdependence of the events in Afghanistan and Tajikistan. Even the supporters of a complete departure from Central Asia were compelled to realize what a completely open border would mean for Russian security. The 201st motorized division was deployed in Tajikistan to guard the borders.

Under the impact of the Tajik civil war, a new CIS agreement, on collective peacekeeping forces, was adopted which modified the latter's mandate to include the functions of collective defence. With further intensification of the war, there was escalation of direct Russian military involvement. However, the important fact was that there was by and large acceptance of Russia's role as an intermediary in the process of conflict resolution. In this the Central Asian response has been significantly different from other Trans-Caucasus states where conflicting parties have opted not to appeal to Russia. The Russian population, within the Russian Federation however, remain wary of the regime's military involvement inside and outside Russia's borders and Russian involvement in Tajikistan has remained fairly unpopular in the Russian mind. However, it was only in June 2004, that a series of agreements between Russia and Tajikistan were signed for the transfer of full authority for frontier security to Tajik forces. The transfer is scheduled to be completed by 2006, when Russian border forces will vacate border posts along the Tajik-Afghan border.[34]

However, coordination of effort between Russia and the Central Asian states in the sphere of defence and security is tending to increase. The constant recurrence of crisis has encouraged consultation and joint action. Enhanced coordination has been planned by way of joint military doctrines and joint exercises like the Friendship 98 exercises. This increase in the numbers of joint exercises can be explained by Russia's concern at the heightened activity of the US military in the region.

To a very large extent the dissolution of the Soviet Union was predicated on the conviction that Russia did not need to continue carrying the economic burden of "alien" republics like Central Asia. As a result the Central Asian states were not invited to Belovezhskaya Pusha. Also, confronted with the ineffectiveness of some reforms at an earlier stage, the Yeltsin government moved to aggressive and protectionist foreign economic policies that created serious difficulties for the newly independent states. Particularly damaging were Russian steps towards establishing world price levels for its oil and gas exports and the "squeezing out" of Central Asian states from the "rouble zone". However, the inadequacies of these measures soon became evident. In the early 1990's it was generally assumed that the rebuilding of relations between Russia and Central Asia would also begin in the sphere of economics. This theme was evident in the speeches of the then Russian Premier Victor Chernomyrdin and the Presidents of the Central Asian states, Akaev, Nazarbaev,

Karimov, and Niyazov, who to begin with, genuinely saw a panacea for all economic and financial ills in the restoration of economic links between their countries and the Russian Federation. Russian technocrats took a more reserved position not forgetting that a large part of Russia's foreign debt went to the Central Asian states and they were in no position to clear the debts.

At the same time, it was also noted that intensive cooperation between Russia and Central Asia could involve the risk of preservation of low standard of technology, labour productivity and product quality in the Central Asian region which had existed in Soviet times. More importantly, it could also lead to the reestablishment of the centre-periphery relations characteristic of the Soviet period. It is now pointed out that the Soviet economic system was created, without taking into account the specific nature of Central Asian society, where economy was principally dominated by agriculture, cottage industry and trade. Industrial work was unknown in the region and the indigenous population remained out of the industrial sectors.

Also, the traditional sectors, where a large part of the indigenous section of the people worked, served the domestic needs of society and did not have too many links with the modern sectors of the former USSR. This traditional sector, that remained separate from the Soviet economic system, provided the material basis for the preservation of traditional behaviour norms in Central Asia. This sector of the economy that has remained self-sufficient has had no need to develop relations with Russia. Even if the development of economic links between Russia and Central Asia become inevitable, it is hardly likely to include traditional pre-industrial production methods. Though with the gradual establishment of training in agricultural produce, the traditional sector could become a factor in economic integration with Russia. There would however be difficulties here arising from problems of transport, taxation and the high cost of Russian industrial production, on the one hand and the fact that with the wide availability of cheap consumer goods from other parts of Asia the requirement for Russian goods would gradually decrease, on the other. A. Akimov, therefore argues that there are few objective reasons for an economic co-operation: they do not deal in similar areas of export, their economies are not mutually complementary, and there is no need for their markets to be merged.[35] However, it was not long before it was realized that Russia could ill afford to sever all economic ties with Central Asia.[36] Even after the commencement of radical economic reforms in Russia, local economies in Central Asia remained important partners for Russian industries.

However, Russia largely failed to translate these economic linkages and ensure its economic presence in the region through investment, purchase of blocks of shares and the creation of joint ventures and financial groups. A rather high level of risk and the lack of any prospect of getting dividends quickly has discouraged private Russian capital from Central Asia, except for oil where Russian companies tried to join in the development of deposits and transport of oil. Russia is also losing its importance as a trade partner. The sharp decline in the volume of trade has not been compensated for since.[37]

Russian Minorities as a Critical Issue in Russo-Central Asia Relations

The programme of "nationalization" of political space in the Central Asian region has meant that a large number of people are now left outside their own national territory or do not have one at all. This also means that in common with each stage of nation-state formation questions of "national majorities" and "national minorities" have come sharply to the forefront, once again. This section examines how the state comes to terms with its minorities in the period of transition.

Soviet nationality policy was based on the assumption that ethnic differences were a relic of the past and was eventually doomed to dissolve under socially engineered programmes of modernization. The "national-linguistic" cornerstone of the territorial divisions based on a core nationality, however, ensured the continuance of the ethnic factor. In some of the Republics this very process of ethnic identification acquired a momentum of its own with identities coalescing around the core group.

The assertion of "ethnic" identity that has accompanied the current stage of state formation, has meant the compelling political need to identify the "other". One of the most familiar ethnic cleavages in the Central Asian region is that between Russians and ethnic Central Asians. Here the cleavage is in terms of both language as well as religion. The majority of these Russians are not recent immigrants from Russia but came to Central Asia in imperial waves of migration in the Tsarist period, then under the expansion of cultivation in the 1920s and 1930s, or later under the Virgin lands programme of Khrushchev. In most cases, they were born in these states. The departure of Russians from Central Asia actually began from the 1980's with the flow of mainly younger educated Russians, in a movement that reversed the flow of earlier migrants.

The complex question of the destiny of the Soviet nationality policy, its success and failure and its claim of having "solved" the national question, forms the background of this section which argues that the question of majorities and minorities often depends on the political unit under consideration and is in essence a variable element in the process of nation-state formation. The ethnic question is geopolitically grounded, as ethnic demands are inevitably territorially based. In the specific case of the former Soviet Union this assumes significance. One of the most dramatic transformations in recent years has been the change in the status of some 25 million ethnic Russians from a majority group into minorities with disputed identities and uncertain futures. The designation of the non-Russians as minorities in the former Soviet Union has changed, through a dramatic reversal of fortunes, where Russians are today the "new" minorities in the post Soviet states.[38]

There are different ways of conceiving what it means to be a Russian in the Central Asian states today.[39] For instance, Russians in Uzbekistan may be understood as being persons of Russian ethnic origin, most of whom speak Russian as their native language, who nonetheless belong to the Uzbek nation, understood as a political territorial or civic nation as the nation of and for all its citizens, regardless of language and ethnicity, not as the nation of and for ethnic Uzbeks. Were this the prevailing self-understanding of Russians in Uzbekistan there would be no Russian "national minority". There would be persons of Russian ethnic origin and persons speaking Russian as a native language but they would not claim to be members of the Russian nation or nationality. However, unfortunately, this is hardly the dominant notion, particularly in the face of the policies of the "nationalizing" state.

The question of "national minorities" thus has to be essentially examined against that of the state, which designates them as the minority. R. Brubaker refers to these states as "nationalizing" states to emphasize that what is being referred to, is once again, a dynamic political stance.

> Characteristic of this stance or set of stances is the tendency to see the state as an "unrealized" nation-state, as a state destined to be a nation-state, the state of and for a particular nation, but not yet in fact a nation-state (at least not to a sufficient degree); and the concomitant disposition to remedy this perceived defect, to make the state what it is properly and legitimately destined to be by promoting the language, culture, demographic position, economic flourishing or political hegemony of the nominally state bearing nation.[40]

The important point about the "nationalizing" state is perhaps the fact that it is not one whose "representatives, authors or agents understand and articulate it as such, but rather one that is perceived as such in the field of the national minority."

The problem in Uzbekistan, as in all the other states, is the creation of a "national identity". Yet, to a very large extent there remains even today a sense of uneasiness about this new found "nationalism" and "national identity". Amidst this uncertainty is a persistent effort to stress on the "Uzbekness" of the nation, particularly in the official political rhetoric "... a feature distinctive of Uzbekistan is its original ethnic structure. Although representatives of more than 100 nations and ethnic groups live on the territory of the Republic, the majority of the inhabitants are Uzbeks".[41]

There is also an attempt to point out that the Uzbek Republic is the homeland of all Uzbeks." Since the territory of Uzbekistan is virtually the only domain of Uzbek national statehood, the Republic is called upon to become a cultural and spiritual centre for all Uzbeks irrespective of their domicile. Citizenship in the Republic is open to all Uzbeks who themselves or whose predecessors had to emigrate from Uzbekistan, during the tragic circumstances of the past."[42] This nationalizing stance of President Islam Karimov was possibly also prompted by a need to neutralize the national character of the opposition platform. Also, scholars like Kadir Alimov have pointed out "there can be little doubt that all the individual Muslim inhabitants of the territory, now known as Uzbekistan, have a strong attachment to their homeland and its Islamic culture".[43] The propaganda of the "titular ethno-nationalists" is based on the fact that there exists an ancient Uzbek nation to which the indigenous population of Uzbekistan belong and that Uzbeks live on the territory of their nation state. Elements of this history, which seek to emphasize a long suppressed and dormant Uzbek identity, have the potential to aggravate relations with the numerous ethnic minorities residing in Uzbekistan. In common with all the new states, Uzbekistan is faced with a difficult conundrum : it must simultaneously promote and implement a rediscovered history to the satisfaction of the people, while restraining those elements from pursuing an overzealous application of Uzbek ethnic identity.

While the need for preservation of national culture is clearly stated, statements with regard to ethnic rights are much more generally worded. "Uzbekistan is a state which ensures the rights and freedoms of all citizens irrespective of their ethnic origin, religious beliefs, social status or political conviction," or "the protection of the interests and rights of ethnic minorities by creating guarantees for the preservation and development of their cultures, language national, customs and traditions and participation in the activities of the government as well as public life".[44] These generalizing statements serve the purpose of ignoring the existence of any ethnic problem.

The ethnic identity of Russians and their attitudes to ethnic relations have changed significantly with the collapse of the Soviet Union. According to Leokadia Drobizheva three factors played a role in this (1) the shock of losing their status as the ruling nation (2) the political struggle in which leading groups want to rely on ethnic patriotism (3) the sharp rise in ethnic competition in the social and working spheres.[45] Whereas the Russians lost their ruling status in 1988-89 and were drawn into the political struggle in the last few years ethnic competition had begun to be felt even earlier. The abrupt end of Russian dominance means that they are now having to think hard about their Russian identity, something they always took for granted. The questions that seem to be uppermost in their minds today are—can they be full citizens of Russia and of another Republic simultaneously? And where exactly do Russia's borders end? [46]

Russian ethnic attitudes in Central Asia today are "complex and tense" for here there have been no great shift in political or economic position with Soviet era leaders having changed stance to retain power. However the fact remains that 36 per cent of the workers in heavy industry are Russians. Russian education standards are higher than Uzbeks, a significant proportion of Russians, 48 per cent are professionals and there is no competition in management. By 1970 Muslims accounted for only 51.15 per cent of all industrial workers in Uzbekistan, 44.3 per cent in Tajikistan, 31.2 per cent in Kyrgyzstan, 31:1 per cent in

Turkmenistan, and 24.1 per cent in Kazakhstan. In Uzbekistan, Uzbeks accounted for 36.25 per cent of the overall industrial labour force, and even less in many essential fields: 18.35 per cent in machine building, 20 per cent in chemical and petrochemical industries and 22.45 per cent in oil refining. 1973 data shows a slight improvement: 39.95 per cent in the total labour force, 20.7 per cent in machine building, 29.5 per cent in oil refining, 26.4 per cent in chemicals and petrochemicals. What is more serious is that no significant progress had been achieved since 1967, inspite of educational advancement.[47]

Results of representative cross-cultural investigations carried out in 1970-71, 1980-81, 1988 and 1991 showed that while previously a majority of Russians had been satisfied with their work and viewed their life optimistically now a majority do not think so. Also a larger percentage now consider working in ethnically mixed groups difficult. About 70 per cent now oppose mixed marriages, twice as much as ten years ago. By the end of 1991, 80-90 per cent of Russians in Tashkent felt that ethnic attitudes had deteriorated, and 70-80 per cent expected further problems. Also Russians feared the rise of Islam and were terrified by the events of Ferghana, Namangan and Osh.[48]

There is also rising ethnic consciousness among Russians whose cultural adaptation has never been very high.[49] That the assimilation of ethnic Russians is weak was reflected in a study conducted in January–February 1992, which recorded the responses of children of old Russian inhabitants and Uzbeks in Tashkent. The author has used the responses of the children to show that children followed ethnic characteristics in their choice. This has been interpreted as a sign of the cultural distance between the two groups.[50] On the other hand despite the presence of large Slavic and other minorities in the state, Uzbeks found it difficult to name even a few social traditions of the another ethnic group.[51] A majority of Russians in Uzbekistan feel that there should be two state languages in Uzbekistan, not just Uzbek.

There is, as Roger Brubaker points out, a triadic relationship between the "national minorities" the "nationalizing states" and the "external national homeland" in the perception of the minority concerned. A homeland is not necessarily where the minority or their ancestors once lived. "Homeland" is a political category. A state becomes an external national homeland for its ethnic diaspora when a claim is made that they belong in some sense to the state and assert that their interests must be protected by the state.[52]

For the Yeltsin government, the problem of the Russian diaspora outside Russia has grown steadily in importance since 1993, and is likely to influence Russia's relations with these states. Through most of 1992 the Yeltsin government showed little or no interest in Central Asia due to political as well as economic reasons. During the next phase (much of 1993) Russia began to assume a major role in the CIS and decided it best to include the Central Asian Republics within the CIS. The third phase was from late 1993 when Russian policies were largely driven by domestic politics.[53]

Yeltsin's role in recasting and redefining the role of ethnic Russians, within the "inner" Soviet empire, has been pivotal. By officially declaring that "it was necessary to put our relations with those republics on a juridical foundation" and thus recognizing the sovereignty and existing boundaries of the republics, he contributed to rendering Russians living in those areas "foreigners". By decisively opting for Russian nation building he also implicitly recognized the other Republics.[54]

Russians in these post Soviet states, who now feel "betrayed" by the people of the state they considered home, are increasingly looking to Russia for assistance. The poem "Where are you, Russian Star?" clearly brings out a strong desire among Russians in the 'near abroad' for intervention on the part of Russia in their favour.[55] For the new reality involves not just such problems as dual citizenship but also ones like that faced by Russian women married into Central Asian families who now feel like foreigners.

That the plight of the Russians in the post Soviet states evokes emotional response is clear from this letter to the editor of the Moscow News, "all present territories and regions, where Russians are numerically predominant in the local population, should be Russia's integral and inseparable parts."[56]

The massive effort at politicization of space that has resulted due to the emergence of "nationalizing" states in Central Asia has meant that a number of changes are now underway in the states. One of the most significant is the proclamation of new language laws in the states, establishing the legal hegemony of local languages over Russian. This has meant that the socio-professional status of the Russian population is seen as being threatened in the newly independent states. It is significant to keep in mind that the integration of the Russian population within the Central Asian societies was low. In particular, most of the Russian population never felt the need to learn the local languages. This today means that in the face of introduction of new language laws, the possibility of discrimination is higher. Here, the most commonly heard complaint is that the possibility of finding jobs and prospects of promotion has been significantly reduced in the aftermath of independence of the Republics. Also there are doubts about the future of children particularly since the ability of acquire the Central Asian languages has now become very important as the use of Russian for all official purposes is likely to be reduced.

This is clearly evident from what Alla Chervova notes:

> The number of Russian schools will be reduced, Russian will no longer be used in business correspondence and so the demand for Russian language teachers will fall. Russian will gradually lose its present social status, particularly the female teachers will have to go for less meaningful jobs.[57]

While the outmigration of Russian population from the Central Asian Republics to the RSFSR had begun by the end of the 1980's, there is also the understanding among the Russian population that Russians in the Central Asian Republics are different from the Russians living in Russia. This is because their domestic lifestyle has assimilated much of what is characteristic of the Central Asian way of life. In fact on migrating to Russia they are identified as "Kyrgyz Russians" or "Uzbek Russians". Life in Russia is difficult and more often than not job prospects are low. Moreover, for most of the migrating Russians, Moscow and Russia were alien regions and their sense of displacement is magnified by the fact that integration into Russian society in Russia is proving to be difficult.

In general the impression is that of not wanting to go anywhere but to continue living in Uzbekistan, since life in Russia is said to be even more difficult. This has led to a tragedy that is reflected in these words of Natasha, a schoolteacher in Samarkand.

> It is not a question of returning to Russia. I have never lived there. I was born and brought up in Samarkand and my parents have lived here most of their lives and are committed to it. I love this place and my whole life is here. I don't look forward to going to Russia. I hardly know it, I hate Moscow... Increasingly we are being looked upon as foreigners and I do not think it will be long before we hear shouts of "Russians go home.[58]

Similar sentiments are expressed by most who now feel displaced:

> I myself grew up in an Uzbek mohallah and the question of where to live has simply not arisen until now. The point is not the state language — to a certain extent it is possible to learn Uzbek, even at my age, the point is different— a question of one's homeland. It would be strange to suddenly find oneself an emigrant, it is something entirely unexpected. Yes, this is our home, we have many people dear to us here, one has passed one's whole life here. But life is just not going to be the same here as it was before....we have many friends, people of many nationalities. And they have passed a good citizenship law. But I see my future as living in

> Russia. Not because someone is making me leave...I am not certain that my opinions will count when decisions regarding my fate are being made. I know that in Russia it would not be easy for me either, because there too are strong vestiges of the old regime. But I believe that nevertheless, I need to be in my homeland, although in my heart I will always retain a great love for Uzbekistan.[59]

A sizeable proportion of the Russian women living in the cities of Uzbekistan today were born in Central Asia. They have memories of their fathers or grandfathers who had fought and sacrificed here during the Revolution and also for most of them their parents or grandparents are buried here. Yet, while recognizing that having been born here, this is their "homeland", most of them also point to the fact that having been infused, since childhood with Russian culture, Russia is also "homeland". In fact many point out that this cultural difference is so significant that the sense of Central Asia being "homeland" is significantly reduced. The ambiguity and uncertainty that pervades is evident from responses to a study that sought to interpret the recent changes in the lives of Central Asian women.[60]

That this sense of duality is being felt by the younger groups of Russian women also and among those who were born in the region is evident from the reply of a young student at the Tashkent Institute of communications, while answering the same question:

> Uzbekistan is my homeland, it is difficult for me to imagine that I could be able to live elsewhere. My home, friends and relatives are all here. But neither is Russia an alien country... I have always found that Russians in Central Asia differ from Russians in Russia itself. My elder sister and her husband left four years ago for the Orenburg region. They are very depressed...I do not want to go anywhere, The main problem for me is the language, even though at the daily level, I do not have any problems with it. But if it came to using Uzbek for my professional work, it would be very

> difficult for me. Life in Uzbekistan differs from life in Russia and is dictated by another way of doing things, another way of thinking.[61]

The last decade has shown that in diaglossic societies, like the Central Asian one, abrupt changes in language usage is improbable. While this largely negates the most significant difficultly identified by the Russian women in the Central Asian region, yet, the sense of displacement, that has now become pervasive, means that most echo the desire to repatriate to Russia. In a process of what is termed as "hidden migration" many of the younger generation are migrating to Russia with the hope of the older members of the families following subsequently. There are other instances of "hidden migration" where Russian women, born and brought up in the Central Asian states, are marrying men settled in Russia in order to migrate. A search for "homeland" thus continues to be one of the fallouts of the politicization of space that accompanies the process of nationalization of states.

There is also a sense of unease about the future of children. Galina Pugachenkova, clearly states "...for my children and grandchildren there is no future here."[62] Vallentina Artemova, similarly notes :

> I have no specific ideas about my future. I would like to leave but my husband and his parents do not want this. The children are growing up, one needs to think about them. But here I have an apartment and interesting work. I love the climate here and the people are also warm. Here things are peaceful. In Russia even though it is my homeland, no one will look out for us and we would have to start everything afresh.[63]

Reiterating the "civilizational" position, scholars like Alexei Malashenko have noted that any evaluation of Central Asian responses to Russia would have to be premised on an understanding of this difference.[64] He points to the inability of Soviet Russia in conducting a dialogue with the Islamic parts of the former Union and to the survival of syncretic Islam in the Central Asian region as significant. The reemergence of this ethno-religious identity in the immediate post Soviet phase was also indicative of a "civilizational" break. Along with this was the reorientation of the historical memory of these people and an increasing cultural difference. Therefore, Malashenko argues, the turning away of Central Asia from Russia began in the very first years after the dissolution of the Soviet Union, with the disillusion with the way the Belovezhskaia Agreements were formulated. It was apparent in the refusal of the proposal for the creation of a Eurasian Union that was mooted by President Nursultan Nazarbaev. At the root of this was apparently the Central Asian confidence about foreign assistance on the basis of the hydrocarbon resources of the region and prospects for the integration within the region. How far such arguments remain valid will now be briefly examined.

"New" Directions for Central Asia: The Central Asian Response

The immediate post Soviet days saw the emergence of a debate around whether the Central Asian Republics would now opt for greater integration with the Turkic world or whether linkages with Russia and the newly independent states of the former Soviet Union, in the form of the CIS, would remain the priority thrust area. Since the Uzbek declaration of independence, for instance, the place of the new state in the world order has been the subject of debate. Can Uzbekistan be considered part of the Turkic world or say the Islamic world? Is it at all a part of the Orient or are the ties with its old political centre, Moscow, still strong enough to warrant its place as part of the western world? This signified once again the duality of perceptions based on a "civilizational" difference between the two regions. In order to examine the so called "new" directions of policy it is necessary to first briefly examine the continuing significance of a "Turkic" dimension of Central Asian policy and the possibilities of the emergence of a "Turkic" confederation.

While "Turkestan" finds appeal among the intelligentsia of the region, due to the renaissance that the Jadidist ideas have received in the region, it is also true that historically the Central Asian region as a whole has never been united, except for brief periōds under Chengiz Khan and then under Timur. The rival Uzbek and Kazakh clans traditionally fought for power, while even within the Khanates there were dissensions. Culturally also the languages of the region diversified and the Soviet policy of creation of separate nationalities has ensured that the language groups now recognize their distinctiveness. While the Turkic languages still share a large vocabulary in common and many basic grammatical features, it is also true that Turkish is no longer the *lingua franca* in the region. Russian is used as a link language today. The unity of the Turks had been rejected even by advocates of Pan Turkism like Zia Gokalp, who in his *The Principles of Turkism*, showed more caution about the form of unity likely to be achieved and pointed out that the immediate goal was the cultural unity of the Oghuz or Turkmen people alone, whose language was closest to modern Turki, thus excluding other groups as the Uzbeks.[65]

In such a background, it was pointed out that a Central Asian federation could only develop on the basis of common economic requirements of the states. Unfortunately in most cases the requirements of the states overlap. As a result there is very little enthusiasm for integration on an economic level. This is also the reason why the arguments put forward for a European Union type integration is not viewed with enthusiasm. The idea of integration is thus most likely to remain a romantic dream with poets like Jamal Kamal, reiterating :

> ...our country is known as Turkestan, we are all Turkish peoples. What is Uzbek/ it is only one branch of the Turkish tree. Our real name is "Turkish". In Great Britain and the West this region is known as Central Asia. But in reality it is Turkestan. .... Turkestan consists of different countries. I hope in future there will be a federation between the republics, economic and cultural.[66]

While this romantic vision of a united "Turkestan" may no longer be viable, even the Uzbek President, Islam Karimov, on the occasion of the opening of Kazakh day in Tashkent, in 1995, reiterated similar visions of a common Uzbek and Kazakh homeland in "Turan". He went on to say that just as in the past the Kazakh/Uzbek boundaries were not divided, God willing, in the future there would be no such divisions.[67] He then went on to say that if the Kazakhs and the Uzbeks stayed together then there could be no power on earth capable of breaking this harmony. He cited the poet Gafur Gulam " ...we are two pages of the same book".[68]

In the background of this discussion about the possibility of the emergence of Turkish identity in the region, an examination of the development of Russo-Uzbek relations becomes interesting. Here once again a change is clearly evident in the changed rhetoric about Russian interests in the region. In the immediate post independence days, the requirement for strengthening its security in the south induced Uzbekistan to enter into a military alliance with Russia. However, while collaborating militarily, reservations were expressed about Russia's June 1994 draft mutual security pact for the CIS and also about Russia's proposals for dual citizenship. Uzbekistan also criticized Yeltsin's attempts to centralize the CIS around Moscow. President Karimov made energy independence a priority and laid more than 600 miles of pipelines a year to lessen dependence on Russia. Steps were also initiated to use the natural gas from Bukhara for local needs rather than pipe it to Russia.[69]

It is also significant to note that the projection of Uzbek policy towards Russia has also been modified over the past decade. It is interesting that writing in 1993, President Islam Karimov had begun his foreign policy initiatives by pointing to the importance of the "... development of direct and multilateral relations with the signatories of the CIS" and the "...development and consolidation of equitable relations with Russia and reliance on its potential".[70] By 1997, this priority had been vastly reduced.

Here, President Karimov begins by pointing to the significance of participation in the UNO, then the international financial and economic organizations, like the IMF and the World Bank, the European Union, the OSCE, NATO, close cooperation with other international organizations primarily from the Asian region bilateral contacts with the United States of America, relations with other European countries, and finally relations that are shaped between the countries of the former Soviet Union. [71]

President Karimov had also voiced his dissatisfaction about comments regarding revision in the status of the post Soviet independent states in certain sections of the Russian press. He also critiqued the projection of intra-regional integration within the Central Asian states as a possible "threat from the south" for Russia. Karimov has quoted Yeltsin's position that "the restoration of the former Union will turn out to be a tragedy" as correct and noted that equal relations between the CIS states should be the foundation of interrelations between Russia and Uzbekistan. He notes:

> Criticizing the great power chauvinism and aggressive nationalism, we, here in Uzbekistan, stand for the development of qualitatively new relations on the territory of the former Soviet Union and first and foremost with Russia. We have centuries old links of friendship, brotherhood and mutual assistance with that country and its great people.[72]

President Karimov's cautious attitude towards the development of integration with the CIS did not go unnoticed. In a message, passed on during a visit to Uzbekistan by the then Prime Minister Viktor Chernomyrdin, the then Russian President Boris Yeltsin remarked, "we are concerned about the position of the Uzbeki side on the issues of integration within the CIS framework and its approach to the function of the bodies and institutions of the Commonwealth. We regard any attempt of our partners to accuse us of imperial ambitions or of intervening in the internal affairs of our friends with sincere pain."[73] The Uzbek state declared in February 1999 that it would not renew its membership in the Collective Security Treaty of the Commonwealth of Independent States. However, it also declared that this would not in any way affect the bilateral arrangements with countries of the CIS. Moscow reacted to this by pointing out that it was the sovereign right of every nation to decide whether it wanted to be a part of any collective treaty. And this was projected as a signal reflecting a more independent stance of politics in the Eurasian region.

However, President Putin's support of President Karimov's hardline policies led to a rapprochement of Russo-Uzbek relations. President's Karimov's hardline anti militant policies have been endorsed by President Putin, who has himself assumed such an approach towards Chechnya.[74] The meeting between Putin and Karimov towards the end of December 1999 made this clear. Karimov publicly stated that he "recognized Russia's interests in Uzbekistan".[75]

In the post September 11 period, with the increasingly active involvement of the United States in the region, Central Asian responses occasionally reflected a movement out of traditional spheres of influence.[76] In this connection an article in the Tajik newspaper *Biznes i Politika*, is interesting. [77] Reacting to State Duma Speaker Gennadiy Seleznev's statement that "Russia must increase its presence in Central Asia", the article questions Russian motives in making such a statement and the methods that Russia would employ to ensure its presence. It also calls for embarking on a qualitatively new level in the relationship.

Despite such variations in policy statements it is, perhaps, significant to take note of the numerous continuing invisible connections that till date remain significant in an examination of Russo-Central Asian relations. All across the territory of the former Soviet Union, for instance, there is still a single Russian speaking elite, which shares a common set of old, political ties and connections. This is an objective reality and remains an important factor in cementing relations between segments of the population in Russia and Central Asia. In fact a nuanced reading of the way relations between the two regions will develop would have to take note of this and other such social patterns that are located below the political surface but which nonetheless shapes the institutional functioning of a society.

It is also significant to keep in mind that there are numerous perspectives on Russia's position in the region. Konstantin Syroezhkin, Deputy Director at the Kazakhstan Institute of Strategic Studies, concludes his study of Russian policy in Central Asia in these words:

> Is this situation hopeless? In the author's view, disregarding the linkage between the limited capabilities of Russia and its changed geopolitical environment, it is not....the internal problems of the states of Central Asia are not likely to be resolved without the participation of Russia. In Russia itself, judging by recent publications there, an understanding is developing of the extent of the threatened loss of its geopolitical influence in the post Soviet space and of the need to strengthen Russia's position in a southerly direction.
>
> The reestablishment and consolidation of the Russian presence in the region and an end to tendencies unfavourable for Russia are possible if a coordinated policy of dynamic and flexible balancing within the framework of a real power balance in the region, taking into account Russia's much reduced capabilities, is pursued.[78]

Rather interestingly Syroezhkin points to Makinder's position of the Central Asian region as the "geographical pivot of history" to demonstrate the geopolitical significance of the region to Russia.

The Tajik position, on developing integration processes within the post Soviet space and specially maintaining close ties with Russia, has been based on the compulsions of internal conflicts within the state and the reality of long borders with Afghanistan. As such Tajikistan has shown interest in strengthening the CIS. Mouzaffar Olimov, Professor at the Tajik State National

University, notes that in general the people of Tajikistan admit that their country is in the Russian foreign policy orbit and in the sphere of Russia's national interests. However, he goes on to note that, since economic, humanitarian and cultural ties are scant and military cooperation very extensive, the long-term prospect of cooperation between the two countries is not very firm.[79]

The continuities and discontinuities in Russia's Central Asian policy, in the transition from a geo-cultural and old imperial mode to a mode dictated by globalization, shows that while elements from the old Russian imperial policy remain active and crucial in today's policy, yet the partial dissolution of the old ties and the "unburdening" of Russia becomes necessary, in the configuration of the new Russianness. Here, the old Soviet ideology is inadequate in defining the new nationalism. Yet, the "unburdening" has not, to date, justified a complete disavowal of the recent past. Hence, the modern dilemma, which is possibly best exemplified in the economic sphere.

NOTES AND REFERENCES

1. Cited from Taras Kuzio and Sergei Blagov, "GUUAM Makes a Comeback Bid—US Support", *Eurasia Insight*, July 7, 2003.
2. For details see Zamira Eshanova, "Central Asia: Diplomatic Visits Highlight US-Russian Competition," *RFE/RL Report*, 3 December 2002.
3. See for instance, Andrei Kortunov and Andrei Shoumikhin, "Russia and Central Asia: Evolution of Mutual Perceptions, Policies and Interdependence", in Yongjin Zang and Rouben Azizan (eds) *Ethnic Challenges Beyond Borders, Chinese and Russian Perspectives of the Central Asian Conundrum*, London: Macmilian in association with St Antony's College, Oxford, 1998.
4. Sergei Gretsky, *Russia's Policy Towards Central Asia*, Washington D.C.: Carnegie Moscow Centre, 1997.
5. Boris Rumer (ed) *Central Asia in Transition: Dilemmas of Political and Economic Development*, New York and London: M.E. Sharpe, 1996.

6. For details of the debates and the key ideas and views underlying the foreign policy orientation see Nicole J. Jackson, *Russian Foreign Policy and the CIS: Theories, debates and actions*, London and New York: Routledge, 2003.

7. See *Nezavisimaya Gazeta*, 12 January, 1994.

8. For a detailed discussion see Jackson, *Russian Foreign Policy and the CIS.* Jackson identifies them as reformists with liberal western orientation, communists with fundamentalist nationalist orientation and centrists with pragmatic nationalist orientation.

9. Irina D Zviagelskaya, "Russia's Policy Options in Central Asia", in Gennady Chufrin (ed) *Russia and Asia:The Emerging Security Agenda*, New York: OUP, 1999.

10. F.M. Dostoyevsky, *Dnevnik Pisatelya: Sobraniye Sochinenii*, Vol 14, cited from Zviagelskaya, "Russia's Policy Options in Central Asia".

11. For a detailed discussion see Gretsky, *Russia's Policy Towards Central Asia.*

12. Igor V. Podberezsky, "Between Europe and Asia: The Search for Russia's Civilizational Identity" in Chufrin (ed) *Russia and Asia:The Emerging Security Agenda.*

13. Podberezsky, "Between Europe and Asia: The Search for Russia's Civilizational Identity".

14. Manuel Sarkisyanz,"Russian Conquest in Central Asia: Transformation and Acculturation", in Wayne S. Vucinich (ed) *Russia and Asia - Essays on the Influence of Russia on the Asian People*, Hoover Institute Press, 1972.

15. Sarkisyanz,"Russian Conquest in Central Asia".

16. For details of Nikolai Truetskoi's writings and the views of other Eurasianists see Madhavan Palat,"Eurasianism as an Ideology for Russia's Future", *Economic and Political Weekly*, Special Number, December 18, 1993.

17. For a detailed discussion of this see Milan Hauner, *What is Asia To Us? Russia's Asian Heartland Yesterday and Today*, Boston: Unwin Hyman, 1990.

18. Podberezsky, "Between Europe and Asia: The Search for Russia's Civilizational Identity".

19. Hauner, *What is Asia To Us*?.

20. For a detailed study see Zviagelskaya, "Russia's Policy Options in Central Asia".

21. For details on why the Central Asian leaders decided to join the CIS see, Bakhtior A. Islamov," Post Soviet Central Asia and the Commonwealth of Independent States", in Beatrice Manz (ed) *Central Asia in Historical Perspective*, Westview Press: Boulder, 1994. Here it is pointed out that the primary reason for this was economic and the result of the administrative command integration, set up in the Soviet period.

22. See *Nezavisimaya Gazeta*, 13 May, 1993.

23. See *Argumenty and Fakty*, 26 June, 1993.

24. Elizabeth Kridl Valkenier "Russian Policies in Central Asia : Change or Continuity," *SAIS Review*, Vol 14, (2) Summer-Fall 1994.

25. Gretsky, *Russia's Policy Towards Central Asia.*

26. Gretsky, *Russia's Policy Towards Central Asia.*

27. Cited from Chufrin (ed) *Russia and Asia, The Emerging Security Agenda.*

28. Chufrin (ed) *Russia and Asia, The Emerging Security Agenda.*

29. Jackson in *Russian Foreign Policy and the CIS*, outlines three key stages through which foreign policy moved. In the first (August 1991-March 1992) debate and policy were characterized by the domination of liberal westernist ideas. In the second phase (March 1992-November 1993) multiple ideas were entertained and pragmatic nationalism became prominent in foreign policy debate. During the third (November 1993-June 1996) debate and government rhetoric were dominated by pragmatic nationalism. There was broad agreement that Russia should remain involved in its "natural sphere of influence" though the negative consequences and costs of this involvement was also aired. Policies were focused on particular interests and specific actions and their success varied depending on the particular case.

30. For details see "Russia Frets Over Islamic Militants", *Asia Times Online*, August 29, 2000.

31. Tamara Makarenko,"Russian Language in Kyrgyzstan: Balancing the Security with Economics", *Central Asia and Caucasus Analyst*, May 10, 2000.

32. For details see Robert O. Freedman, "Russia and Central Asia Under Yeltsin", *Central Asia Monitor*, No 4, 1996.

33. Zviagelskaya, "Russia's Policy Options in Central Asia".

34. For details see Kambiz Arman,"US Geopolitical Position Takes Hit in Tajikistan", *Eurasia Insight*, July 21, 2004.

35. A. Akimov,"Rossiya- Tsentralnaya Azia: Perspectivy Ekonomichiskoi Integratsi", *Aziya i Africa Segodniya*, No 6, 1994.

36. For a detailed examination see Ichiro Iwasaki, "The Initial Phase of Transition of Russo Central Asian Economic Relations- An Institutional Approach", *Islamic Area Studies Working Paper Series*, No 11, Islamic Area Studies Project, Tokyo, Japan.

37. For detailed figures of Russia's trade with the Central Asian republics (1991-1996) see Zviagelskaya, "Russia's Policy Options in Central Asia".

38. C.A. Macartney points out

> in almost every aspect of social existence, there will be found a majority and a minority ..... Practically every state in the world contains minorities. But so long as the state confines itself to strictly political functions thus serving equally all nations belonging to it, it is impossible to speak of the national minority in the true sense of the term. A minority becomes a "national minority", properly speaking, only when its national aspiration conflicts with those of the state." Thus notions of majority and minority are highly variable.
>
> (C.A. Macartney, *National States and National Minorities*, London: Oxford University Press, 1934.)
>
> Roger Brubaker in the course of his detailed discussion of the situation in Yugoslavia points out:
>
> "A national minority is not something that is given by facts of

ethnic demography. It is a dynamic political stance or more precisely a family of related yet mutually competing stances not a static ethnodemographic condition. Three elements are characteristic of this political stance or family of stances 1) the public claim to membership of an ethnocultural nation different from the numerically or politically dominant ethnocultural nation 2) the demand for state recognition of this distinct ethnocultural nationality and 3) the assertion on the basis of this ethnocultural nationality of certain collective cultural and or political rights...."

(Roger Brubaker, "National Minorities, Nationalizing States, and External National Homelands in the New Europe", *Daedalus*, Vol 124 (2) Spring 1993.)

Similarly, A. Khazanov points out :

"Minority and majority statuses are more than just a matter of the arithmetic proportion of various ethnic groups within a certain state. It is also a matter as to who holds the political power, and whose language and culture occupies the dominant position in the state. Ethnic minority statuses is an empirical reality based on the non dominant, and at times the outright subjugated position of an ethnic group (nationality) in a state as well as on its wish to preserve and enhance its separate status and, as a rule, on the state's recognition or non recognition of this status."

(Anatoly Khazanov, *After the USSR- Ethnicity, Nationalism and Politics in the Commonwealth of Independent States*, London: The University of Wisconsin Press, 1995)

39. Conversation with Russians in Tashkent clearly indicated this. A series of informal meetings, of the present scholar, with one of the departmental heads of the *Fundamantalnaya Biblioteyeka* of the Academy of Sciences, (name withheld on request) an ethnic Russian, clearly brought this out. She was born in Uzbekistan and has lived in Tashkent for most of her life. More significantly her father and grandfather are buried here. But she does not speak the local language, though this, according to her, did not affect her relations with the local people. Her sense of belonging, however has been affected in recent times.

40. Brubaker, "National Minorities, Nationalizing States and External National Homelands".

41. Islam A Karimov, *Uzbekistan— The Road of Independence and Progress*, New Delhi, 1993.

42. Karimov, *Uzbekistan— The Road of Independence and Progress.*

43. Kadir Z. Alimov, "The Rediscovery of Uzbek History and its Foreign Policy Implications", in Fredrick Starr (ed) *The Legacy of History in Russia and the New States of Eurasia*, New York: M.E. Sharpe, 1994.

44. Karimov, *Uzbekistan—The Road of Independence and Progress.*

45. Leokadia Drobizhyeva, "Russian Ethnic Attitudes in Changing Political Situations," *Economic and Political Weekly*, Special Number, December 18, 1995.

46. Conversation with Dmitri A. Trofimov, the Russian First Secretary, at the Russian Embassy in Tashkent on 12 March, 1998, at the Russian Embassy in Tashkent, clearly indicated Russian attitudes towards Central Asians.

47. Michael Rywkin "Cadre Competition in Uzbekistan, Ethnic Aspects," *Central Asian Survey*, Vol 5, No 3\4, 1986.

48. Drobizhyeva, "Russian Ethnic Attitudes".

49. This proved to be correct in the course of conversations with Russians in the city. There seems to be general dissatisfaction with the economic situation, which Russians realise is being faced by Uzbeks also. But whereas the Uzbeks see this as an inevitable process in the course of transition, the Russians view it in less optimistic terms.

50. A. Selebyerstova, "Deti Russkikh Starozhelov v Uzbekistane" *Vostok*, No 2, 1994.

51. Reuel Hanks, "The Islamic factor in Nationalism and Nation Building in Uzbekistan- Causative Agent or Inhibitor?", *Nationalities Papers*, Vol 22 (2), 1994.

52. Brubaker notes:

   ....the concept of external national homeland...denotes a dynamic political stance or again a family of related yet competing stances - not a static condition - not a distinct "thing". Common to homeland stances are the axiom of shared nationhood across the boundaries of state and citizenship and the idea that this shared nationhood makes the state responsible, in some sense not only for its own citizens but also for ethnic co-nationals who live in other states and possess other citizenship.... But there is a great variation among particular homeland stances, great variation in understandings of just what the asserted responsibility for ethnic co-nationals entail. Should ethnic co-nationals, living as minorities in other states, be given moral support? What sort of ties and relations with the homeland or mother country should be fostered? What sort of immigration and citizenship privileges, if any, should co-ethnics abroad be offered? What sort of stance should they be encouraged to take vis-a-vis the states in which they live. And what sort of stance should the homeland adopt towards those states. How forcefully should it press its concerns about their policies towards minorities? What weight should those concerns be given in shaping the homeland state's overall relations towards the states in which co-ethnics live?

(Brubaker, "National Minorities, Nationalizing States and External National Homelands")

53. Valkenier "Russian Policies in Central Asia : Change or Continuity" .

54. For Yeltsin's views see John Dunlop," Russians Confronting A Loss of Empire— 1987-1991," *Political Science Quarterly*, Vol 108 (4) Winter 1993-94.

55. Where are you Russian Star
Will you hide long in the mist Russian star
Or by some optical trick
Will you reveal yourself forever.

FBIS-SOV, May 2, 1995.

56. *Moscow News*, No 5, February 4-10, 1994.

57. Alla Chervova, in Marfua Tokhtakhodjaeva and Elmira Turgumbekova, *The Daughters of Amazons: Voices from Central Asia* (translated from Russian by Sufian Aslam), Lahore: Shirkat

Gah Women's Resource Centre, 1996.

58. Trevour Fishlock, *Out of Red Darkness, Reports from the Collapsing Soviet Empire*, London: John Murray, 1992.

59. Elena Topornina in Tokhtakhodjaeva and Turgumbekova, *The Daughters of Amazons: Voices from Central Asia.*

60. Tokhtakhodjaeva and Turgumbekova, *The Daughters of Amazons: Voices from Central Asia.*

61. Olga Egunova, in Tokhtakhodjaeva and Turgumbekova, *The Daughters of Amazons: Voices from Central Asia.*

62. Galina Pugachenkova in Tokhtakhodjaeva and Turgumbekova, *The Daughters of Amazons: Voices from Central Asia.*

63. Vallentina Artemova, in Tokhtakhodjaeva and Turgumbekova, *The Daughters of Amazons: Voices from Central Asia.*

64. Alexei Malashenko,"Turning Away from Russia: New Directions for Central Asia", in Bruno Coppieters, Alexei Zverev and Dimitri Trenin (eds) *Commonwealth and Independence in Post Soviet Eurasia*, London: Portland; Frank Cass, 1998.

65. Zia Gokalp, *The Principles of Turkism*, Leiden: E.J. Brill, 1992.

66. Cited from Antony Hymen, "Turkestan and Pan Turkism Revisited", *Central Asian Survey*, Vol 16, No 3, 1997.

67. Islam A. Karimov," Yedinstvo Proshlovo i Budushyevo" in *Turkestan Nash Obshei Dom*, Tashkent: "Uzbekiston", 1995.

68. Karimov, "Yedinstvo Proshlovo i Budushyevo".

69. For details see, S. Frederick Starr, "Making Eurasia Stable", *Foreign Affairs*, January/February Vol 75 No 1, 1996.

70. I.A. Karimov, *Uzbekistan: The Road of Independence and Progress.*

71. Islam A Karimov, *Uzbekistan on the Threshold of the 21st Century: Threats to Security, Conditions of Stability and Guarantees of Progress*, Tashkent: Uzbekiston, 1997.

72. Karimov, *Uzbekistan on the Threshold of the 21st Century.*

73. "Poslaniye Prezidentu", *Pravda Vostoka*, Tashkent, December 31,

1997, cited from Vitaly V. Naumkin, "The Emerging Geopolitical Balance in Central Asia: A Russian View" in Chufrin (ed) *Russia and Asia:The Emerging Security Agenda*.

74. Birgit Brauer, "Central Asia Readjusting to Life in Putin's Orbit", *Central Asia and Caucasus Analyst*, March 29, 2000; also see Sophie Lambroschini, "Central Asia: Russia Sanctioning Anti-Islamic Crackdown" *RFE/RL Report*, Moscow, 2 August, 2000.

75. See Robert M. Cutler," Russia Slouches Towards Central Asia," *Central Asia and Caucasus Analyst*, April 12, 2000. For further developments in Russia's relations with Uzbekistan see Chapter 3.

76. For a more detailed discussion on this see Chapter 3.

77. "Central Asian Nations May Prefer USA to Russia- Tajik Newspaper", *Tajikistan Daily Digest*, January 24, 2002, source *Biznes i Politika*, Dushanbe, January 18, 2002.

78. Konstantin Syroezhkin, "The Policy of Russia in Central Asia: A Perspective From Kazakhstan", in Chufrin (ed) *Russia and Asia: The Emerging Security Agenda*.

79. See Mouzaffar Olimov, "The Policy of Russia in Central Asia: A Perspective from Tajikistan", in Chufrin (ed) *Russia and Asia: The Emerging Security Agenda*.

Chapter 2

China, Central Asia and the Re-emergence of "Turkestan"

The "new international politics" of the region, that was historically known as Turkestan, is today once again portrayed as a reversal back to the politics of the mid 19th century, when a shadowy game for control over the region was played between two imperial powers, which was immortalized by Kipling as the "Great Game". The projected "geopolitical vacuum", that the region is now seen as facing, in addition to its unexplored mineral resources, and its predominant Islamic culture, meant that it was immediately identified as an arena for numerous "little games" in the post Soviet era.[1] The only difference is in the changed identity of the new players, among whom China is now seen as important.

In China, the new geopolitical landscape in Central Asia has been viewed as a mixed blessing. Three out of the five Central Asian Republics of the former Soviet Union now border China and China's common border with Russia has been significantly reduced, particularly in the northwest. While, on the one hand, the newly independent Central Asian states were seen as significant markets for Chinese goods, on the other, they were viewed as potentially destabilizing factors for China's Xinjiang Uighur Autonomous Region, which in turn was viewed as threatening to China's national security and territorial integrity. China was also faced with the problem of having to settle its territorial disputes with the newly independent states. On the other hand, China's regulated economy and secular status was projected as an attractive model for the pragmatic Central Asian regimes. China could also provide transit options that the states could exploit thereby cutting down Central Asian dependence on trade and transit routes through Russia.

Most writings examining developments in the relationship of the Central Asian states with China, in the years immediately following the declaration of their independence, therefore typically emphasized:

> China lost no time in recognizing and establishing diplomatic relations with all the five Central Asian states, which were seen as presenting opportunities as well as challenges. Beijing looks towards the region as a vast market for Chinese exports and has proposed joint venture projects and offered liberal economic aid and investment... Politically China seeks to exploit the inter-regional rivalries and contradictions to establish a strategic environment favourable to the Chinese interests. Strategically the challenge before China's defence planners is to secure their country's northwestern and southwestern frontiers, which are no longer as secure as they were in the days of the Soviet Union... Therefore China's main interest is to stop instability spilling over into the strategically important Muslim majority province of Xinjiang, which borders the Central Asian states.[2]

This rather neat summing up of the situation, however, ignored the nuances of changed political situations in the Central Asian region as also compulsions inherent in the definition of China as a player in this new "great game". As an onlooker's perspective of developments, it also failed to empathize with certain finer aspects of Central Asian reality, where imperatives of transition to newer forms in a vastly changed international context determined the direction that politics in these states assumed. A more realistic assessment of trends in the development of relationships would have to move beyond such definitions to an examination of linkages and identities between eastern and western *Turkestan*.

For China, the reemergence of the concept of *Turkestan* is

said to have assumed significance today in terms of development of its relationship with the Central Asian region. This is because both Chinese economic and strategic interests in the region are based upon the supposed fact that the populations in eastern Turkestan, i.e, Xinjiang and western Turkestan, i.e the Central Asian Republics share a common Turkic identity. This also stems partly from the fact that organizations and movements that today seek greater autonomy, in the Inner Asian regions, once again define themselves as a movement for *Eastern Turkestan*. While on the one hand the reemergence of this Turkic identity could revive linkages with kin groups across the borders and promote separatism, on the other the projection of these linkages could increase the significance of Xinjiang, as point of contact for increased economic and trade linkages. Most of the Uighur settlements have also historically been based along China's borders with the Central Asian states and this makes Xinjiang critical in China's engagement with the Central Asian region.

What is undeniable is that there is, today, remarkable fluidity across the region that was identified as Turkestan. Cross border contacts have achieved unprecedented levels, trade has boomed, inter ethnic relations have changed their nature and dimensions, transfrontier migratory movements have resumed and new transportation networks have begun to emerge. With changing economic patterns, a shifting strategic balance and a new geopolitical context, a number of issues along the borderlands of Turkestan have once again emerged as significant. The significance of this borderland is exemplified by the fact that Xinjiang's total international border is almost 5,600 kilometers long, which is a quarter of China's total land frontier. It shares 56 km with Russia, 1718 km with Kazakhstan, 980 km with Kyrgyzstan and about 450 km with Tajikistan.[3]

However, the emergence of a significant trend towards pan Turkism is suspect, both in the former Soviet Republics as well as in the Muslim lands of China. Pan Turkism had historically been confined to a minority of the population in the Khanates of

Central Asia. The oases of the Taklamakan had defined themselves as separate entities, with separate identities and Islam itself had numerous trends in the region. The opening of trade and intellectual borders today, seems to have reinstated the traditional hostilities between the oases and local identities have reemerged as significant rather than the emergence of any significant common pan Turkic identity. Also, economic linkages have their limitations as the regions on either sides of the border have competing rather than complimentary interests.

Since the Central Asian Republics are now independent states, with different and sometimes divergent foreign policies, flexible policies are now required to meet regional challenges. However, it is significant that while Central Asia became increasingly important in China's national security strategy and in the economic development of China's underdeveloped northwest, it remains peripheral to Chinese foreign policy. A major policy consideration here is recognition of Russia's interests in this region, which neither China nor the Central Asian Republics themselves can ignore.

It is in this background that China's position in the Central Asian region will be assessed. It is undeniable that China's policy towards the states of Central Asia is significantly influenced by developments within the Xinjiang Uighur Autonomous Region, as the province that shares its borders and ethnic patterns with the Central Asian states, and as such is capable of influencing the stability of political and economic environment of both the regions. Xinjiang is significant for China because of its strategically important geographical location and also as one of the largest oil bearing basins in the world. Xinjiang also has the potential to play an important role in the development of bilateral trade and economic link with the states of Central Asia. This is also partly because the different ethnic groups in Xinjiang share the same ethnicity with ethnic groups across the borders in the Central Asian states.

The chapter, therefore, begins by briefly examining pan Turkic trends in western and eastern Turkestan, Han Chinese presence in the region and a look at the ethnogenesis of the Uighurs before moving on to an examination of compulsions of Chinese policy in the region. Here, once again an emphasis on multilateralism is evident, with the Chinese recognition of the Russian influence and US presence in the region.

The Significance of Pan-Turkism and Activism in Eastern Turkestan

Historically, the Central Asian region was referred to as *Turkestan*, a term used by Persians to define the land of the Turks, which was discontinued on ethnographic basis in the post national territorial delimitation period in the 1920's. The frontier of Turkestan was variously defined, to include all lands outside Persia or the area where the Turks dwelled in the region since the ancient times. However the borders between Iran and Turan changed, geographically with the shifting of the Oxus, and politically with the changing fortunes of empires.[4]

Debates on the viability of demarcating this essentially cultural unity of pan-Turkism into the reality of a political unit had begun by the turn of the century in Central Asia. In the first decades of this century some pan-Turkic visionaries, like Mustafa Chokaev, subscribed to the view that "Turkestan" was a nationally and linguistically homogenous unit.[5] However, it has to be recognized that this was a debate that was principally confined to a group of reformers who were known as the Jadids. Identity for the majority of the people of the region was defined in local terms. For the most part the uniting bond was Islam. However, it would be an exaggeration to conclude that the Muslims of Russia formed a homogeneous community, even from the purely religious point of view. Within the broad Muslim identity, differentiations existed, chiefly along regional lines.[6]

Pan-Turkism was introduced in such a background of segmented identities. The father of pan-Turkism in Russia was

Ismail Bey Gaspirali, who wielded, the hitherto diffuse reformist thought into a coherent ideology. In his *Terjuman* he advocated the unity of the Turkish peoples around a common literary language, a common culture and a common political organization. In much of this there was little success as by the time these efforts began, differences between the various Turkic groups had become significant.

With the emergence of the Central Asian Republics, as independent entities, once again a search for pan Turkic linkages began as the politics of the new post-Soviet era encouraged pan Turkic ideas. It received a boost from western policies that supported pro Turkic tendencies against a reemergence of Iranian interest in the Turkic regions of the former Soviet Union. Turkey herself was not reluctant to adapt itself to this new international atmosphere and forged new links with the countries in this region. The Balkans, the Caucasus and Central Asia were revitalized, as having once been significant regions within the Ottoman territory or, as having close relations with the Ottomans.

During the first years of independent existence, relations with Turkey was an important aspect of the Central Asian foreign policy. This is rather interestingly displayed in a booklet published from Tashkent, where small comprehension passages are used to describe the most significant events of the months immediately following independence in Uzbekistan. A large number of these passages deal with the visits of the then Turkish President Turgut Ozal to Tashkent and to the visits of Uzbek delegations to Turkey.[7] Similarly, the Uzbek President in his book points to a number of organizations and states as significant and these include, the UN and its organs, International Financial and Economic Organizations, the European Union, NATO and OSCE, international organizations of the Asian region particularly *Turkish language speaking countries*, other European countries, the CIS and the Central Asian countries.[8]

The debate on Turkey's emerging relationship with these

states was clearly divided between those who pointed to Turkey's interest in Central Asia that peaked in the days of the leadership of President Turgut Ozal and Prime Minister Suleiman Demirel and others who pointed to a growing trend towards regionalism. This, combined with the decline in the interest shown by Turkey in the region since the death of President Ozal in April 1993, was used to indicate that the euphoria of the initial years which was now over. However, it was also noted that while the progress in economic relations proved to be less spectacular than expected, steady mutual contacts in the cultural and educational fields have been sustained.

It remains undeniable that while the viability of economic linkages is questionable, to a very large extent it was the bridges that the Ataturk had pointed to — *dil*, *inach* and *tarikh* or language, belief and history, which form the linkages. Given this, it would be interesting to move away from examining economic linkages to an examination of the dynamics of a cultural relationship, that is defined as pan-Turkism. However, this linkage needs to be critically examined as numerous scholars have pointed to the fact that identities in the Central Asian region were based on local bondage. The larger pan identities were a later phenomena, that developed as the region was opened to the influence of newer ideas from the west and from Turkey. In any case these larger identities were subscribed to by a small minority of enlightened Jadids. However, given their reemergence in the present context, both in political rhetoric as well as in intellectual circles, their significance cannot be completely ignored.[9]

The politics of the new post-Soviet era also encouraged pan Turkic ideas. It received a boost from western policies that supported pro Turkic tendencies against a reemergence of Iranian interest in the Turkic regions of the former Soviet Union. Turkey herself was not reluctant to adapt itself to this new international atmosphere and forged new links to the countries in this region. The *Black Sea Economic Cooperation Organization* (BSEC) was founded in 1992. The BSEC handled small projects and sought to develop transportation, communication and environmental projects. The *Economic Cooperation Organization*, initially founded by Turkey, Pakistan and Iran during the late 1960's was expanded by the addition of the five Central Asian States, Azerbaijan and Afghanistan in 1993. This became a catalyst for building private sector banking, for building infrastructure and scientific technical cooperation. The Turkish world was expanded from Europe to Eurasia.

In the light of these developments, the *Turkish Cooperation and Developmental Agency* was founded as a semi official agency devoted to regional cooperation. It funded a number of projects and helped communication between the countries of the Caucasus, Central Asia and the Balkans. Also the *Eurasian Chamber of Commerce and Industry* was founded in 1993. The Balkans, the Caucasus and Central Asia were revitalized, as having once been significant regions, within the Ottoman territory or as having close relations with the Ottomans. The Turkic Republics of Central Asia had a special place in the course of this development. Turkey's cultural and historical affinities, with the peoples of Central Asia, provided opportunities for Turkey to regain regional power status. A change was evident in the new trend for the study of this extended Turkic world in Turkey.

Turkey proved attractive to the Turkic Republics, not just as a model to be emulated but also as a counterbalance to the linkages with the Russian Federation. However, the inadequacies of Turkish economic means to meet the demands of the Republics soon became evident. Tensions also arose between the Russian Federation and Turkey, over the issue of the proposed oil and gas pipelines from these Republics. Turkey's proposed route from Baku to Ceyhan on the Mediterranean was countered by Russia's proposal of the Novorossiisk-Turkish Straits route.

It was, thus, to cultural and educational spheres that significance was attached as realism pointed to the problems in economic linkages. However, even here differences in the political goals of the various Turkic Republics became evident in the course of the yearly Congress of Turkic states under the name of *Friendship, Brotherhood and Cooperation*. While visiting Central Asia, as Prime Minister in 1992, Suleiman Demirel had referred to the prospects of forming an "association of independent Turkic states". This association, however, failed to materialize.

Turkish scholars today point to Turkey's cultural retreat from the Soviet Turkic world, during a phase of extreme anti-communism of the Turkish authorities in the Cold War era, as a major deterrent to any active involvement of Turkey with the former Turkic Republics of the Soviet Union.[10] The rejection of Ottomanism also meant that Republican Turkey was determined to limit itself to the political territory of Anatolia. The projection of ethnic, religious and cultural homogeneity within its borders was supplemented by lack of interest in the regions that Turkey had cultural and historical ties with.

The most significant spatial factor, that limits the sweeping definitions of Turkish lands extending across Asia from the "Adriatic to the Great Wall of China", is the fact that Turkey is no longer geographically contiguous with the regions it claims as being historically and culturally contingent. In fact Turkey can only access the Central Asian region either via Iran, or through the Transcaucasus and the Caspian Sea or across Transcaucasus and Russia. While the significance of geopolitics is restrained, the significance of geoculture, or common cultural linkages between groups inhabiting different states, may well become significant, in the case of Central Asia's relationship with Turkey. How far this "cultural pan Turkism" emerges as crucial remains to be seen. For the moment pragmatism ensures that both Turkey and the Central Asian Republics focus on the Eurasian reality as more significant. There is also recognition of the criticism that sweeping definitions of "Turkic lands" evokes from other states. The remarks of the Turkish Defence Minister, Turhan Tayan, to the effect "that many living (in Xinjiang) are our relatives and that we will always be interested in those people's welfare...our government is and will continue to be sensitive over the plight of our Turkic and Moslem brothers throughout the world", evoked strong resentment from the Chinese authorities. Similarly, possibilities of Turkish involvement in the region through numerous *East Turkestan* Organizations, active in Turkey and the Central Asian republics, is now suspect.

The most prominent of these is the *Eastern Turkestan Foundation*, which was established in 1978, by the acknowledged leader of émigré Uighurs, Isa Yusuf Alptekin. Alptekin met the then Turkish Prime Minister Suleyman Demirel and other senior political figures, on a number of occasions. Alptekin was received by the Turkish President Turgut Ozal in 1992 and presented him with a traditional Uighur coat and a Eastern Turkestani flag, symbolizing the handover of the Eastern Turkestani cause to him. President Ozal is reported to have said:

> I declare that I have taken delivery of the Eastern Turkestani cause. The Turkic Republics under former Soviet rule have all declared their independence. Now it is Eastern Turkestan's turn. It is our desire to see the ancient homeland of the Turkic peoples as a free country.[11]

However, by 1998, this position had seen a shift with the premiership of Mesut Yilmaz of the *Motherland Party*, who urged ministers and government officials not to take part in any political activities organized by the East Turkestan and Uighur organizations based in Turkey, since Xinjiang was part of the territory of China and émigré activities were creating difficulties in Turkey's relations with China. Similarly, the official Chinese news agency, *Xinhua*, reported that the speaker of the Turkish Parliament, Hikmat Cetin, reiterated Turkey's opposition to separatist activities and this was reinforced in a meeting Li Peng held with the Prime Minister Bulent Ecevit.[12]

Similarly, numerous Uighur organizations functioning in the Central Asian region have received support from Kazakh parties like the *Kazakh Nationalist Party*, which asked for reunification with the Kazakh nation in Xinjiang. *Uighur Liberation Committees* have been set up in Kazakhstan, Kyrgyzstan and Tajikistan together with an *International Uighur Union* for Uighurs living throughout the CIS. The *Inter Republic Uighur Association* is frequently engaged in all kinds of activities in Kazakhstan. The *United National Revolutionary Front for Eastern Turkestan* is also active in Kazakhstan and openly advocates the independence of Xinjiang. Similarly, the *Nevada Semipalantinsk Movement* in Kazakhstan has a separate department to mobilize opinion against the Lop Nor nuclear tests. People to people contact has multiplied. In 1991, visas were abolished for citizens of China and Kazakhstan, visiting each other's country, which led to significant migration of people from Xinjiang to Kazakhstan.

The response of the Central Asian leadership to émigré Uighur organizations in region has been similar to that shown by Turkey and it is unlikely that any of these Organizations will emerge as significant in the near future. The Central Asian leadership is unlikely to encourage the separatist movement in Xinjiang and this was recently reaffirmed when the Kyrgyz government handed over Uighur separatists to the Chinese government. The *Voice of Eastern Turkestan*, published in Russian from Almaty, has reflected frustration at such responses and noted that because of the Shanghai agreements the Central Asian states have failed to support the Uighur cause in Xinjiang.[13]

The separatist movement in Xinjiang, which had remained dormant for over twenty years, gradually reappeared in the post Maoist era, though the first major incident of resistance to CCP control over Xinjiang is generally acknowledged to have been the Khotan uprising of December 1954, in southern Xinjiang, by a pan Turkic organization known to Chinese authorities as Amin group.[14] The Aksu and Kashgar riots in April 1980, in which several hundred civilians and security forces were reported to have been killed or wounded, marked the revival of the separatist movement in Xinjiang. Uighur academics, intellectuals and literary figures voiced their dissenting views on the historical, cultural and socio-economic life of the province. Turgbun Almass, an Uighur expert on local history and culture published three books *The Uighurs*, *A Short History of Xiongnu* and the *Literature of the Uighurs* between 1986 and 1989, which created, ripples in Xinjiang. The author was accused of manipulating history, in order to ferment "secession from China".[15]

The 1990's witnessed further ethno-religious resurgence. The Seventh Xinjiang Uighur Autonomous Regional Peoples' Congress, held in March 1990, at Urumchi identified the ethno religious separatist movement as the greatest danger facing Xinjiang. However, it was only after violent riots rocked the Baren township in Kashgar in early April 1990, that the Chinese authorities made a through reappraisal of the situation.[16] The anti-Chinese riots were reportedly sparked off after the local authorities banned the construction of a mosque near Kashgar airport on the occasion of Ramazan. The riots, which soon spread to other towns, were described as armed counter-revolutionary rebellion. Activists and supporters of the *Islamic Party of Eastern Turkestan*, aspirants for the establishment of an independent Islamic Republic in Xinjiang, proclaimed *jihad* to "eliminate infidels" from the province.

The collapse of the Soviet Union in 1991 and the emergence of the new Turkic Republics inspired the Uighur Muslims to intensify their movement for an independent Uighuristan or Eastern Turkestan.[17] The situation in Xinjiang became more volatile since 1991 and the local authorities admitted the emergence of subversive forces in the region. There was an abortive Islamic uprising in the town of Baren in 1992. The same year Ibrahim Rouzi, Director of Xinjiang's Religious Affairs Bureau, ordered a government probe into the mushrooming of unauthorized mosques and Koranic schools in the region, which he said were being opened "with funds received from abroad".[18] The bomb blasts in Kashgar in 1993 and some other towns, demonstrated the persistence of organized movement by Islamic militants against the Chinese authority in Xinjiang. There were disturbances in six towns in the Ili region of northwestern Xinjiang in April 1995, demonstrations in Khotan in July 1995 and a number of incidents in four counties of the Aksu region in 1996 with links to the separatist struggle.[19] The biggest riot in Xinjiang occurred in February 5-6 1997, during Ramazan when a large number of people demanding independence, paraded the streets and indulged in arson and beating. Three bomb explosions in Urumchi occurred in three buses on three separate roads in February 1997.

Since pan Turkism in both western and eastern Turkestan was closely aligned to pan Islam, religious identities in the region remain significant. Here, differences between the oases in relation to responses to religion is evident. The Muslims of Kansu, for instance, are mainly Chinese by blood, language and culture, with a few communities that remained Turkish in language and predominantly Central Asian by blood. Similarly, like in all other frontier regions, Sufism had a substantial impact and various Sufi sects were prominent.[20]

This brief account of the history of separatist movements in Xinjiang brings to the forefront the necessity of an examination of Han Chinese presence in Xinjiang and subsequently a look at a group identified by them as Uighurs.

The Chinese in Xinjiang and the Ethnogenesis of the Uighurs

Ancient Chinese historical records make frequent references to Central Asia. Among the official histories dealing with Central Asia is the *Memoir on Dayuan*, which is sometimes translated as Ferghana. There is a reference to numerous tribes and peoples who inhabited the Ferghna Valley in ancient times.[21] Official histories of Sima Qian and other historians from the Han Dynasty to the Tang Dynasty also provide detailed accounts of Central Asian history. In addition, information about Central Asia is available in Chinese records about Buddhism. Similarly, an entire body of records is to be found in ancient Chinese poetry written by either Chinese officials and soldiers sent to the frontiers of the empire or literary figures who had first hand experience of the region.[22] These records illustrate, that the Central Asian region, sharing vast stretches of frontiers with China, had always been significant to the Chinese Empire.

The expression "Sinkiang-Uighur Autonomous Region", is a translation of the Chinese *Hsin-chiang Wei-wu-erh Tzu-chih-chu.*[23] *Hsin-chiang* is generally translated into English as "new dominion" or "new province" and Xinjiang was thus designated in Chinese, after control over the region was reinstated after the rebellions of Yakub Beg, in the late 19th century. The character *chiang*, however, is more correctly translated as "frontier". *Hsin-chiang* was part of a much larger entity often referred to in Chinese history and literature as *Hsi-yu* or the Western Regions. Hsin-chiang referred to the newly acquired or newly consolidated territory beyond the Han settled parts of northwest China where the Empire held the line against the outside world. That it was given a Chinese name, unlike other border areas like Mongolia or Tibet, is an indication of the special interest that the Chinese have had in the region. As a frontier region, it is remarkable, for the great distance that it penetrates into Central Asia away from China proper.

In its relationship with the external world the Chinese Empire had developed a concept of dual, inner and outer, frontiers. Prior to 1884, Xinjiang was considered as a part of the intermediary zone, separated from China proper by the Gansu corridor. It was in the context of conflict, with the western world in the 19th century, that China began to adopt western concepts of sovereignty, which meant that boundaries had to be precisely demarcated.[24] The need to make sovereign rule coincide with actual frontiers meant that the region had to be formally annexed to China. Xinjiang was formally annexed in 1884.

In 1863, the revolt of Yakub Beg had led to the establishment of an independent Eastern Turkestan by the overthrow of the

Qing rulers, a brief experiment that was eventually crushed by Chinese armies. The Qing dynasty had annexed this region in 1759 and had given it the name of Xinjiang, yet successive Chinese rulers had "never directly controlled its new province because of the dearth of Han Chinese available to govern it".[25] This meant, that like in the case of Tibet, the region had been allowed by the Chinese rulers to rule themselves under the supervision of Chinese representatives. The Uighur population revolted against the Chinese rule again in 1933 and then again in 1944, when the East Turkestan Republic was formed from the three northwestern provinces of Xinjiang (Ili, Chevchek and Altai) with Yining as its capital. Once again it had a short existence. Yet the "Three Districts Revolution" stands as an illustration of a successful Turkic independence movement in China and visions of its reemergence, in what is today Xinjiang, remains alive in Chinese official thinking.

Since the incorporation of Xinjiang within the Peoples' Republic of China in 1949, Xinjiang's spatial and cultural boundaries changed. Kashgar's and Ili's westward orientation towards Central Asia was largely eliminated. In 1962, the Sino-Soviet split effectively sealed borders and cross border communications came to a halt. At the same time demography was altered and there was an increase of Han migration. This changed in 1985 when Xinjiang's borders were reopened and traditional trade and cultural ties were sought to be reestablished.

With the opening of Xinjiang's borders, traditional trade and cultural ties with the outside cultures have been reestablished causing rivalries between the different oases to resurface and leading to fragmentation of Uighur identity. Uighur intellectuals are now competing to place historical events or personages relating to their home oasis into prominence and each now claims that the figure or event he has chosen is the most significant. These competing historiographies are actually undermining the possibility of a cohesive intellectual leadership and a pan-oases ethnic unity. Self-identification is now also delineated along social lines. Thus, the three social groups in the Turpan oasis, intellectuals, merchants and peasants, hold diverse conceptions of identity. Uighur intellectuals, who reside mostly in Urumchi define themselves, in opposition to the Han and identify with the larger Turkic world of Central Asia and Turkey. Middle income and poor peasants who do not travel outside the Turpan region, identify strongly with Islam and maintain strong oasis identity. Uighur merchants, who trade with China and wealthy peasants benefiting from China's developmental policies, identify themselves as citizens of the Chinese state.[26] Differences are also evident due to uneven economic developments and differences in attitude towards Islam and its clergy. For instance the power of the mullah has grown stronger in Turpan, while Kashar Uighurs, who have not experienced economic growth, are more resentful against the Chinese.

Aware of their strategic position as the hub of Trans Asian trade and also its vast economic resources the Uighurs have been poised to assert their socio-economic and political position. To China the secession of Xinjinag would cause irreparable loss of economic resources and strategic position. Given the strategic location of Xinjiang the Chinese authorities have viewed the entire northwest region as an important growth centre. In 1992, Xinjiang's annual allocation was doubled and it was accorded the right to conduct preferential trade policies and free economic zones. Xinjiang was converted into a new prosperity zone that would attract investment from Hong Kong, Taiwan as well as domestic investment from coastal provinces. China's concern in Xinjiang is not only about the ethnic and religious revivalism but also about the protection of the regions, 30 billion tones of proven petroleum, which is critical to China's energy security. Xinjiang has become militarily important to China as it houses the nuclear experimentation centre at Lop Nor. It also serves as the buffer against Russia.

Eastern Turkestan lies in the heart of Asia, bordering on the south west, west and northwest, Pakistan, Afghanistan, Tajikistan,

Kyrgyzstan and Kazakhstan. A majority of the people belong to the Turkic-speaking groups but distances were so great that primary loyalties were to kinship groups, rather than to nationalities, as such. Scholars trace the ethnic origin of the Uighurs to the Uighur Empire, that dates from 8th and 9th centuries and locate it in northwestern Mongolia. By the end of the eleventh century, at the latest, the Turkic languages had by and large spread through the entire Tarim basin as the lingua franca.

Uighurs constitute about 7.2 million of the Muslim population of China, according to the 1990 Chinese census. In addition in Xinjiang there are about 6,82,900 Huis who have historically played the role of a buffer between the Uighur and the Han population, who have increased their numbers from 2,50,000 in 1949 to 6 million in 1990's.[27] This has been the result of large resettlement of Han-Chinese population in the region during the initial years of the PRC's dealing with the region. This resettlement has resulted in persistent Uighur complaints about discriminatory policies and restrictions on Uighur cultural development.

The Uighurs form a fairly compact population in China's northwestern autonomous region, officially named after them because they are the dominant minority in the area. Although they reside chiefly in Xinjiang, according to Eden Naby, the Uighurs fall into two fairly distinct and historically separated communities that even today do not mix readily.[28] Those living north of the Tien Shan mainly from the Lli Valley have looked to Soviet Central Asia and even China for stimulation and contact. They tend to be educated, in accordance with western standards, politically and bureaucratically involved in the running of the region and they represent a more secular part of the Uighur ethnic group. This group of Uighurs migrated to Urumchi more readily. The second group, on the other hand, still focuses on Kashgar and the predominantly Muslim culture that the city represents. Terrain dictates this kind of separation as does past history.

Geographically the Tien Shan cuts Xinjiang into two unequal

parts. The smaller northern part consists of the Dzungarian basin, which tends to slope westward so that access is easier from the Soviet side rather than from the Chinese side. The larger southern part forms an oval, almost entirely ringed with mountains, and is largely composed of sandy desert. The plain tends to tilt upwards, towards the west until it ends before the barrier of the Pamir plateau.[29] It was not till the mid 1930's that the Chinese government defined the Uighur ethnic group as oasis dwelling Muslims in the Tarim basin of Xinjiang. Prior to this the name, Uighur was not used as an ethnic label and relations between the oases of Xinjiang were characterized by political, religious and armed rivalries.[30] In fact the inhabitants of these Muslim regions of China were not all Turkic. The Hui, who are a significant section of the population, are Chinese speaking and are closer to the Han Chinese than to their Muslim brethren.

The use of the term Uighur, however, papered over a whole host of internal differentiations among the separate oases of the Tarim Basin. Contrary to the common views of Xinjiang as a single entity, it is actually composed of four distinct geographical regions, each influenced by a different bordering culture. While the geography of flat desert wastelands, between the individual oases of Xinjiang, appear free of obstacles, historically contact across borders was more frequent and important than contact between the oases themselves. This fostered distinct and separate oasis identities.[31] Eventually, all the oases were linked by a road system, which was later identified as the Silk Route. This geographical legacy has influenced the nature of Uighur identity. Lattimore points out:

> While the oases of the Taklamakan had a strong generic resemblance to each other, they remained invincibly separate from each other... There was no compulsion whatsoever towards trade between the oases. For this reason the people of the different oases could be homogeneous in race, language and culture and yet almost totally indifferent towards each other.[32]

Historically the region west and north of the Tarim basin from Kashgar towards Kucha, was influenced by Western Turkestan, particularly the peoples of the Ferghana Valley, including Andijan, Kokand, and Osh. The northwestern Zungarian Basin was oriented to the Semireichiye region, that today is Kazakhstan and parts of western Central Asia and was influenced by nomadic Mongolian and Turkic tribes. The region in the southern Tarim Basin, from Yarkand past Khotan to Keriya was strongly influenced by Indian culture. Finally the eastern part of Xinjiang, including Turpan and Hami was closely tied to China.

Writing about the ethnogenesis of the Uighur, Dru C. Gladney notes that despite geopolitical maneuvering on the Inner Asian frontiers the Uighurs have retained much of their ethnoreligious identities, though new expressions of identity have evolved in interaction with the nationality policy and socio-economic change.[33] It has been emphasized that the peoples of Inner Asia have been particularly resistant to Han cultural assimilation, despite having been brought fully into the Chinese nation state. A correct understanding of the modern Uighur identity in China must take into account this dialectical recreation and reinterpretation of the past to account for the present interactions and identities on the Inner Asian frontier. In its turn, this would have a significant impact on the development of China's relationship with the Central Asian republics.

China and the Newly Independent Central Asian Republics

Two prominent examples illustrates the current Chinese involvement in the Central Asian region: China's leadership in creating the Shanghai Cooperation Organization, in partial defiance of Deng Xiaoping's dictum that "in international affairs China should keep a low profile and avoid taking the lead" and China's October 2002 military exercise with the Kyrgyz military, the first combined exercise in the history of the Peoples' Republic of China.[34] In fact China has had a threefold interest in Central

Asia since ancient times, ensuring physical security along China's border with Central Asia, ensuring that no empire hostile to China occupied the Central Asian steppes or river valleys and ensuring that China had unfettered access to the natural resources of the region. Three factors have been identified by Chinese scholars as compulsions for seeking active engagement in the region. These include the fact that Central Asia neighbours, China's troubled Xinjiang Uighur Autonomous Region where a segment of the ethnic Uighur population are striving for independence, China wants assured access to Central Asia's hydrocarbon resources and Chinese manufacturers covet a share of the Central Asian market.[35]

This led China to follow, what is referred to as the "Three C's" to ensure Beijing's three enduring national security interests along its Central Asian frontier; co-opting, conquering and colonizing. This strategy often meant "legitimizing" local kingdoms in Central Asia, conquering their territory outright or Sinification of the indigenous people. During the Cold War and the Sino-Soviet rivalry, all of China's key security interests in Central Asia were challenged: China's western border was under direct threat, an empire hostile to China controlled Central Asia and Beijing had no access to the resources of the region.[36]

With the end of the Cold War, China and Russia were able to settle many of their border disputes and security differences. However, China's border, with the newly independent Central Asian states, still generated concern. With the collapse of the Soviet Union, China suddenly found herself sharing common borders with the new Central Asian states. Given the fact that these states, with their numerous problems, bordered the Xinjiang region of China, the initial Chinese reaction to the developments in Central Asia was surprisingly cautious. The first official reaction, described developments in Central Asia as well as the other Soviet republics as the "internal affairs" of the region. Officials in Beijing, confirmed that they would respect choices made by the people in these countries. Notwithstanding this official line there was clear appreciation in Beijing of the significance of the changes in terms of Chinese security.

China's compulsions for seeking active engagement with the Central Asian states may be categorized as both, threat based compulsions as well as ambition based compulsions, though they overlap in most cases. Among threat-based compulsions, China was faced with the presence of unaccounted nuclear weapons, missiles and fissile materials across unstable borders. The emergence of ethnic nationalism, in the newly formed Central Asian Republics was visualized as a potential factor in recharging separatism in the bordering regions of China. Also, given the situation in Afghanistan, terrorism became a critical concern. Certain ambition-based compulsions have also guided Chinese engagement with the states. The most important is the long-term policy of ensuring access to the energy resources of the Central Asian region. The significance of this may be gauged from the fact that while during 1999 China imported 40 million tones of crude oil, which was about 20 per cent of the total consumption, in 2000 this went up to 50 million tones, i.e, 25 per cent of the total consumption.[37] China is also concerned about the engagement of other states in the region, including Russia, the United States, Turkey and France.[38]

Among threat-based compulsions, the projected rise of ethnic nationalism in the Central Asian Republics and the possible impact of these events in Xinjiang was the most significant. Overlapping ethnic communities, across ill-defined borders, was the most decisive factor determining the course of evolution of Sino-Central Asian relations. Xinjiang has strong ethnic ties with the Central Asian region and Kazakhstan and Kyrgyzstan providing home to a quarter million Uighurs. The Xinjiang region itself is host to a million Kazakhs, often with strong ethnic ties with Central Asia. This places China in a special category, as far as states dealing with the Central Asian Republics is concerned. While Hong Kong, Macao, Taiwan and Tibet may be the most cited examples, Beijing has always been more concerned with the continued unrest in its expanded inner core in Tibet and Xinjiang, which remain the most important factors determining its views on the Central Asian region.[39]

On the diplomatic level, China recognized the independence of the Central Asian states in December 1991. In January 1992, China signed different communiqués on the establishment of diplomatic relations with the five states. In the same year Presidents of three Central Asian states, Uzbekistan, Kazakhstan and Kyrgyzstan visited China. In 1993 the President of Tajikistan also visited the country. These visits considerably deepened the relations between the states. During Li Peng's visit to the four Central Asian states, in April 1994, Beijing proposed four principles as ground rules for promoting ties between them. These included; 1. maintaining good neighbourly relations and peaceful coexistence; 2. promoting mutually beneficial co-operation and seeking common economic prosperity; 3. respecting the choices made by the Central Asian peoples and never interfering in their internal affairs and 4. respecting other countries' independence and sovereignty and contributing to the regional stability.[40]

While these formed the basis of the relations, the Chinese government also took steps to specify some particular principles, which are specifically applicable to China's relations with countries of the CIS. In July 1994, the Chinese Foreign Minister Qian Qichen elaborated these principles as follows: 1. respect the choices made by the peoples in those countries and respect and understand foreign and domestic policies made by those countries in accordance with their own circumstances and international environment and never interfere in their internal affairs; 2. maintain that differences in social systems, ideologies and development models should not stand in the way of resolving problems in bilateral relations; 3. adhere to the principle of equality and mutual benefit in conducting trade and economic cooperation in accordance with the norms of international economic exchanges and strive for common economic development and prosperity; 4. sincerely hope for domestic stability of all CIS states and for peaceful solution of all conflicts among all CIS states, so as to realize the regional political stability of the former Soviet Union. He also stated that the development of China's relations with the CIS states was not directed against any third country.[41]

Beijing was also successful in promoting its one China policy. The Central Asian states reiterated that the government of the People's Republic of China is the sole legal government of China and that Taiwan is an inalienable part of the Chinese territory and affirmed that they would not establish any form of official relationship with Taiwan.[42]

A new image of Central Asia began to emerge for China where Beijing wanted a stable and economically prosperous Central Asia where stability would be maintained through economic development. This signaled the beginning of Chinese economic and commercial penetration of the Central Asian region and trade ties deepened considerably as traders from both sides started to travel extensively. On the official level the Chinese central authorities signed several agreements on Chinese credits to these countries. The Chinese model of development also attracted the attention of the Central Asian leaders who started to talk about adopting the Chinese model of market economics for their own. Also the Chinese route began to be used by the states for trade. In interviews, officials from Kyrgyzstan said that they plan to export energy and minerals to third countries via northern Chinese ports. Similarly economists in Uzbekistan have noted that their country hopes to ship items of daily use through China to cut costs and Turkmenistan plans to lay a natural gas pipeline through China to Japan.[43]

The proximity of Central Asia meant that the success of the economic boom in Xinjiang would depend on stability in the entire region and developed transportation links. The opening up of the Trans Eurasian railroad through Central Asia in 1990 and the linking of Almaty and Urumchi by railroad in 1992 ensured a long term role for China in Central Asia. A joint Central Asian - Chinese initiative of reviving the Silk Road and steps in this direction has also brought in dramatic change in the relation. The most ambitious plan of cooperation between China and Central Asia is the proposed construction of a pipeline that would carry Central Asian oil to China.

China's policy towards post Soviet Central Asia is now determined by a number of factors.[44] The most important is, of course, the geo-political location of the region, which borders Russia, Iran, Afghanistan and China. The internal alignment of the political factions in the newly independent states and the possibilities of the leadership to control internal economic and social situations is also identified as significant. Along with this is the possibility of revival of Islamic organizations and the issue of Uighur diaspora in the Central Asian states. Geo-economic factors, including the growing energy needs of China, is also emerging as a significant factor in China's relationship with these states.

According to Professor Ma Jiali, of the China Institute for Contemporary International Relations, the following strategic concerns have been the main guiding parameters of China's policies with the five states. Firstly, considering that China shares about 4,000 km of joint borders with the states, the foremost strategic concern has been to ensure the stability of the northwestern frontier so as to create a more favourable external environment. Secondly, in view of Washington's attempts at using issues like Tibet, Taiwan and human rights to seek its goal of weakening China, it becomes imperative for China to ensure that any engineered social unrest does not affect its security and stability. By strengthening ties with the states China must suppress these elements by handling separatists and religious extremist infiltration from these countries. Thirdly, China's engagement with the Central Asian states provides Beijing with a buffer zone against the eastward expansion of the NATO. Since the war in Kosova, in the mid 1990's, China has felt herself squeezed both from the west, by the NATO's eastward expansion and from the East by the US-Japan military alliance. And finally, the fourth strategic concern is to seek stable and reliable energy supplies.[45]

China has demonstrated significant commitment towards exploring Central Asian energy resources. One of the more ambitious projects signed by China with the Central Asian states includes a $11 billion 5,730 km long gas pipeline project between Turkmenistan, Uzbekistan, Kazakhstan and China in which a consortium of companies from United States, Japan and China are participating. This projects plans to exploit gas deposits from the right bank of the Amu Darya and is expected to provide an alternative to the gas pipeline from Russia's east Siberian region.[46] Other pipelines are under study, including one that is expected to link the natural gas oilfields in Russia's Irkutsk region with Rizhao in the eastern Chinese province of Shandong. It would later be extended to the Republic of Korea and Japan to make it commercially viable. The other pipeline is expected to run from West Siberia to Shanghai via Xinjiang.[47]

Chinese scholars now emphasize the strategic significance of the Central Asian region, which shares long borders with China.[48] The frontiers of China's North West have traditionally been perceived as the most vulnerable to defend and this has put security issues as significant in terms of her relationship with these states. Here four issues are identified as significant: the nuclear security issue, border disputes, defence and military cooperation and Central Asian multilateral security arrangements.[49]

One of the fallouts of the disintegration of the former Soviet Union was to make Kazakhstan a quasi-nuclear state. And China was naturally concerned about the emergence of a nuclear power along its borders. In the immediate post independence period, Kazakh ambiguity towards its nuclear status had become a cause for concern. However, by 1995, Kazakhstan announced that it had either handed over all its warheads to Russia or destroyed them. This was followed by assurances from the Chinese government not to deploy nuclear weapons on Kazakhstan.

Chinese leaders are aware that promoting this new strategy in the Central Asian region is not easy. There remain certain areas where problems and misunderstandings continue. The Central Asian leaders, particularly the Kazakhs and the Kyrgyz, are unhappy with continued nuclear testing at Lop Nor to the east of the Kazakh border. Water rights and environmental issues also exist. In January 1993 Kazakhstan and China agreed to build a water conservancy works over the Horgos river along their border, to address hydropower, flood control and navigation interest. Alteration of the river flow affects both the signatories and Uzbekistan, located downstream on the river. On the Chinese part, authorities in Beijing continue to worry about the ethnic issue with fears that Xinjiang's Muslims may link up with their fellows in the former Soviet Union. Pressure from China has forced Kazakhstan and Kyrgyzstan to ban parties and activists fighting for an independent Uighuristan.

China's relations with Central Asia was also complicated by territorial claims made by China on a number of areas of present day Kazakhstan and Kyrgyzstan. Though, officially the problem was resolved by the legal registration of the border in 1994, the actual demographic and geopolitical situation may raise the issue again. China is also faced with the problem of large numbers of Uighurs in Kazakhstan and Kyrgyzstan, a fact that has prompted the signing of the Shanghai Treaty between China and the neighbouring states of Central Asia, to establish a "demilitarized zone" of eight thousand kilometers in length, along the borders adjoining Central Asia and China.

Border disputes, therefore, proved more difficult to resolve. Tensions and military confrontations along the Sino Soviet border had been hallmarks of Sino Soviet relations. The disintegration of the Soviet Union changed the context of the ongoing negotiations for the settlement of disputed borders. China's border disputes with the former Soviet Union now became China's disputes with four independent states, Russia, Kazakhstan, Kyrgyzstan and Tajikistan. How to settle the border disputes with the newly independent states became an important aspect of China's security relations with the Central Asian states and consequently one of the major thrusts of Chinese foreign policy was aimed at settlement of these border disputes. This was pointed to as integral to China's search for security of its North Western frontiers.[50] China moved towards the settlement of her borders with these states on the basic principles of respect for results already achieved in Sino Soviet negotiation, existing treaties as the basis of the negotiations, settlement in accordance with the established rules of international law and mutual consultation and accommodation on equal footing. The Central Asian states themselves were eager to negotiate for the settlement of disputes as regional peace and stability was crucial for them in their state building efforts. China has negotiated border agreements with Kazakhstan and Russia and it is unlikely that this will prove to be a major obstacle in the near future.

China with her geographical proximity, policy emphasis on promoting trade and economic dynamism, dramatically expanded its economic role in the region. With continued economic growth and expansion of transportation links, China's influence will continue to grow. What is important is an examination of how far China's influence in Central Asia might expand. China, however, has never expressed any interest in extending an exclusive sphere of interest in the region. China's main policy priority involves avoiding of instability in the region, securing access to energy resources and expanding economic cooperation.

Another important dimension of the new security relations between China and the Central Asian states was the need to develop bilateral and multilateral defence and military co-operation. This would include enhancing confidence building measures, reducing troops and military forces along common borders, disarmament in the border areas, and increasing the significance of border defence. While the Central Asian states have been keen to build their own defence and military forces they are still largely dependent on Russia for their defence. In the field of military and defence co-operation between China the Central Asian States and Russia, the signing of the Five Nation Agreement on Confidence Building in the Military Forces in the Border Areas on 26 April 1996, in Shanghai, at a summit meeting among leaders from China, Kazakhstan, Kyrgyzstan, Russia and Tajikistan, was the most significant step. Under the agreement the military forces of both sides stationed along the borders promise not to attack each other. This multilateral agreement has significantly increased transparency of border defence on both sides. In addition, bilateral military agreements have been signed with Kazakhstan and Russia.

The multilateral security arrangements which the Central Asian states have entered into also have implications for security relations with China. In the course of the last decade, a number of significant multilateral security arrangements have been signed by the Central Asian states, both within the framework of the CIS and outside it. The most significant among them was the Treaty on Collective Security signed by Russia, Uzbekistan, Kazakhstan, Kyrgyzstan, Tajikistan and Armenia. China has keenly kept note of these agreements and impact that these could have on its northwest. Outside the CIS the Central Asian states are today members of the Partnership For Peace Programme. However, China and the Central Asian states recognize that none of these are aimed at China.

This encouraged China to take the lead in forming the Shanghai Cooperation Organization. China's goals in forming this organization were: (1) resolving the long standing border issues with Russia and the newly independent Central Asian nations (2) creating a security mechanism for containing the chaos on the other side of its borders and isolating its own problems in Xinjiang (3) laying the groundwork for trade with and access to the key economic resources of Central Asia, including energy resources (4) establishing itself as a significant player in Central Asian affairs before the United States becomes too entrenched, through NATO and the PfP, and before Russian efforts to reassert itself into its "near abroad". In addition to this the SCO also became a platform from which China could advocate its multilateralist vision of a "new security concept" in contrast to the US led alliance based security structures.[51]

China and the Central Asian Economies: "Political Stability through Economic Cooperation"

China now views Central Asia as a huge energy resource and market for its consumer goods and also as a continental bridge, which would extend China's reach through Iran to the Persian Gulf. China not only opened Xinjiang to cross border trade and traffic with the Central Asian Republics but has also been evincing keen interest in the project for revival of Silk Route by extending the Urumchi-Almaty rail upto Iran. Since the 1990's China's traders have been busy in the Central Asian region and according to some estimates upto 50% of Kazakh consumer goods were coming from China. In fact, China's trade with Kazakhstan exceeded that with Turkey.[52] It is undeniable that if the current rate of growth in China is sustained the stream of goods, money and migrants may force Russia out of Central Asian economy, politics and demography, thereby pulling the region towards East Asia. Since Russia is now establishing itself as an exporter of raw materials and China is increasingly becoming involved in the import of raw materials, China may prove more attractive to the importer economies of Central Asia.[53]

Continued strong economic growth is an obvious prerequisite for almost any scenario in which China is able to project its influence beyond its borders. Sustained economic growth will provide China with the financial resources necessary to further expand its economic presence in Central Asia. For the countries in the eastern part of Central Asia, China represents a dynamic and accessible market and a vital non-Russian conduit through which the region can move goods to the broader international marketplace. China's geographical proximity to this otherwise remote region is significant. Due to its landlocked nature, Central Asia is not an easily accessible market for countries of the developed world. The smaller Central Asian countries on China's border, Kyrgyzstan and Tajikistan, are the most likely candidates to move gradually from Russia's sphere of economic influence to that of China. The process is already evident in Kyrgyzstan. In 1994, China was Kyrgyzstan's largest official export market.[54] Some observers note that China may dominate Kyrgyz economy within the next five years if unofficial trade, potentially quite large given the common use if barter is counted. China also offers Kyrgyzstan road links to ocean ports in Pakistan by way of the Karakoram highway.[55] The renaming of Lenin Avenue to Deng Xiaoping Avenue in Bishkek indicates that China's political influence is beginning to follow, in the wake of its economic influence.

Some qualifications regarding China's potential economic role in Central Asia in general should be noted. China will play a large, perhaps dominant, role in the region as a source of imports and market for exports. However, most of the states like Kyrgyzstan also require foreign capital to successfully complete its transition to a market economy. Because Kyrgyzstan does not have large amounts of oil or gas reserves, China is unlikely to become a significant source of foreign investment. China's economic influence in the country will therefore be limited in this respect.

Similarly China's economic relationship with Kazakhstan will also inevitably grow.[56] Kazakhstan is already China's largest trading partner in Central Asia with official bilateral trade in 1997 totaling to $500 million.[57] Ethnic ties between Kazakhs in Kazakhstan and those in China should facilitate further expansion of Sino Kazakh trade. The opening of the Almaty Urumchi railway line, grating Kazakhstan access to the Chinese ocean port at Lianyungang, for trade and its large investments, in the western

Kazakh oil fields further bolster China's economic importance to Kazakhstan. China's economic role in Kazakhstan extends beyond commercial trade. China is committed to significant investments in Kazakhstan's energy industry and provides a non-Russian transport corridor through which Kazakhstan can ship its goods to world markets.

Two major factors will constrain China's economic influence in areas of Kazakhstan that do not lie near the Sino-Kazakh border. The first is Kazakhstan's large ethnic Russian population particularly those living in the predominantly ethnic Russian region in northern Kazakhstan along the Russo-Kazakh border. The Russian ethnic and political presence here predates that of other parts of Kazakhstan, to say nothing of the rest of Central Asia. Kazakhstan's industry, in this region, remains closely integrated with the Russian industry in southern Siberia.[58] This is not to say that Russians in this area of Kazakhstan will avoid profitable opportunities for economic interaction with China. The point is that the region's stronger ethnic affinity and economic orientation towards Russia renders it less susceptible to Chinese economic domination, particularly those lying near the Chinese border.

The second factor limiting the potential growth of Chinese economic influence in Kazakhstan is the existing and growing presence of large multinational corporate interests from developed countries. China's investment of $9 billion to develop the Uzen oilfield is significant but considerably smaller than Chevron's $20 billion investment in the Tengiz oilfield. Other large corporations that have entered agreements with Kazakhstan include British Gas, Mobil, Shell, Total, Agip, British Petroleum and Statoil.[59] China's role will be limited as long as there are many large capital-intensive multinational corporations interested in the region.

Uzbekistan and Turkmenistan are both geographically separated from China. Turkmenistan's proximity to the western or southern routes will mean an economic orientation towards Iran to the south or Azerbaijan and Turkey to the west. The limited Chinese influence in the western regions of Central Asia demonstrates the general point that as one moves away from the Sino-Central Asian border the influence of economic and political players in the region increases with not just traditional powers like Russia, Turkey, Iran and Saudi Arabia in the fray but also the growing influence of the United States. Individual Central Asian countries are developing economic and political links and affiliations that are appropriate to their particular location and economic and political needs. Insofar as China represents only one of a number of potential markets and sources of capital for the new states its ability to play a role in the entire region will be limited.

China's trade with the Central Asian states has traditionally been dominated by barter trade. While this trade started since the mid 1980's, over the last few years various diversified trading channels have expanded the bilateral trade, border trade, local trade, border residents markets and the tourist purchases are now flourishing in towns like Yilin and Urumchi.[60] In the course of the last decade economic and technical cooperation has increased significantly between China and Central Asia. In addition, a number of joint ventures are now in operation, and Chinese entrepreneurs have signed a number of agreements, contracts and letters of intent with their counterparts in Central Asia.

The most important factor in the development of bilateral trade is that both Central Asia and China's North West are located in Inner Asia and are completely landlocked. In addition operation of antiquated barter trading practices, delay in implementation of trade agreements, the inadequate investment environment in Central Asia also create problems.[61] The operation of rail and road linkages, like the second Euro-Asian continental bridge, will therefore be crucial for the operation of trade. The opening of a Khorog-Kashgar road link between China and Tajikistan is also significant in this context. The road route is expected to promote a significant expansion in trade between Tajikistan and China over the medium to long term and boost the share of Chinese goods in the Central Asian market.[62]

On the energy front, China has been an importer of oil since 1993, and its demand for oil is now far exceeding domestic production. China imports nearly half the oil it uses, most of it from the Middle East. With demand growing and domestic production unable to meet its needs China now sees Central Asia as a vital energy source. China is engaged in intensive exploration and production of oil in the Xinjiang region. At the same time China has acquired the right to develop three oil fields in the Aktyubinsk region of Kazakhstan. Besides Sino-Kazakh accords included the rehabilitation of the large Uzen oil fields in western Kazakhstan and the construction of two oil pipelines from western Kazakhstan.

The recent conflict in Iraq has increased the potential of Chinese role in the energy sector in the region. Following the US-British ouster of Saddam Hussain's dictatorship in Iraq, the outlook for Caspian Basin energy exports specially for the Baku-Tiblisi-Ceyhan (BTC) pipeline has become suspect. US experts and officials have suggested that expanded Iraqi oil exports could hurt Western demands for BTC oil. Washington's envoy for Caspian energy issues, Steven Mann, recently indicated that the increased competition could put pressure on Caspian states, specially Azerbaijan, Kazakhstan and Turkmenistan.[63] The recent resurgence in China's interest in the Central Asian region and intensification of its diplomatic activity in the Caspian Basin in order to secure reliable energy supplies to fuel economic development is significant in this regard. Central Asian states like Kazakhstan have welcomed Beijing's higher regional profile as China offers an export alternative in an uncertain Caspian Basin energy development environment.

During his visit to Kazakhstan President Hu Jintao focused on the development of energy related projects. Kazakhstani officials announced on June 5, 2003, that the China National Petroleum Corporation had purchased a 25% stake in an energy venture known as CNPC-Aktobenumaygaz. In addition officials discussed several pipeline projects including the China-Atasu-Alashankou oil route and a gas link to Turkmenistan via Kazakhstan.[64] A pipeline from Kazakhstan to China would help alleviate potential supply problems, specially if such a route can tap into resources in Iurkmenistan and Azerbaijan. At present China does not control enough oil in Kazakhstan to make the pipeline economically viable. Nevertheless, national security interests are likely to compel China to proceed with the pipeline project.

Implementing their new strategy of "political stability through economic cooperation and development", the Chinese authorities were quick to assure the Russians that they had no intentions of threatening Moscow's interests in the region China considers Russia a significant player in the region. Russia and China share a common interest in deterring an ethno nationalist resurgence in Central Asia. At a 1992 meeting between Russian and Chinese Foreign Ministers, the Russian foreign Minister noted, "Central Asia should remain a CIS sphere of influence and not a sphere of extremist forces, and in particular of Islamic fundamentalism." The Chinese Foreign Minister replied that Russia and China "have common interests in preserving stability in the Central Asian region," that Chinese policy towards Central Asia would take into account the close ties that had been established between Russia and the region."[65] The recognition of Russia's natural interests in the region was also evident during discussions in Shanghai in April 1996, following which Russia, China and the Central Asian states, bordering China, signed a confidence building treaty involving the demilitarization of their frontier. From the Chinese point of view the Treaty transformed this long contested area into "a region of peace, friendship and cooperation."[66]

While China has been quick to reassure Russia that China's

expanding economy should not be viewed as a threat, it has been pointed out that Chinese and Russian interests in the region do not always coincide. For instance, the Russians are interested in promoting the Trans-Siberian railway as the main connecting link between Asia and Europe. The Chinese are believed to be rather cool towards this idea. They prefer the southern route to Europe across Central Asia-Transcaucasus-Turkey to the Mediterranean coast. According to analysts this will provide China's western regions "a new geostrategic importance" since it will expand Chinese influence from Xinjiang to the Caspian Sea. Francesco Sisci, for instance notes:

> It will project China into the Middle East, the Mediterranean as well as South Asia, including India. The proposed Chinese railway from Qinghai in the far west to Tibet will not only link the restive Tibetan region to the rest of China, it will also link China's economic heart to India, through roads and railways that could one day move passengers and goods from Lhasa to New Delhi.[67]

There have also been reports of China and Pakistan developing the Indus Basin corridor that would provide the latter with an access to Central Asia. Possibilities of China and Pakistan joining the GUUAM have also been indicated as a possibility.[68]

Central Asian Responses

In the light of the above discussions, it has been observed that Chinese-Central Asian relationship will develop into what is being termed as "periphery-periphery" relations, i.e, relations that are confined between the peripheral areas of China and the former Soviet Union, Xinjiang and Kazakhstan/Kyrgyzstan. It has been noted that:

> ...these relations will not be of priority significance due to the fact that Kazakhstan will be attracted by the weak peripheral areas northwest of China (Xinjiang). The interaction of the two peripheral areas can hardly lead to any

> significant diversification and intensification of these relations. In the mutual attraction of the two peripheral systems, their relations will not acquire the depth and scale once characteristic of Kazakhstan's relations with Russia. This is evident now, when China is supplying cheap consumer goods rather than its technologies, know how and other serious productions.[69]

Here too, there are difficulties as trade is not the only thing that Xinjiang requires. It also requires investment and the opening up of its mineral resources. Here, the Central Asian Republics will be of little assistance. The Republics are themselves in need of large amounts of investments and are themselves competitors in terms of mineral endowments. And Xinjiang, like the Central Asian Republics, is landlocked. So Xinjiang will have to look further afield. Here, while China is the obvious choice, the most important sources of foreign investment would be either the oil rich Muslim states in the Middle East or Western oil multinationals or Japan. Also transportation linkages with China remain crucial.

In reality, developments within China's Inner Asian frontiers is likely to become a more significant issue. Here, the difference in the economic situation between the eastern and the western parts of China is likely to emerge as significant. The sharp cuts in economy encouraged the turn towards linkages with markets in other regions. While the South Asian markets were explored, the turn was principally towards the markets in the CIS. However, the idea of counterpoising the opportunities for an opening to the west for Xinjiang, as against developing links with markets in China to the east may be simplistic. On a broader scale it has been argued that Xinjiang's opening to the northwest could not have been conceived, without a similar expansion of its integration into the national economy, as a whole.

As China's testing ground for nuclear weapons (Lop Nor) Eastern Turkestan remains significant. A second factor that has strengthened the hand of Xinjiang in its dealings with China was the realization that China's existing oil reserves are reaching a point where they can at best only meet her domestic demand. Here, the large deposits of proven oil reserves in Xinjiang, though the exact figures for this are disputed, could become significant for China's energy security.

Sustained ethnic or religious unrest in Xinjiang is the most obvious potential source of conflict between Beijing and the governments of Central Asia. An exchange between China and a Kyrgyz newspaper in Bishkek hinted at the potential divisiveness of this issue. In 1997, China protested to the Kyrgyz Foreign Ministry that the newspaper *Res Publica's* coverage of Uighur riots in the Chinese city of Yining represented "impudent interference in China's internal affairs" and "seriously offended the feelings of the Chinese people". For its part the *Res Publica* responded sharply asserting that its editorial office "reserves the right to publish materials without sharing the authors, opinion and also publishes opinions expressing opposing opinions." Res Publica went on to note that it was willing to publish an article from the Chinese embassy expressing its position on conditions in Xinjiang, "provided it does not insult the feelings of people living in Kyrgyzstan." [70] This incident demonstrates that China is sensitive to the appearance of outside support for Uighur separatist movement but also that there is a certain amount of interest in the fate of the Uighurs in Kyrgyzstan.

Any increase in separatist activity in Xinjiang or political instability in Central Asia will mean that pressure will build within the Chinese leadership to restrict activity along China's Central Asian border. This will be more likely if Beijing concludes that its economic policies are allowing greater financial or material support for separatist elements to enter the country from outside. The closing of the borders may mean that a primary foundation of the current Sino Central Asian relationship is withdrawn.

There are other potential issues that could disrupt China's

relations with the Central Asian states. The perception of Chinese economic exploitation of Central Asian markets and China's nuclear tests in the Lop Nor region of Xinjiang have led to confrontation between Beijing and the Central Asian governments. Central Asian consumers have often complained that Chinese merchants frequently sell products of low quality. However, Chinese officials point out that it is often the Central Asian merchants who purchase low quality, but inexpensive goods in China for resale in their home countries. Similarly, Kazakhstan has launched official protests with China expressing its concern over the potential harmful impact of the tests on the ecology of the region.

Murat Mukhtarovich Auezov, currently Director-General of the National Library of Kazakhstan and former Ambassador to China, while emphasizing that the Central Asian states need to maintain their relationship with China very seriously, also points to certain difficulties in China's relationship with Central Asia when he notes:

> In the days of the Soviet Union, there was a certain balance of power between Russia and China, which took account of Central Asian interests. For instance, when China claimed the right to the waters of the Black Irtysh, the Soviet Union threatened to cut off the Kyzyl Su waters that provide water to the Kashgar Valley. But since the collapse of the Soviet Union, Central Asian countries have had to move to a principle of bilateral relations with China on these issues. There is no doubt that China has been the winner against Central Asian countries on a number of contentious issues concerning border territories and trans-border rivers and the latter have lost a lot. Now every drop of the Kyzyl Su that flows from Kyrgyzstan to Uzbekistan and Kazakhstan is counted, but there is no account of the waters that flow into Chinese territory. Similar is the case with the waters of the Black Irtysh. Many such problems with China can be recounted.[71]

On the Central Asian side, there has also been some unease about a possible Chinese influx that could result from large scale Chinese economic penetration into the region. Chinese bilateral agreements on joint ventures with all the states has led to large scale resettling of Chinese in the Central Asian states. Many Chinese who came to give economic assistance then stayed on after the expiry of their visas. Some married local women and acquired property. Central Asian authorities have not moved to expel the illegal settlers for fear of antagonizing the Chinese government but a degree of concern is evident from a reading of local newspapers.[72]

However, not all opinions are critical and some Central Asian analysts echo the Chinese position when they clearly state that there is no connection between the growing economic power of China and its penetration into neighbouring states, on the one hand, and the perception of China as a threat, on the other.[73] In this context, Virina Galyamova notes that Kazakhstan, for instance, has developed increased immunity to problems of external influence and that in any case the main focus of China is economic cooperation with the Asia-Pacific region, which puts development of relations with the Central Asian states in second place.[74]

On the whole, significance of links with China has been acknowledged by the Central Asian leadership. For instance, in the course of addressing Kazakh diplomats, the Kazakh President Nursultan Nazarbaev noted:

> In Asia, the key priority is towards China. In the context of the processes of economic integration and development of partnership with the region's countries, the effective employment of communication channels connecting Kazakhstan with the region through China is extremely important.[75]

Such statements lend credence to the future prospects of Sino-Central Asian engagements. Acknowledging this Irina D Zvyagelskaia writes:

China moving gradually towards a leading position in the struggle for influence in the post Soviet era has geographical advantage. It also has far fewer limitations than its Middle Eastern (Muslim) rivals. A regulated economy, which is more compatible with the secular state and available financial means are also in the plus side. China offers the Central Asian states the use of its territory to gain direct access to the Pacific and on the Far East and Southeastern Asia.[76]

At present China's policy towards Central Asia seems to be a two fold one of keeping its political presence restricted and expanding its economic opportunities and developing a large Central Asian market. In all of this a multilateral approach is clearly evident. Establishment of a stable neighbourhood and maintenance of economic reforms are identified as basic priorities. Here, internal developments and linkages of the recent past may assume as significant a role as historical or ethnographic legacies in determining the direction China's relationship with the Central Asian states will assume. China's strategy towards the Central Asian region seems to be to influence the developing economic life of the region and to maintain political stability through mutual cooperation.

While the two previous chapters examined the Russo-Central Asian and Sino-Central Asian relations the next chapter moves on to examine the trilateral Russo-Sino-US relationship and how developments in these relationships affect the Central Asian region.

NOTES AND REFERENCES

1. See for instance Diane L. Smith, "Central Asia: A New Great Game?", http://www.writersg.com/milnet/pentagon/centasia/cenasap5.htm
2. Dr J. Mohan Malik," China, Central Asia, India and Pakistan Now Come Face to Face with Vigorous Separatism", *Defence and Foreign Affairs Strategic Policy*, 30 September, 1993.

3. For a detailed account of the nature of Xinjiang's western borderlands see Witt Raczka, "Xinjiang and its Central Asian Borderlands", *Central Asian Survey*, Vol 17, No 3, 1998. Raczka contrasts the natural north-south divide of the region with the imperial east-west divide and suggests that the north-south divide is far less arbitrary than the imperial China/Russia border.

4. V.V. Barthold, *Turkestan Down to the Mongol Invasion*, (reprint) London: Lowe and Brydone, 1968.

5. Mustafa Chokaev, "Turkestan and the Soviet Regime", *Journal of Royal Central Asian Society*, Vol 28, 1931.

6. Geoffrey Wheeler, *The Modern History of Soviet Central Asia*, London: Weidenfeld and Nicolson, 1964.

7. V.V. Sovslyev, O.A. Pidayeva and A.I. Markova, *Uzbekistan—Nezavisimi Kronika Sovetii*, Tashkent: Uzbekiston, 1993.

8. I.A. Karimov, *Uzbekistan on the Threshold of the Twenty-First Century, Threats to Security, Conditions of Stability and Guarantees of Progress*, Tashkent: Uzbekiston, 1997.

9. For a detailed analysis see Anita Sengupta *Frontiers into Borders: The Transformation of Identities in Central Asia* (published for Maulana Abul Kalam Azad Institute of Asian Studies) Delhi and London: Hope India Publications and Greenwich Millennium Press Ltd, 2002.

10. Busra Ersanli Behar, "Rediscovering Multidimensionality: Turkey's Quest for Partnership with the Turkic Republics", *Private VIEW*, Winter, 1997.

11. *Eastern Turkestan Information*, Vol 2, No 2, March 1992, cited from Michael Dillon, *Xinjiang — China's Muslim Far Northeast*, London and New York: Routledge Curzon, 2004.

12. Cited from Dillon, *Xinjiang — China's Muslim Far Northeast.*

13. For details see Dillon, *Xinjiang — China's Muslim Far Northeast.*

14. For details of the beginning of opposition to Han Chinese control see Dillon, *Xinjiang — China's Muslim Far Northeast.*

15. Cited from L.K. Choudhary, "Islamic Militancy and Terrorism in Xinjiang: China's Anxiety and Concerns", *India Quarterly*, Vol

LVIII, No 2, April-June 2002.

16. For details see Dillon, *Xinjiang — China's Muslim Far Northeast.*
17. See Lillian Craig Harris, "Xinjiang, Central Asia and the Implications for China's Policy in the Islamic World", *The China Quarterly*, No 133, March 1993.
18. As reported by Ahmed Rashid, "The Chinese Connection", *The Herald*, December 1995 cited from Choudhary, "Islamic Militancy and Terrorism in Xinjiang.
19. For details see Dillon, *Xinjiang — China's Muslim Far Northeast.*
20. For a detailed examination of Islam in the region see Dillon, *Xinjiang — China's Muslim Far Northeast.*
21. See Cui-Yi Wei, "Ancient Chinese Historical Records About Central Asia", *Central Asian Survey*, Vol 5, No 2, 1986.
22. For details of the poetry see Wei, "Ancient Chinese Historical Records About Central Asia".
23. See W.J. Drew, "Sinkiang: The Land and the People", *Central Asian Review*, Vol XVI, No 3, 1968.
24. Raczka, "Xinjiang and its Central Asian Borderlands".
25. Felix K. Chang, "China's Central Asian Power and Problems", *Orbis*, Vol 41, No 3, Summer 1997.
26. Owen Lattimore, *The Inner Asian Frontiers of China*, (reprint) Hong Kong: Oxford University Press, 1988.
27. Justin Ben-Adam, "China", in David Westerlund and Ingvar Svanberg (eds) *Islam Outside the Arab World*, London: Curzon Press, 1999. For details also see Yuan Qing-Li, " Population Changes in the Xinjiang Uighur Autonomous Region (1949-1984)", *Central Asian Survey*, Vol 9 No 1, 1990.
28. Eden Naby, "Uighur Elites in Xinjiang", *Central Asian Survey*, Vol 5, No 3/4 1986.
29. Drew, "Sinkiang: The Land and the People".
30. Jon Justin Rudelson, "Uighur Historiography and Uighur Ethnic Identity Change", in Ingvar Svanberg (ed) *Ethnicity, Minorities*

and Cultural Encounters, Uppsala: Centre For Multiethnic Research, 1991.

31. Justin Jon Rudelson, "The Uighurs in the Future of Central Asia", *Nationalities Papers*, Vol 22, No 2, 1994.

32. Lattimore, *The Inner Asian Frontiers of China*,.

33. Dru C. Gladney, "The Ethnogenesis of the Uighur", *Contemporary Central Asia*, Vol 9, No 1, 1990.

34. David Finkelstein, "China's Emergence in Central Asia: Security, Diplomatic and Economic Interests", *CSIS Forum on the Current State of China-Central Asia Diplomacy and Implications for US Foreign Policy*, Wednesday, February 5, 2003.

35. See for instance, Virina Galyamova, "Vozrozhdayushiesya Gigant i Kitaiskaya Ugroza v Istorichiskoi Retrospektive", *Kazakhstan i Sovremennie Mir*, Vol 1, No 2, 2002; Shiping Tang,"Economic Integration in Central Asia: The Russian and Chinese Relationships", *Asian Survey*, Vol XL, No 2, April 2000. See also John Calabrese, "China's Policy Towards Central Asia: Renewal and Accommodation", *Eurasian Studies*, No 16, Autumn-Winter 1999 and James P Dorian, Brett Wigdortz and Dru Gladney, "Central Asia and Xinjiang, China:Emerging Energy, Economic and Ethnic Problems", *Central Asian Survey*, Vol 16, No 4, 1997.

36. Finkelstein, "China's Emergence in Central Asia: Security, Diplomatic and Economic Interests".

37. Zhao Shaoqin, "Nation May Import 50 million tonnes of crude Oil in 2000", *China Daily*, July 3, 2000.

38. Sun Zhuangzhi, "US Strategy in Central Asia", *Beijing Review*, Vol 43, no 26, June 26, 2000.

39. Ross H. Munroe, "Central Asia and China", in Michael Mandelbaum (ed) *Central Asia and the World*, New York: Council on Foreign Relations Press, 1994.

40. *Renmin Ribao*, 19 April 1994 cited in Guangcheng Xing, "China and Central Asia: Towards a New Relationship", in Yongjin Zang and Rouben Azizian (eds) *Ethnic Challenges Beyond Borders: Chinese and Russian Perspectives of the Central Asian*

Conundrum, Oxford: Macmillan in association with St Antony's College Oxford, 1998.

41. *Renmin Ribao*, 4 July 1994, cited in Xing, "China and Central Asia: Towards a New Relationship".

42. See Foreign Ministry of China documents on agreements with the Central Asian states. All of them agree that Taiwan is an integral part of China.

43. "China Provides Trade Gateway for Central Asia", *China Daily*, June 9, 1999.

44. For a detailed discussion see Limanov Oleg,"China's Policy Towards Central Asia in the Post Soviet Era", in P Stobdan (ed) *Building A Common Future: Indian and Uzbek Perspectives on Security and Economic Issues*, New Delhi: Knowledge World in association with IDSA, 1999.

45. Ma Jiali "Central Asia: Geostrategic Situation and Big Powers' Policy", *Contemporary Central Asia*, Vol 3, No 1, April 1999.

46. "Turkmenistan, China Discuss Gas Pipeline Project", *FBIS-CHI-2000-0706* dated July 6,2000.

47. Shao Qin, "Experts Call for Oil Strategy", *China Daily*, January 10, 2000.

48. Guangcheng Xing "Security Issues in China's Relations with Central Asian States" in Zhang and Azizian (eds) *Ethnic Challenges Beyond Borders*.

49. Xing "Security Issues in China's Relations with Central Asian States.

50. Xing "Security Issues in China's Relations with Central Asian States.

51. Finkelstein, "China's Emergence in Central Asia: Security, Diplomatic and Economic Interests". Also see Li Jingjie, "Pillars of the Sino Russian Partnership", *Orbis*, Vol 44, No 4, Fall 2000.

52. John Anderson, *The International Politics of Central Asia*, Manchester and New York: Manchester University Press, 1997.

53. The growing economic power of the Chinese in the Central Asian

market was attested to by Dr Dostym A. Satpayev, (Director Assesment Risks Group) in the course of a conversation with the author in Almaty on December 3, 2003.

54. *Economic Intelligence Report*, "Kyrgyzstan Country Report", 4th Quarter, 1996.

55. "Akaev on Trade Developments with China. Pakistan", *Kyrgyz Radio First Programme*, Bishkek, December 13, 1994.

56. For details see Victor Krivonogov, "Kazakhstansko-Kitaiskie Togovo, Ekonomicheskie i Nayuchno-Tekhnicheskiye Otnosheniya" *Kazakhstan i Sovremennie Mir*, No1(4), 2003.

57. *International Monetary Fund Direction of Trade Statistics Handbook*, August 1998. Also see Dai Xaiohua, "China-Kazakhstan Trade and Economic Cooperation Promising", *Beijing Review*, Vol 41, No 20, May 18-24, 1998 and Yasmin Melet," China's Political and Economic relations with Kazakhstan and Kyrgyzstan", *Central Asian Survey* Vol 17, No 2, 1998. Melet provides detailed statistics of trade figures between China and the two states for 1992-1995.

58. Martha Brill Olcott, "How New is the New Russia? Demographic Upheavals in Central Asia", *Orbis*, Fall 1996.

59. Rosemarie Forsythe, "The Politics of Oil in the Caucasus and Central Asia", *Adelphi Papers* No 300, London:Oxford University Press, 1996.

60. Qingjian Liu, "Sino-Central Asian Trade and Economic Relations: Progress, Problems and Prospects", in Zang and Azizan (ed) *Ethnic Challenges Beyond Borders*.

61. Liu, "Sino-Central Asian Trade and Economic Relations: Progress, Problems and Prospects".

62. Kambiz Arman, "US Geopolitical Position Takes Hit in Tajikistan", *Eurasia Insight*, July 21, 2004.

63. Ted Weihman, "China Making Diplomatic Push in Central Asia", *Eurasianet*, June 9, 2003.

64. Weihman, "China Making Diplomatic Push in Central Asia".

65. *FBIS-SOV*-229-95, November 27, 1992.

66. Michael Yahuda, "China's Search for a Global Role", *Current History*, September 1999.

67. Francesco Sisci "China Eyes Silk Road All the Way to the US", *Asia Times*, June 18, 2001 cited from Jyotsna Bakshi, *Russia-China Relations, Relevance for India*, Delhi: Shipra, 2004.

68. Bakshi, *Russia-China Relations.*

69. A. Smagulov, "China in the Foreign Economic Strategy of Kazakhstan", *Novoye Pokoleniye*, No 16, Almaty, 1994, cited in Yuiry Kulchik, Andrey Fadin and Victor Sergeev, *Central Asia After the Empire*, London and Chicago: Pluto Press, 1996.

70. *Res Publica*,"The Uighur Question is Not only China's Internal Affair", April 27, 1997, Bishkek in *World News Connection*, April 29, 1997.

71. Murat Mukhtarovich Auezov, "India, Russia and China in the Emerging Dynamics of Central Asia", in K. Santhanam and Ramakant Dwivedi (eds) *India and Central Asia: Advancing the Common Interest*, New Delhi:Anamaya Publishers, 2004.

72. For one such report see Dillon, *Xinjiang — China's Muslim Far Northeast*. Details of this penetration is also available in Akihiro Iwashita, *A 4000 Kilometer Journy Along the Sino- Russian Border*, Slavic Research Cenre, Hokkaido University:Sappora, 2004.

73. See for instance, Galyamova, "Vozrozhdayushiesya Gigant i Kitaiskaya Ugroza v Istorichiskoi Retrospektive".

74. Galyamova, "Vozrozhdayushiesya Gigant i Kitaiskaya Ugroza v Istorichiskoi Retrospektive".

75. "The Kazakh President defines the Republic's Foreign Policy", *Kazakhstanskaya Pravda*, February 16, 1995 cited in Melet, "China's Political and Economic relations with Kazakhstan and Kyrgyzstan".

76. Irina D Zvyagelskaia, "Central Asia and the Caucasus: New Geopolitics", in Vitaly Naumkin (ed) *Central Asia and Transcaucasus: Ethnicity and Conflict*, Westport, CT: Greenwood Publishing Group, 1994.

Chapter 3

Russia-China-United States

Three "Bilateral Relations" in Central Asia

In terms of the changed global environment in the aftermath of 9/11, the development of parallel Sino-US relations and Sino-Russian relations is being advocated within China. Su Ge, Deputy President of the China Institute of International Studies elaborates on this in these words:

> Facing the new international situation, we need "to advance with the times". Under the new international environment, we should recast the old ideology of "zero sum game" and foster a new security concept of gaining security through mutual trust and cooperation. With the development of the international situation, China, the United States and Russia will increase the convergence of their national interests. The gain of one side should not necessarily mean the loss of the other two sides. And, vise versa, nor the loss by either sides, not necessarily the gain of the third party. If properly coordinated it is probable that a "win-win-win" or "win-win" result will appear in the relations among the three countries. Hence it would seem improper to view Sino-US-Russian relations under the new situation with the traditional concept of "triangular relationship.
>
> It would be more apt to view the new Sino-US-Russian relations as three parallel "triangular relationships". The three bilateral relations, i.e, Sino-US relations, Sino-Russian relations and Russian-US relations are mutually related and at the same time mutually independent. The nature of the "trilateral relations" is entirely different from that of the

"triangular relationship" during the period of the Cold war. Firstly, the new trilateral relations feature non-confrontation. For instance, out of their respective national strategic interests, while maintaining friendly relations with each other, neither China nor Russia want to confront the US. The US also endeavours to maintain cooperative relations, with both China and Russia, even if there are differences, it tries to prevent contestations from escalating into confrontation. Secondly, the "trilateral relations" have the feature of coexistence of cooperation and competition. Each of the three countries has its specific strategic intentions and goals and adjustment of the relations among one another is still underway. But all of them can still try to seek the convergence of their national interests, i.e, to maintain regional and world peace and development. Thirdly, the "trilateral relations" have "non-symmetrical" characteristics. As the comprehensive strength of the US is much stronger than that of China and Russia, the trend of US global strategy and foreign policy will to a great extent affect the changes of the trilateral relations.[1]

Strategic writings from within China today stress the significance of maintaining cooperative relations with Russia and the United States which take into account "specific strategic intentions and goals".[2] With this is the clear realization that the "comprehensive strength" of the US is stronger than Russia and China and that Sino-Russian relations are bound to be affected by US global strategy. In fact, a section of analysts from the Central Asian region itself have emphasized this in the post 9/11 scenario. Talgat Ismagambetov, Deputy Director of the Institute of Russia and China in Kazakhstan notes:

> After the events of September 11 and October 7, 2001, USA has become the key player in the region. It is the USA that has been acting with the greatest consideration for the specifics of the country's geopolitics. One example of this strategy has been the intention to establish military bases near Karshi, Uzbekistan and at the airport in Bishkek,

Kyrgyzstan. By so doing they are controlling the heartland of the region — the south of contemporary Uzbekistan.[3]

This is also clearly evident from Russian strategic writings on Sino-Russian relations. Yuri V. Tsyganov, commenting on Sino-Russian strategic partnership notes:

> Rapprochement is motivated by the external logic of the "triangular" strategic relationship and the main value of their cooperation is determined by a shared need to meet real or perceived challenges from the West.[4]

Similarly strategic writings from China stress that the presence of the US factor is undeniable in Sino-Russian relations.[5] This is most particularly true in so far as Sino-Russian relations with respect to Central Asia is concerned. The American factor is not merely the result of the presence of American troops and the establishment of bases in the region that is generally projected as a deterrence to Russian and Chinese influence. It developed over the course of the evolution of Sino-Russian relations from being purely endogenous to an exogenous one.

The transformation in Sino-Russian relations took place during the visit of the Russian President Boris Yeltsin to China in April 1996 when China and Russia announced the establishment of a strategic cooperation partnership and created the Shanghai Five as a dialogue mechanism. The formation of the Shanghai Five was an important turning point in the externalization of Sino-Russian relations and also marked the beginning of the expansion of bilateral relations to a multilateral one, with the recognition of common interests in the Central Asian region as the pivot. It has been noted that the growth of the US factor in Sino-Russian relations is an outcome of this transformation.[6]

It is undeniable that the Central Asian region forms a significant part of the interaction between Russia, China and the United States today. This became more particularly so in the aftermath of September 11 with the recognition of the significance of the region in any "war against terror". As American presence increased and the US was offered basing rights by the Central Asian states, an entirely new set of geopolitical relations was seen to be emerging where traditional areas of interest were projected to have been transformed. Accepting the position that the Russo-Sino-US interaction should be dealt with as a set of three bilateral relations this chapter examines ways in which they have been transformed in the course of developments in the recent past. General developments within each of them and the international environment that affected their relations will form the background against which their interactions over the Central Asian region will be examined.

Reflecting on the interplay between China, Russia and the United States in the Central Asian region, former National Security Advisor Zbigniew Brzezinski notes:

> The United States will be favourably positioned between Russia and China: one whose influence is receding, but whose influence, in its residual fashion, may actually even be more attractive to Central Asian countries because it will be less threatening: and one whose influence is rising but whose ambitions may make the Central Asian states nervous... US interests by and large are benefiting from the fact that instead of monolithic control over the region a more complicated set of bilateral relationships between an expanding indirect Chinese influence and a receding but less threatening Russian presence is developing.[7]

Events following 9/11 also seemed to indicate that certain premises of international politics would also have to be reexamined to take into account recent transformations in the relations between states. For instance, traditionally, interactions between states has been assumed to be reflective of a desire to further national interests as defined by them. Alternative non-rationalist interpretations now emphasize that states not only pursue their national interests in interactions among themselves but also seek to establish identities for themselves. Relations between states should therefore be examined not just in terms of advantages of victory but simply in terms of privileges of winning.

This chapter attempts to examine the usefulness of such interpretations in the set of three bilateral relations i.e, Russo-US, Sino-US and Sino-Russian, particularly in terms of their interaction over Central Asia. It examines the "three bilateral relations" in terms of not just interests but a search for identity. It begins by looking into what is now defined as the "new" Russo-US rivalry in the region before moving on to examine the rhetoric and reality of Sino-US interactions. It then examines Sino-Russian relations in terms of emerging realities in the region and in the background of their position on the necessity of multilateralism.

The Recognition Game in Central Asia

Elaborating on his alternative identity based model for interaction between states, Eric Ringmar notes:

> The problem with traditional explanations of relations between states is that they focus on matters of interests and pay insufficient attention to matters of identity. (This discussion can be improved) by providing a formal discussion on the role of recognition. World politics is best described as a recognition game rather than a prisoner's dilemma.[8]

Ringmar goes on to prove the applicability of this argument through an analysis of the relations between Soviet Russia and the West and attempts to define a number of important events of the twentieth century in a new fashion. In fact, he notes, questions regarding a state's identity must always be more fundamental than questions regarding its interests.

Ringmar argues that the confrontation between capitalism and communism, democracy and dictatorship, the arms race and the threat of nuclear annihilation, were not primarily the consequences of mutually incompatible interests, but instead the result of mutually incompatible descriptions of self and the other. He goes on to state that throughout most of this century Soviet Russia was the unrecognized party and the West (and after the Second World War the United States) was the recognized party. During the entire era, the Soviet state had to fight to be accepted. In the 1920's the Bolsheviks sought recognition as a "legitimate state", under Stalin recognition as a "great power", during the Cold War the position of a "superpower" and during the Gorbachev era to be acknowledged as a part of the "common house of Europe".

Ringmar concludes his article with the mid 1980's. Most recent writings on Russia's relationship with the United States, in the post September 11 era, seem to extend Ringmar's arguments to note that it was actually 9/11 that provided Russia with the perfect opportunity for "recognition". Post September 11, in President Bush's view, the world was divided into two groups, those countries supporting the United States in its war against terrorism and those that were not. In this black and white world Russia was seen to clearly emerge as a supporter of the war against terrorism. Therefore in President Bush's view, Russia became a "partner, a friend and even an ally" of the United States in the global war against terrorism.[9] And finally the trajectory of integration into a "common House of Europe" and of recognition as a partner was assumed to have been achieved.

A significant part of this recognition involved Russian acquiescence to the entry of the United States forces into Central Asia. As the "soft underbelly" of the Russian state Central Asia has always been crucial in Russia's strategic perspective. The stationing of US forces in the region was, thus, seen as a major concession. While it is true that as members of the Partnership for Peace (PfP) initiative the Central Asian states were already part of the NATO, yet, it was September 11 that actually saw the entry of the American troops and the use of Central Asian air bases. While these states had been recognized as geopolitically significant ever since Mackinder named them the "heartland"

and Kipling portrayed a "great game" for influence, it was actually the post 9/11 era that seemed to highlight their significance as major players in the "war against terrorism".

The Central Asian response to this new geostrategic significance varied, depending on the level of dependence on Russian military assistance. Uzbekistan, for instance, had already opted out of the Collective Security Agreements of the CIS and was the first to offer air bases and use of air space to the US. In return the US declared that the *Islamic Movement of Uzbekistan* that had proved problematic to the Uzbek state was a terrorist organization. It was hoped that further concessions would accrue.[10] It was thus assumed that a new era had arrived in the US partnership with the post Soviet space where a neutralized Russia would recognize the US position in the region.

However, very soon there were disagreements on how long American troops would stay on in Central Asia. Russian Parliamentary Speaker Gennady Seleznov warned, "Russia will not approve of permanent US military bases in Central Asia."[11] While the Bush and Putin administration also disagreed on a number of other issues and even on the definition of terrorism, it is on the issue of extension of influence over Central Asia that there appears to be a definite change in the Russian stance.

Illustrative of the Central Asian response to these changed situations is Uzbekistan's interactions with Russia and the US in the post 9/11 era. Though it would be more correct to define the foreign policy orientation of each state separately, the Uzbek case is interesting as both the exception and, in some cases, the rule. In the immediate post 9/11 period Uzbekistan had shared close collaborative relations with the US. Uzbekistan had already moved out of the Collective Security Agreement of the CIS in 1999 and this coupled with its close alliance with the US was seen as illustrative of a cooling off of its relations with Russia. However, disappointment with financial incentives received from the US led to reinstatement of relations with Russia and in June 2002, Uzbekistan became a member of the SCO.

Russia also revived attempts to reintegrate Uzbekistan within a common economic bloc and during a visit to Uzbekistan, on August 6, 2003, President Putin attempted to convince Uzbek President Karimov to enter the single economic zone, that currently includes Russia, Belarus, Ukrain and Kazakhstan.[12] However, President Karimov refused to be co-opted into the single economic zone and only recognized that Russia had a legitimate interest in what went on along its southern border. He also offered only limited support in the Shanghai Cooperation Organization's efforts to build a counter terrorism force.

However, it is also true that when the GUUAM (the organization of Georgia, Ukrain, Uzbekistan, Azerbaijan and Moldova) was recently revived, with active US assistance, as a counter to Russian attempts to revive the Eurasian Economic Community, Uzbekistan preferred to opt out of it. Uzbek Foreign Minister Abdulaziz Komilov noted that the Uzbek position was based on the fact that Uzbekistan was finding it more convenient to trade through non-GUUAM countries than through GUUAM mechanisms. It was, of course, later clarified that Uzbekistan had not withdrawn from GUUAM but merely "suspended" its participation in the grouping.[13] In March 2002 Uzbekistan signed a Declaration of Strategic Partnership with the US.[14]

Subsequently, while speaking at the opening of the Fall Parliamentary Session on September 1, 2003, President Karimov stressed the importance of bilateral relations with Russia but pointed out that this would not mean a deterioration of relations with the US.[15] Similarly, in the aftermath of the March 28-31, 2004, militant attacks in Tashkent and Bukhara, Uzbekistan sought to boost economic and political ties with Russia. The Uzbek and Russian Presidents negotiated a Uzbek-Russian strategic cooperation pact though no desire was shown to downgrade relations with the United States.[16] However, an announcement in July 2004 that the US would withhold its economic assistance to Uzbekistan coupled with an expanded economic partnership with Russia, in the oil and gas sector, could well herald a change in priorities.[17]

Similarly, Kazakhstan's relationship with Russia, its largest neighbour and main foreign trade partner, has not prevented it from expanding its military-technical cooperation with the United States. In accordance with a five year plan signed by the two states in September 2003, the US will develop Kazakhstan's military infrastructure, provide military hardware and arms that meet modern standards, train and equip Kazakhstan's Kazbat peacekeeping battalion and assist in the creation of a professional army. However, US presence in the region is not accepted without criticism. Olga Zakrzhevskaya, Professor of International Relations Chair of the Kazakh University of International Relations and World Languages, clearly states:

> The line taken by USA, which has taken on itself the role of the main actor in the war against international terrorism, is proof of its endeavors not towards the consolidation of strengths and activities of countries, in the first place, nor of its interest in eliminating and eradicating international terrorism but actually to use this in their interest in implementing its own geopolitical plans i.e, widening its presence, including the military one in Central Asia, weakening the role and influence of Russia and China in the region and ultimately to use the situation prevailing in post-war Afghanistan to consolidate the unipolar world order while preserving only the American centre of power.[18]

Kazakhstan has also taken advantage of the preferential terms afforded to Collective Security Treaty Organization members, for the purchase of Russian military hardware and arms. Tajikistan has also welcomed western cooperation and aid while becoming more assertive regarding the reorganization of the Russian troops stationed on its territory. While this has been interpreted by some analysts as a distinct move towards the US, though not all analysts agree.[19]

In 2003 President Askar Akaev released Kyrgyzstan's new foreign policy doctrine where he states that in view of

Kyrgyzstan's geographical location Kyrgyzstan has the need and the opportunity for simultaneously developing fruitful relations between Kyrgyzstan and the neighbouring countries, Kyrgyzstan and Europe and Kyrgyzstan and the East and South-East Asia.[20] A spate of activity in foreign policy terms indicates that this has been put into practice. President Akaev has stressed that security in Central Asia cannot be achieved without Russian influence and help and there has been an agreement with Moscow to raise Russian troop levels in Kant to one thousand, by the end of 2004. At the same time Kyrgyzstan has sought to increase cooperation with the US and an agreement has been reached extending military cooperation for another five years to 2010. Kyrgyzstan's military cooperation has not stopped with Russia and the US alone. Britain has stepped up its commitment to provide language training to the Kyrgyz military and France has signed a cooperation agreement for annual officer exchanges between the two countries. On the non-military front Kyrgyzstan has also increased trade cooperation with Iran.

The response of the Central Asian states to the Iraq crisis also differed, indicating not just domestic considerations but also the balance of power between the Russia and the US. Despite the presence of the largest US base in the region, Kyrgyzstan denied the US and allied forces permission to use Kyrgyz bases to launch operations against Iraq and expressed support for the German-French-Russian position on the crisis as did Kazakhstan and Tajikistan. The only state to support US action was Uzbekistan while Turkmenistan, maintaining neutrality did not officially react to the situation. While the Kyrgyz position was based on the fact that support could prove potentially dangerous to the ruling regime, the Kazakh position reflected a desire to minimize the risk of loss of income due to any flood of cheap Iraqi oil in the market leading to a post war slump in oil prices.[21]

This prompts one to argue that Ringmar, in his analysis of world politics, had failed to take note of the fact that the "recognition game" often involves an independent set of actors, recognition from whom and recognition of "special interests" over whom becomes crucial in determining the final outcome. As independent actors in world affairs today, the Central Asian states are themselves engaged in a combination of the "recognition game" and a search for the best way to achieve their national/ special interests and it is important to take this into consideration. The recognition of a "special interest" in its near abroad has always played a significant part in the Russian recognition game. The duality that Russian foreign policy displays in its westward orientation, on the one hand, and an attempt to reemerge as a significant power over its 'near abroad' in Central Asia, on the other, is reflective of the fact that while "recognition" is important, a set of core *special interests* remain equally crucial.

It would be interesting to extend Ringmar's argument and examine the interaction of Russia and the United States in the Central Asian region in the aftermath of 9/11 within the framework of a "recognition game". Most Russian actions in the immediate aftermath of September 11 seemed to indicate that the Russia had in fact decided to further its recognition in the West through active involvement in the "war against terror". It was equally evident one year after that what continued to be crucial was the recognition of Russian special interests in the Central Asian region. In fact, Central Asia has always been critical in the Russian search for identity and this has defined Russia's relations with the Central Asian region since the nineteenth century. Moves made by Russia in recent months, to counter US presence in the region particularly through reinforcing existing CIS agreements is reflective of this. Yet, along with this there remains the recognition of the presence of other powers in the region and an indication of this is the active Russian involvement in the SCO.

Sino-US interactions in the immediate post September 11 era similarly illustrates that while "recognition" was a significant part of relationship yet certain core issues of interest remained significant. After an initial period of reluctance China extended support to the US "war against terror" by offering to share information and support the US effort in post war reconstruction of Afghanistan. For China, as for Russia, Central Asia has increasingly assumed significance over the last decade.

Independence, not only created the need to define borders with the new states but also threw up the question of the significance of emerging pan-Turkic ideas in western and eastern Turkestan. On the other hand the region, with long common borders and unexplored markets, offered immense economic opportunities. The recognition of this significance meant that Chinese reactions over American and NATO presence in the region had moved through various phases from an initial one of reservation to acceptance and back to a position of reservation about the long term American presence in the region. While on the one hand China recognizes the significance of American presence in the region as a stabilizing factor on the other there is recognition that long-term presence may reduce her own influence. There is therefore a move towards multilateralism evident in most Chinese actions in the region.

Russia and United States in Central Asia: The "New" Rivalry

The "new" rivalry between Russia and the US is particularly interesting since it was assumed that the cordial atmosphere that had developed in the immediate aftermath of the September 11 events would herald a new era in Russia-US relations, particularly as far as policy towards Central Asia was concerned. The 9/11 events were seen to "spark a Russian pivot" to which the West was seen to have responded very positively. President Vladimir Putin was noted, as the first foreign head of state, to have called President Bush and then followed it up with a whole string of actions that amounted to a wholesale reorientation of Russian foreign policy.[22] From September 11 onward, often acting without the support of his foreign and defence advisers, Putin was seen to have recognized the primacy of the US even within the strategic borders of Russia.[23] In fact many American scholars admitted that in the "war against terror" in Afghanistan the contributions made by the Russians exceeded those made by all the NATO allies of the United States combined. [24] Apart from that, Russia in order to improve relations with the United States, also made concessions on other important issues. For instance, it tacitly consented to the unilateral withdrawal of the United States from the Anti ballistic Missile Treaty signed in 1972 and abandoned the limit which it had set on the NATO's eastward expansion, thus removing the barriers to the three former Soviet Baltic states joining NATO. Russia also closed, on its own accord, its military bases in Cuba and Vietnam.[25]

This was reflected in statements that noted:

> The war on terrorism has brought Washington and Moscow closer and has seen the development of a personal relationship between President Bush and President Putin. Before the 2001 terror attacks on the United states few would have thought that Russia would sit by while America established a military presence in four of the Soviet Union's successor states, given Moscow's earlier reactions to United States criticism of Russian conduct in Chechnya. Yet Russia seemed to acquiesce to America's movement into Central Asia and even remained quiet when American troops landed on Russia's border in the Caucasus.[26]

However, the fact that such depictions were not entirely correct is evident from the fact that when the United States began contacting the Central Asian states about basing rights in early October 2001, officials in the Russian military and Putin's government are supposed to have privately exerted pressure on the Central Asian governments to decline the American requests. It was only with the realization that most of the Central Asian governments would agree to host the American troops that Putin publicly stated that Russia had no objection to what was now a *fait accompli*.[27]

In fact, when President Bush had called President Putin on

the weekend of September 22, 2001, and asked if the Russian President would use his influence with the Central Asian states to help the US obtain basing rights, President Putin had replied:

> I am prepared to tell the heads of government of the Central Asian states that we have good relations with and that we have no objections to a US role in Central Asia as long as it has the object of fighting the war on terror and is *temporary and not permanent*. (emphasis mine) If it is that then we have no objection and that is what I will tell people.[28]

It is not surprising therefore that a year later there was a reversal of trends with reports of a growing disillusionment in Russia about the strategic partnership agreements concluded with the US and other western allies over the past year. In fact there have also been adverse reactions to the presence of the NATO forces in Central Asia, which is now seen as "the penetration of a strategic region that undermines the security not only of Russia but also of China".[29] While those close to the Russian army were most vocal about expressing their displeasure, it was also reflected in the Russian press with the *Nezavisimaya Gazeta,* referring to the presence of American troops in Afghanistan as a backward step for Russian influence in the region.[30] In response to this the Russian Foreign Minister Sergei Ivanov, insisted on a clear operational deadline for the American troops in the region arguing that they would have to leave once their objective of defeating terror, per se, had been achieved.[31]

In addition, the two countries have significant differences regarding the definition of terrorism and a number of other issues. The issue of Iraq is a prime example where US claims of Iraqi violation of a ban on the development of weapons of mass destruction has been negated by Russia, with President Putin pointing out that Russia does not have any intelligence proving that Iraq possessed weapons of mass destruction. Russia is also at odds with the United States, over its relations with Iran, and is dissatisfied with the attitude of the US government towards Georgia. Furthermore, Russia still has differences with the United

States regarding implementation of the treaty on the reduction of strategic offensive weapons, the US missile defence programme and other issues.

Russia and five other CIS countries, Armenia, Belarus, Kazakhstan, Kyrgyzstan and Tajikistan, in a summit held on April 28, 2003 formalized a security alliance that could help boost Moscow's presence in Central Asia by creating the Collective Security Treaty Organization (CSTO) which will attempt to provide a more efficient response to the strategic problems confronting member states, specifically terrorism and narcotics trafficking.[32] The CSTO is an outgrowth of the 1992 Collective Security Treaty, which sought to promote greater strategic Cooperation among the signatories. The Organization is now committed to creating permanent institutions, responsible for budget management and strategic military planning. The bulk of the organization's attention and resources will be initially concentrated in Central Asia with rapid deployment force to be stationed at the Russian military facility at Kant.

Russian policy makers believe that the CSTO has the potential to help Moscow reestablish its high strategic profile in what traditionally has been its sphere of influence. According to a report in the Russian daily *Nezavisimaya Gazeta*, some CSTO summit participants pressed Kyrgyz officials to curtail basing rights, given to the US forces in Manas. President Putin downplayed the notion that Russia seeks to utilize the CSTO to reduce US influence in the region, saying that the organization would strive to contain the flow of drugs coming out of Afghanistan and counter the threat posed by radical Islamic organizations in Central Asia.[33] Some political analysts believe that the impetus for the formal creation of the CSTO is concern over the US tendency under the Bush administration to take a unilateralist approach on strategic issues as recently underscored by the American campaign against Iraq.

President Putin has also sought to resurrect Russia's

diminished influence in post Cold War global politics. In addition to signing a nuclear arms treaty with Washington and setting up a new joint council with NATO, he has courted American adversaries, including China, North Korea and Iraq and extended economic ties to what the US refers as the "axis-of-evil" namely Iraq, Iran and North Korea. In addition, as already noted, Russia has stationed troops and warplanes in Kyrgyzstan.[34]

Similarly the Russo-Turkish relationship and particularly cooperation over the Central Asian region is once again attaining a positive note. Following the September 11 events diplomatic activities between Russia and Turkey were also initiated for elaborating a common approach to the problem of fighting terrorism. In a telephone conversation between the President of Turkey, Ahmet Necdet Sezer and the Russian President Putin, both heads of state pointed out "the need to step up efforts of the international community in the struggle against this phenomenon (terrorism)."[35] Subsequently an important agreement between the two countries was reached during the meeting between the Minister of Foreign Affairs of Russia, Igor Ivanov and the Minister of Foreign Affairs of Turkey, Ismail Cem, on 16 November 2001, when both ministers signed a "Plan of Action to Develop Cooperation Between the Russian Federation and the Republic of Turkey." This Plan of Action "calls for the formation between Russia and Turkey of partner relations in regional and international affairs, above all in Eurasia". The document created a new mechanism for consultations—the high level Joint Working Group, consisting of the Ministers of Foreign Affairs. The areas of cooperation have been defined very widely to include the political resolution of conflict situations, reinforcement of stability and the creation of conditions for sustainable development in Central Asia.

Consequently Russo-Turkish Cooperation assumed a new political momentum. Both countries were keen to play an important role in the new strategic and geopolitical framework in order to achieve their political objectives at the domestic and international level. For Russia these concessions include limitation of US military presence in Central Asia, cessation of criticism against Russian military action in Chechnya, Russia's WTO entry to be expedited and reduction of the Soviet debt. Similarly Turkey has been keen to assist the US since it assumes that this will make western assistance more forthcoming in terms of issues like EU flexibility over Turkish objections to NATO asset sharing with the proposed EU rapid reaction force, or a more open EU viewpoint on Turkish opposition to Cyprus's expected membership to the EU in 2004. An alliance between Russia and Turkey at this point also creates the possibility of a counterbalance to US interests in Central Asia.

In the light of these developments an important reason for Turkish-Russian collaboration in Central Asia and Caucasus is the common concern in promoting and consolidating stability and peace in the region. While Turkey seeks a more peaceful environment for the promotion and expansion of the Turkish economic sector, Russia desires stability not only for economic reasons, but also political and security considerations.

It has been noted that the recent Russian foreign policy moves may undermine the alliance between Moscow and Washington.[36] The $40 billion economic agreement with Iraq, sale of five nuclear reactors to Iran and public demonstration of warm feelings towards Kim Jung II have all been noted with apprehension in the US. Balancing these relationships with Russia's desire for a reliable partner in the Caucasus and Central Asia may prove to be difficult. Southern Caucasus also remains an area of friction between state interests and different ethnic groups and military factions. It remains to be seen whether denying the Chechens a "strategic rear" in the Pankisi Gorge and beyond and escalating pressure on Georgia will bring the Chechen conflict to an end. However, escalation of pressure on Georgia may well further exacerbate friction with Washington. Similarly, Russia insists that its war in Chechnya is an extension of the "war on terrorism". The Chechen issue, however remains a potential area of disagreement between Russia and the West. Also Russia's inability to bring the conflict to a close also has an effect on attitudes towards Russia in Central Asia.

While Russia's role in central Eurasia remains ambiguous, political analyst Ahmed Rashid notes that, a number of factors are now actually leading Russia to regain her influence over the region, not the least of which is the US administration's inability to come up with a coherent aid programme for the region. Rashid notes that another significant reason is the fact that in the post September 11 period the Central Asian elite is very seriously divided. In Turkmenistan the former Foreign Minister Boris Shikhmuradov has moved to Moscow and set up an opposition group, along with a number of other leading Turkmen political figures. In Kazakhstan the current leader of the opposition is the former Prime Minister, Akezhan Kazhegeldin. In Kyrgyzstan, similarly, many members of the former elite are in jail and now form the opposition. Because a large part of this dissident elite is now in Moscow, Rashid notes that this will allow Russia huge leverage in Central Asia.[37]

It is in this connection that Aleksie Malashenko, Professor at the Moscow Institute of International Relations points out that Russian efforts to set up a permanent Russian base in Kyrgyzstan may be significant. Kyrgyzstan is now faced with a political crisis where President Askar Akaev has accused opposition protesters of trying to destabilize the country and has indicated that he has no intentions of responding to calls to for his resignation. Malashenko has noted that the Russian military presence in the country will serve, first and foremost to maintain the rule of President Akaev, who is considered to be pro Moscow. Malashenko notes:

> The kind of developments that have taken place in Kyrgyzstan in October and November (2002), in my point of view, exactly point out that the current Kyrgyz political elite is very much interested in cooperation with Moscow. At least cooperation with Moscow, including military cooperation gives some

> confidence to Akaev's regime, while the American presence, in my opinion, in no way influences its stability or its future.[38]

In the aftermath of 9/11, Kyrgyzstan had indicated complete support for the "war against terrorism". The September 11 terrorist attacks were, in Kyrgyz President Askar Akaev's words, a turning point for the international perceptions of political and security developments in the region. President Akayev immediately expressed his condolences to the American people and his full support for the US action against international terrorism and extremism.[39] He also offered Kyrgyz airspace for the American action in Afghanistan.[40] The United States government in its turn indicated that it valued Kyrgyzstan's support and that it would extend economic and military assistance to the Republic. In December 2001, the US established a permanent military base near Bishkek airport.

The establishment of a US base in Kyrgyzstan was in many ways an unprecedented step since it was projected to mean among other things a radical reorientation of security arrangements from Russia to the US. Some political groups and the Russian military were highly critical of the US bases and this meant that Kyrgyzstan had to search for a delicate balance between the interests of the two major powers prompting analysts to note:

> After 11 September 2001, Bishkek's foreign policy makers had to find a balance between the long standing security arrangements with Russia and the newly established regime of anti-terrorist cooperation with the United States which brought a US military presence to the outskirts of Kyrgyzstan's capital. In November 2001, US personnel hastily began building the Republic's first ever American military base, just a few miles away from a Russian sponsored CIS anti-terrorist centre. Moreover the visitors were talking about extended cooperation with the independent Kyrgyz defence forces, outraging Russia's generals and political hawks.[41]

However, Kyrgyzstan is not the only Central Asian state that will be host to both Russian and American forces. In December 2002 Tajik President Imomali Rakhmonov met the US President George Bush. One of the main issues under discussion is supposed to have been the creation of a permanent US military base in Tajikistan. Tajikistan is already host to some 25,000 Russian border guards.[42] In addition, there have been talks of establishment of a permanent Russian base in Tajikistan.[43]

While Malashenko notes that President Putin's visit to Kyrgyzstan and President Rakhmonov's visit to the White House is indicative of a new military reapportionment of Central Asia with the US and Russia as the main players and will eventually result in the stability of the region, others like Alisher Abdimomunov, a deputy in the Kyrgyz Legislative Assembly and head of the Parliamentary Committee of International Relations expressed his reservations about the presence of competing powers in the state who may well be chasing different geopolitical interests.[44] It should also be kept in mind that China is also seeking to extend her influence through an alliance with Russia and through the Shanghai Cooperation Organization.

Observers believe that with Central Asian security conditions becoming more complex, countries in the region are eager to engage in cooperation with all the regional powers including China, Russia and the United States. Kazakhstan, in particular is eager to pursue a "multivector policy" as Maulen Ashimbaev, Director of the Kazakh Institute of Strategic Studies pointed out in an interview with the *Express K* newspaper.[45] Similarly, in the aftermath of the late March 2004 militant attacks in Tashkent and Bukhara, Uzbek President Karimov once again stressed the need to strengthen bilateral cooperation with Russia. Commenting on this, the Uzbek Foreign Minister Sadiq Safayev pointed out that "After deep analysis and considering prospects for bilateral relations both sides agreed that it was important that Uzbekistan and Russia sign a strategic partnership agreement in the near future".[46] In the light of such statements it appears that in perusing close strategic ties with both Russia and the United States,

Uzbekistan is following a multivector policy that Kazakhstan, Kyrgyzstan and Tajikistan already follow.

Another recent development is the reemergence of the GUUAM with active American support. The GUUAM which is a group consisting of Georgia, Ukrain, Uzbekistan, Azerbaijan and Moldova saw a revival in a meeting held on July 3-4 2003, in Yalta. It is being pointed out that much of the support needed to promote GUUAM is coming from the United States.[47] In addition to lending diplomatic encouragement, the US government is also reportedly providing economic assistance to foster GUUAM development.

Officials in Moscow have remained silent about recent GUUAM developments. But, Russian media left little doubt that Moscow views GUUAM prospects as limited. A commentary in the *Nezavisimaya Gazeta* pointed out that only two heads of state, those from Georgia and host Ukrain attended the summit. A primary source of tension between GUUAM and Russia is competing trade interests. GUUAM states have supported a trans Caucasian transport corridor known as TRASECA, which would link countries in the Caspian Basin and the Black sea regions, effectively bypassing Russia. At the same time Moscow is seeking to promote the so called North-South transport corridor. Moscow has been promoting the Eurasian Economic Community as an alternative to GUUAM.[48] What will reduce the significance of the GUUAM is the fact that Uzbekistan has decided to opt out of it though it clarified that this was a temporary measure and that Uzbekistan could rejoin the grouping, at a later date.[49]

The US position in Tajikistan has also faced challenges with the establishment of a permanent Russian military base in Tajikistan and the opening of the Khorog-Kashgar road link between Tajikistan and China. Tajik political experts have noted that US policy in Tajikistan and particularly US policy to engage in discussions with the Tajik opposition has had a significant part in this.[50] Along with the establishment of a permanent base,

Russia has also worked out details for the transfer of border security to Tajik troops. Similarly, the opening of the Khorog-Kashgar road link will significantly expand trade between Tajikistan and China and also create jobs in the Badakshan region of Tajikistan. For China, the expansion of a share in the Central Asian market has been seen as a way of expanding Chinese geopolitical influence in the region.

However, even within this framework of a "new rivalry" other issues require attention. The US and Russia have now embarked on an energy partnership with announcements about imports from Russia for the US Strategic Petroleum Reserves. At a commercial summit meeting in Houstan, Texas, in October 2002, industry leaders and officials came together to further the energy dialogue, declared by President George W. Bush and President Vladimir Putin at their Moscow Summit in May 2002.[51] While this will help to build the US emergency stockpile it is also expected to help keep Russian output of crude high at times of sagging world demands. These are issues that could well become crucial in determining the contours of the relationship and its subsequent impact on Central Asia.

Energy security remains a significant part of the US policy towards Russia and the Central Asian region. Here, it has been observed that a truce has also been declared in the "battle of the pipelines". John Erickson notes that there is in the making a form of "geostrategic-geoeconomic trade off" between Russia and the United States. In return for the agreed admission of the American military into Uzbekistan and Tajikistan, albeit viewed in some military circles as a security threat to Russia, Moscow anticipates acceptance of Russia as a secure conduit for oil and gas pipeline from the Caspian.[52] Russia's resumption of its role as a leading oil producer in the late 1990's coincided with the political and strategic changes that followed 9/11. Developments since then have deepened the United State's sense of vulnerability to imported oil supplies particularly from Saudi Arabia. Within this context an energy partnership slowly developed between the

US and Russia. This emerging cooperation was based on American oil companies, providing badly needed financial resources to Russia's energy industry and in return Moscow presented itself as a stable oil supplier to the United States.[53]

However, it is unrealistic to expect that Moscow can replace Riyad as the principal supplier of oil in the near future. Russian oil industry is still restrained by economic, political and geographical obstacles. These include hesitant reform, lack of foreign investment, inadequate transportation infrastructure and a relative shortage of proven reserves, compared to the Middle East. Russia's future level of oil production will be defined by the ability of oil companies to discover and develop oil deposits in the Arctic region, eastern Siberia and Sakhalin Islands. At the moment oil production from deposits is exceeding its rate of discovery, of new reserves, by a significant margin. The depletion of existing oilfields raises fears that Russia's current oil boom might be followed by a sharp decline in the foreseeable future. Also shipping to the US is costly because of the great distance between the two countries and the lack of Russian deep water ports.

It is undeniable that 9/11 had significant strategic impact on US relations with Russia. The war in Iraq further intensified the US efforts to reduce dependence on Middle East oil and secure supplies from other regions. However, the sheer quantity of Persian Gulf reserves ensures that Riyad will continue to have a significant impact on the world's petroleum supplies and prices. This in its turn will reflect on future developments in the region and future Russo-US interaction in the Central Asian region.

Post Beslan, there was reemergence of the debates on the limits of Russian and US power in the Caucasus and Central Asian region. It was argued that since chances of the establishment of either Russian or the US, as the dominant power was slim, it would best serve the purpose of both to increase cooperation in the two regions. The threat of renewed conflict in South Ossetia and the recent cases of radical violence in Uzbekistan have helped sharpen this viewpoint. The debate in Russia, however, is still sharply divided between those who are opposed to confrontation with the US, given the fact that Russia does not have the ability to prevent the redeployment of US troops to these regions and in any case now share a common concern about the containment of radicalism and others who continue to believe that Russia can roll back US influence in Caucaus and Central Asia.[54]

Summing up the scenario in the region, Erickson comments:

> The formation of the international coalition to wage war on terrorism transformed what has been long standing "Eurasian maneuvers", competition for political and economic influence, jostling for privileged positions to exploit huge regional energy resources.... The sanctity of the "Heartland" was not only invaded some of the invaders were actually invited in...
>
> The post September 11 rapprochement between Russia and the US provided a virtual guarantee of non interference in Russian affairs and an acknowledgement of Russian primacy in Central Asia. Washington publicly affirmed that it had no intention of "squeezing Russia out of Central Asia". However, US military presence in Central Asia must of necessity cause concern in Beijing. That development when coupled with warming US-India strategic relationship and US troops in South Korea and Japan could intensify Chinese fears of encirclement.[55]

China and the United States in Central Asia: Rhetoric and Reality

It is generally argued that most of the economic and political considerations that underlie China's policies towards the Central Asian states has little or no direct relation to its relationship with the United States. China hopes to extend economic influence, primarily through border trade, with the states. Increased trade between China and the five Republics has the potential, over the long run, to increase overall stability and economic strength of the region. Stability and economic development of the Central Asian region, as an antidote to the emergence of extremist forces in the region, is also the professed American strategy. In many ways China's role in Central Asia actually complements US policy goals for the region since China supports stable secular regional governments.

Serious conflict between China and the US over Central Asia is imaginable only if Chinese actions in the region begin to restrict international access to energy resources. This seems unlikely since the major oil bearing regions lie far from the Chinese border. However, China's support for the extension of pipeline routes from Central Asia through Iran has the potential to generate conflict between Beijing and Washington. China's oil agreement with Kazakhstan included a Chinese pledge to help construct a pipeline from Kazakhstan to the Kazakh-Turkman border with the goal of eventually extending it through to an Iranian port. This could run counter to the current US policy of denying Iran access to Central Asian oil. Despite these possibilities it is argued that China's relationship with the countries of Central Asia does not carry the same potential threat to US interests as its relationship with Russia does.

However, it is undeniable that the strategic aspect of Beijing's relationship with Moscow, which now includes the formation of a multilateral alliance along with the Central Asian states through the Shanghai Cooperation Organization, could challenge US position in the region. It is also evident that China's policy towards Central Asia is a component of a broad policy intended to gradually reduce China's vulnerability to US power and move the world towards a multipolar international order. China's reactions to the post 9/11 deployment of US forces in Central Asia is reflective of this. Beijing first evinced shock and worry over US intentions in the region and how this would affect immediate and long Chinese interests. In the next phase Chinese analysts concluded that successful US operations in Central Asia might actually stabilize the region and serve Beijing's near and mid term interests. These include destroying radical forces which threaten China and laying the foundation for regional economic development that will assist China in pursuing future trade policies in Central Asia. The identification of *Eastern Turkestan Forces,* as part of the global terrorist movement, by the US proved to be an important incentive for China to support US actions.[56] Subsequently, however, Chinese analysts reverted back to expressing concerns about long term US involvement in the region.[57]

This Chinese concern about the presence of US troops in the Central Asian region also became evident when a group of Chinese and US experts convened at the Centre for American Studies, Fudan University in early January 2002, for a strategic dialogue on regional security issues.[58] During the course of the dialogue there was recognition that each state feared that the other was trying to push it out of regional spheres of influence in Central Asia. The Chinese reservation about US troops in Central Asia was evident from the fact that the Chinese side clarified that while the US military presence was an issue between the US and its allies, in principle China did not endorse military deployment outside national borders. In particular, the Chinese side expressed reservations about the nature of the American anti-terrorism campaign and its subsequent impact on South and Central Asia.

Prior to an examination of the Sino-US interaction over the Central Asian region it would be interesting to examine the development of Sino-US relations in the post Cold War period. US policy towards China, in the immediate aftermath of the Cold War, was an extension of its policy of containment against the Soviet Union. During the course of the Chinese civil war of the late 1940's the US government expressed reservations about the emergence of a pro-Soviet Chinese Communist Party. The US government therefore adopted a policy of "non-recognition" of the People's Republic of China and intensified efforts to set up a "defence parameter" against China. However, during the end of the 1960's differences in ideology emerged between the Communist Parties of China and the Soviet Union which gradually evolved into a conflict of national interests between the two countries. The deployment of massive troops along the China-Soviet Union border following the Zhenbaodao Island incident was seen as a threat to Chinese security.

This led to a transformation of relations within the Soviet-China-US triangle with China moving closer to the US. This change was reflected in a report submitted by four Chinese marshals to the Premier Zhou Enlai in 1969, which pointed out that the contradictions between China and the Soviet Union were greater than that between China and the United States and the contradictions between the United States and the Soviet Union were greater than that China and the Soviet Union. This led to a transformation in Sino-US relations and was symbolized by the visit of President Nixon to China in 1972. The counter hegemonism embodied in the Shanghai Communiqué embodied the new Chinese strategic thinking.

By the end of the 1970's the international situation had undergone further changes, symbolized not just by the transformation of Soviet-US relations but also the emergence of multiple independent forces in world politics. On the other hand China was not taking too kindly to the repeated US interference in its internal affairs. A more independent stance emerged in Chinese foreign policy. With the end of the Cold War a new environment emerged with the US now eager to consolidate relations with its former allies and also seek new multilateral security arrangements.

In this new atmosphere Sino-US relations underwent changes with imposition of sanctions on China. On the other hand increased Russian military supplies were seen as a threat to US interests, especially to the security of Taiwan. There was also apprehension that US policies were driving Russia and China together.[59] However, the attraction of the Chinese market ensured that the US policy of "engagement" towards China continued. In the meantime, with the disintegration of the Soviet Union, a dialogue on cooperation began between Russia and the United States. Sino-Russian relations also entered a new stage with Russia clearly indicating that it would attach equal importance to Europe and the Asia-Pacific regions. This was clarified in the course of agreements on confidence building, along the border between China and the Soviet successor states in 1996. This was further strengthened with consensus on common issues of concern like the eastward expansion of the NATO, maintenance of global strategic stability and the role of the United Nations.

With the events of September 11, 2001, the global scenario changed once again with massive US efforts to strengthen coordination with its allies to deal with the threat of international terrorism. In 2001, Sino-US relations underwent a number of changes In early April the mid air collision of a Chinese fighter with a US Navy EP-3 plane seriously undermined relations. Raising the quality and quantity of the arms sales to Taiwan by the US also jeopardized Sino-US relations. However, after September 11, a dialogue was resumed with the recognition that international terrorism could only be combated through cooperation.

However, in the days and weeks after September 11, China became increasingly concerned that its strategy for expanding its presence and influence in Central Asia through the Shanghai Cooperation Organization (SCO) was in jeopardy. It was noted that the US efforts to build and lead an international coalition against terrorism had been swift and effective. The US was seen to have seized the initiative from the SCO and provided the SCO members with an alternative for addressing the issue of regional terrorism. The willingness and the level at which SCO members offered their support and cooperation to the US was noted with concern by Beijing.

China's plans to expand its influence throughout the Central Asian region was thus seen to have been put on hold by the events following 9/11. Prior to September 2001, China had been well on its way to expanding her presence over the Central Asian region. According to some western analysts, by Spring 2000, both China and Russia seemed poised to take advantage of what was viewed as US indifference towards the region. As an example of this indifference, they point to the $16 million dollar combined aid to three states, Uzbekistan, Kazakhstan and Kyrgyzstan which was seen as a "declaration of disinterest" towards the region. Analysts argue that this sent a signal to China regarding Washington's perceived "ambivalence" towards the region.[60]

Although the United States had delivered around $1.5 billion in aid to the region between 1992 and 1998, this assistance had been accompanied by pressure on the states to establish pluralistic and democratic societies. The Central Asian states on the other hand were more concerned about security and the consolidation of their secular governments than on the establishment of democracy and pluralism. The Chinese position on democracy and pluralism, on the other hand, was closer to that of the Central Asian regimes. China provided military and technical aid to Uzbekistan, Kazakhstan and Kyrgyzstan and also increased trade and economic relations with the states hoping to ensure access to valuable Central Asian oil and gas reserves. China was also utilizing the SCO to develop closer ties with Russia. This was enhanced by the signing of the declaration for the establishment of the Shanghai Cooperation Organization, the Shanghai Covenant on the Suppression of Terrorism, Separatism and Extremism and the Sino Russian Friendship Pact signed with Moscow. An important component of this process was the development of a potential Sino-Russian counter weight to closer ties between Russia and the United States.

However, since September 11, the eagerness of some member states to assist the United States bilaterally in the war against terrorism raised a number of questions about the future of the SCO and China's plans for spreading its influence and presence in the region. Similarly the absence of the SCO as a regional player in the war against terrorism has been noted.[61] It has been argued that, the SCO had been involved since 1996 in the fight against what it calls the "three evil forces" and could have used this collective experience to offer multilateral regional support to the war against terrorism. Instead it appears that the multilateral option had been put on hold as each of the states opted for the bilateral option. Chinese strategic writers, of course, noted that since the US is not a SCO member, the SCO could not join in the war against terrorism.

The events of September 11 and their aftermath changed Chinese security calculus. In response to the shifting strategic landscape, Beijing launched a concerted effort towards her neighbours. Before the attacks, China had viewed its strategic situation as gradually improving. Relations with China and Central Asia were gradually deepening and tensions between Washington and China were receding. However, with the events following 9/11, and expanded US presence in the immediate neighbourhood of China, Chinese security analysts had to reexamine their position.

Despite the recently signed Sino-Russian Friendship Treaty and the professed unity in it to oppose hegemonism, Russia extended broad support to America's military campaign. China's Central Asian neighbours also offered their bases and airspace to the US despite being part of the Shanghai Cooperation Organization. Uzbekistan and Tajikistan offered invaluable assistance to American forces and Kyrgyzstan seemed willing to support long term support to US military presence in the region. In Afghanistan, a relatively pro American government was seen to be emerging.

In the course of the campaign against *Al Qaeda*, American troops and some of its biggest guns were deployed in China's backyard. Moreover the conflict marks the first time that US combat forces have fought on China's borders since the Korean and Vietnam wars. With US troops in South Korea, Japan and Central Asia, there is apprehension in China that the US is "encircling" China.[62] This does not imply that China opposed America's response to the terrorist attacks. Chinese leaders share US concerns about terrorism. Areas where the US could seek Chinese cooperation against terrorism include intelligence sharing, use of Chinese airfields and airspace to support humanitarian aid or combat, diplomatic support in the United nations, export controls for small arms that may reach terrorist groups and sanctions against states that refuse to cooperate with anti terrorist methods.[63] However, there are obstacle to this on both sides. The US will not support China's tendency to equate terrorism with separatism and China is concerned about setting precedents for open ended US military intervention and wants the United Nations to authorize any expansion of US military responses.

In an attempt to stabilize the fluid situation Beijing is pushing for a comprehensive diplomatic agenda to strengthen ties with the key regional players. As a part of this strategy, President Hu Jintao visited the Central Asian states as part of his first foreign engagement. He met the Kazakh President and members of the Kazakh Parliament, in June 2003.[64]

On the other hand there is little consensus among US specialists regarding the trends and outlook in US policy towards China.[65] Many US specialists on China argue strongly that the Bush administration needs to change its recent policy in order to avoid damage to US interests as a result of growing differences with Beijing, caused by the recent US tilt towards Taiwan. It is argued that only by curbing US military cooperation with Taiwan, resuming active military and strategic dialogue with the PRC and seeking closer interaction with the PRC leaders the US goals of regional peace and development will be possible.[66] A somewhat different perspective is offered by specialists who stress that the anti-terrorism campaign after September 11 has added pressures on the Bush administration to modify differences with China and seek closer relations, through high level leadership contacts with the Chinese administration.[67]

However, it is undeniable that the Bush administration displays a view of China that is different from that followed by the Clinton administration which had expressed the hope that US "engagement" with China would lead to an eventual change in Sino-US relations. The Bush strategic vision of China is more focused on China as a competitor and strategic adversary and Taiwan as the key area where these differences have been played out. [68] China is seen as rising economic and military power that seeks to confront the US not only over Taiwan but also the strengthening of US-Japan defence alliance, US missile defence plans and works against US interests in Asian and world affairs. One of the manifestations of this confrontation, particularly in the Central Asian region, is through the Shanghai Cooperation Organization.

The rebalancing of the US stance in the US-PRC-Taiwan triangular relationship in a direction favourable to Taiwan thus far has not elicited much domestic debate in the United States. Debates over China policy related issues has been muffled as a result of US preoccupation with the anti-terrorism campaign which appears to have much more salient implications for American interests. Mainstream opinion in Congress, the media, and in public opinion remains skeptical of China and more positive regarding Taiwan and US support regarding Taiwan. However, US business interests remain a powerful domestic force in favour of avoiding disruptive controversy in US-PRC relations, but their concerns appear to be met by the Bush administration's careful emphasis on maintaining mutually advantageous economic relations with China despite differences over other issues.[69] Meanwhile PRC leaders have been reluctant to express strong dissatisfaction with the Bush administration to tow the line on US relations with Taiwan and other sensitive issues.[70]

The low level of attention that the US leadership devotes to China appears broadly understandable at home and abroad given the many other more pressing US foreign policy concerns which include its preoccupation in the Middle East, the war in Iraq,

NATO expansion, NATO Russian relations and US ballistic missile defence efforts. Similarly, the preoccupation of the Chinese leaders with other policy priorities appear likely to continue through the transition of leadership in 2002-2003. Newly installed Chinese leaders will probably not seek out a major reevaluation of policy towards the United States unless pressed by events. Also they will seek, under most conceivable circumstances, short of military conflict to preserve the advantageous economic relationship with the United States.[71]

Sino-Russian Relations and the Significance of Multipolarization

The establishment of a dialogue mechanism between Russia and China heralded a new development within Russian policy thinking and the circumstances under which this happened remains significant.[72] This is particularly significant since in the immediate post disintegration period, Russia had turned to the West in an attempt to seek strategic partnerships. Russian democrats, who came to power at the end of 1991, perceived the West as the principle ideological and political ally, the main source of aid urgently required for successful reforms and a model of development. However, it was not before long that profound divergences appeared between Russia and the US.

A number of developments in this period led to this divergence. Internally the failure of "shock therapy" delivered a blow to the radical reformers and nationalist and communist forces who won the parliamentary elections of 1993. In 1994, NATO made a strategic decision for eastward expansion. The US also attempted to strengthen its support for countries on the territory of the former Soviet Union. The influence of the US and NATO also penetrated into the Caucasus and Central Asia and the Partnership for Peace (PfP) was extended to almost all these countries. The crisis in Yugoslavia, the Kosovo war and the war in Iraq also revealed strategic contradictions between the US and Russia. As cleavages developed with the West there appeared changes in Russian relations with China.[73] Since 1993, China emerged as Russia's most natural cooperation partner. Apart from the growing gap of perceptions and alienation from the west several other factors contributed to this. First, Sino-Russian relations in the 1990's did not suffer significant setbacks. The second key factor was the expansion of Russian arms sales to China, that increased military-technical cooperation.[74]

Within Russia four major trends emerged, in the post disintegration period, reflecting differing attitudes towards foreign policy and the attitude towards China was fully reflected in these.[75] The first camp consisted of westerners for whom China continued to pose a communist and geopolitical challenge. They warned that the PRC was turning into a superpower that would begin by bullying Taiwan and the south east Asian countries but would then turn their attention to Russia, whose empty spaces in Siberia and the Far East were highly tempting to overcrowded China. The second camp, radically opposed to the first, rejected the notion that the West and Russia could be friends. Those who shared fears about the western threat advanced various alternatives on how to combat the West. Quite a few suggested an alliance with China. It was also quite popular among communists and communist sympathizers to talk about an alliance between Russia, China and India. Communists pointed out that an alliance between Moscow and Beijing was inevitable, for ideological reasons as well. However, an interest in aligning Russia with China was also found outside the communist ranks, among nationalists and conservative circles.

A third school of thought in Russian foreign policy debates united those who called on their compatriots to keep the country closed to external influence. China was included among such countries, particularly since China was suspected of encroachment on Russia's Far East. This alarmist view of China was, therefore, particularly strong in the Russian Far East, where China was blamed for crime, unemployment, housing shortages, contaminated goods, counterfeit money, stealing natural resources, price fixing and territorial expansion in the North. The fourth set of views expounded in national debates in Russia called for a balanced strategy in the world. Elaborating on this Yevgeny Primakov stated that conducting a diversified active policy, where Russian interests are involved, was a vital necessity in order to create optimal conditions for dynamic internal development.[76] The proponents of this view pointed out that while an alliance with the PRC was impossible it would be equally harmful to treat China as a potential adversary, since China did not pose any threat to Russia.

Since 1996, the balanced open approach started gaining momentum in Russian foreign policy. With his victory in 1996, President Boris Yeltsin reshuffled his government to include a large number of young liberal reformers who pushed for a pragmatic economic oriented strategy of the world that could not ignore China. Another important reason was the emergence of a strengthened executive branch which managed to push through its own policy on external strategy despite the communist and nationalist opposition in the legislature.

As part of this open approach Russia announced in 1996 the establishment of a strategic cooperation partnership with China. The rationale for evolving such a mechanism of cooperation was based on a number of factors. First, both sides recognized the dividends of a strategic partnership and Beijing has been consistent in nurturing it with good results. The Moscow-Beijing bipartisan consensus was in favour of evolving a multilateral strategy to combat threats to regional security. This was the outcome of a strong and increasingly stable bilateral entente between the two states.[77] Second, as part of a growing convergence of interests, Moscow and Beijing have pledged not to interfere in each others domestic affairs. China has defended Russia's use of military force in the Caucasus. Moscow now defends Beijing's policy towards Taiwan, Tibet and Xinjiang. To craft issues of national interest around regional security appears to be the Sino-Russian agenda. Third, and most important, the two share a resentment against a unipolar system dominated by the United States. Anxiety about the expansion of US military and economic intervention in Central Asia and the inevitable clash of interests has helped in forging a Sino-Russian entente in the Central Asian region. This alliance, projected as "constructive strategic partnership" is essentially a counterweight to American power that is aimed at restoring multipolarity to the international system.[78]

While this is a dominant view among most analysts, others have presented a more pessimistic impression and pointed out that the Sino-Russian "strategic partnership" is actually detrimental to Russia's interests. It has been noted that the Chinese penetration into the Russian Far East is a distinct possibility and that China constitues the most significant threat to Russia's security. Therefore Russia should unite with the West, against Chinese aggression. Some have pointed to Japan as Russia's best partner in Northeast Asia.[79] Still others have moved away from both the overtly optimistic or pessimistic positions to point to the reality of Russia's deep rooted distrust of China and the bilateral problems indigenous to the "partnership". They note that both Russia and China want to establish state power on a firm footing and require stability along their border areas. This is what leads to the significance of the partnership.[80]

Sino-Russian cooperation is also based on a number of other factors. The first is the number of common interests shared by the two, including border stability and peripheral security, economic interests and international cooperation. They also face a number of domestic problems and the core task of their foreign policy is to create and maintain a benign peripheral environment. The security situation in Central Asia constitutes one of the most important common interests of China and Russia in maintaining regional security. In addition, economic, trade, scientific and technological cooperation is becoming increasingly important. Here, China is one of the major trade partners of Russia. Another area where China and Russia share common interest is international cooperation. Russia and China have other common aspects of foreign policy, including a declared support for the UN, criticism of the NATO and the rejection of US plans for a new missile defence system. Both profess concern at what they see as strategic American dominance. Beijing feels that the proposed missile defence plan by Washington is directed against it and it has made no secret of the fact that it would accelerate its own strategic arms build up in response. Similarly, in spite of US assurances to Russia that the programme will not make the latter's nuclear deterrent ineffective, Moscow is severely critical of the plan. More importantly, there is growing Sino-Russian military cooperation.

Russia and China therefore discussed the possibility of developing a joint missile defence system if the United States ignored their objections and went ahead with a national anti-missile shield. The related prospect of developing a joint regional missile shield was discussed during January 2000 visit to Moscow of Chinese Defence Minister Chi Haotian and Russian Deputy Foreign Minister Ilya Klebanov's talks in Beijing in February 2000. Russia has offered to help China develop a manned space programme and has allowed Beijing use of its Glonass global satellite navigation system for various purposes.

China is also a huge market for Russian machines and equipment and arms supplies continues to dominate Russia's exports to China. China has been buying Russian fighter bombers and building a factory to assemble them, purchasing guided missile destroyers and submarines and consistently procuring Russian small and heavy arms. Over the past years the scale of Russian arms exports to China has more than tripled and now accounts for more than one third of the annual turnover and almost 70% of China's arms purchases in the foreign market.[81] A number of agreements have been signed on Russia's participation in modernization and construction of large enterprises, specially energy and transportation facilities. There are plans to create special economic zones along the common border and to share the water and resources of the border rivers.

For some time to come, China will also continue to be an important supplier of cheap consumer goods and labour to Russia, specially its eastern regions. These endeavours are also useful to China as is import of Russian raw materials. Economic and trade cooperation have also made significant headway. Food and consumer goods that flow into Russia via the border trade with China are essential to the residents in the Siberian and Far Eastern regions of Russia. On the other hand abundant oil and gas resources in Russia are attractive to China, which has come to depend on imported oil. Russia and China share a common interest in laying oil pipelines from Siberia to China. Russia is interested in getting access to China's energy market. China is also trying to diversify its fuel and energy import pattern. Russian companies regard it, economically profitable, to sell oil from central and eastern Siberia to China in contrast to markets in Europe because of long distances involved. A number of agreements have been signed between Russian and Chinese oil companies and it is expected that major energy deals will also boost bilateral trade.[82]

Certain factors are likely to result in the continuation of Sino-Russian relations as active partners but not necessarily at the expense of relations with other countries. There is realization that, as states sharing long borders, there remains the necessity to deal on a daily basis with numerous bilateral issues like the movement of people across frontiers, the sharing of river resources, shipment of goods and dispositions of military units. Both also remain dependent in the stability and development of each other, as a condition for their own security and progress. Also as Evgeniy Bazhanov, Director of the Institute of Contemporary International Studies of the Russian Ministry of Foreign Affairs, points out the ideological differences that affected the relationship have virtually lost all ground. The present Russian elite respects the achievements of the Chinese Communist regime and Beijing realizes that a weak Russian democracy is ideologically no challenge to it.[83]

The historiography of borders and the relationship between

the neighbouring countries is a sensitive issue that is closely tied to questions of sovereignty and legitimacy. This has been particularly true about the Sino-Russian border. It was therefore considered important that it be clearly defined and not left dependent on the character of the political relationship between the two countries and the newly independent Central Asian states.[84] It has also been considered important to determine the border not in military terms alone, as in the past, but in terms of economic interdependence. Historically, Russia has sought her security in Asia by stressing the need to control the Kazakh steppes which in turn required further advance into the heart of Central Asia. China, similarly argued that her security depended on the control of Mongolia and Tibet, which implied China's presence in Xinjiang.[85] In both cases geopolitical ambitions and civilizing myths and missions have played a part.

It was in this background that Moscow and Beijing fixed over 4000 kilometer long border and in November 1997 agreed on joint occupation of several disputed islands. However, certain problems remain that may emerge as significant in case certain regions of Russia disputes the present demarcation or if a future Chinese government resurrects its demands to restore certain territories.[86] They have also made significant progress on military confidence building measures in bilateral relations. The two sides have signed agreements on 'no first use of nuclear weapons' and on 'non targeting of missiles' on each others territory. Russia and China along with Kazakhstan, Kyrgyzstan and Tajikistan signed an agreement on confidence building measures, on the border zone. This agreement forms the basis for complementing policies in Central Asia. Again, while these agreements signal complementarily, a future ultra-nationalist Russian government may dispute Chinese presence in the Central Asian region and China will not accept Russian control of Mongolia and Central Asia.

On July 16, 2001 Russia and China signed a twenty year Treaty of Neighbourliness, Friendship and Cooperation. Both sides emphasized that the Treaty was a treaty of alliance. The principal motive behind the signing of the Treaty was to consolidate the long border between the two and endorse each others sovereignty and territorial integrity. All the main themes evolved in the course of the development of Sino-Russian relations in the past decade find expression in the treaty, including the aspiration for a multipolar world and strategic stability. The two sides also agreed to develop cooperation in trade and economic, military-technical, research- technological power engineering and aviation spheres.

The new Sino-Russian Treaty will have diverse effects on a number of issues of common concern. One such significant issue is the change that the Uighur question will assume. It has been claimed that the development of relations between China and Russia has always been connected with the Uighur issue.[87] In an article "Uyghur Separatism-A Common Problem", the Russian politician Alexander Sobyanin also noted that the Uighur question is a dilemma for both Russia and China and that for the sake of safeguarding its southern borders Russia was amenable to a convergence of position with China on this issue.[88] It has been pointed out that this is an important guarantee for the continuing development of Sino-Russian strategic partnership.[89]

Since the September 11 incident, China and Russia have cooperated closely in all international organizations and have consulted and supported each other on a number of issues. The two countries have cooperated very closely over the issue of anti-terrorism. They have also held that cooperation in anti-terrorism among various countries should be based on the United Nations Charter and other norms of international law and that the role of the UN in the struggle against terrorism should be strengthened. They have also expressed similar views on the Iraq issue and opposed the depiction of Iran, Iraq and the Democratic Peoples Republic of Korea as the "axis of evil".

China and Russia have also strengthened their cooperation in Central Asia within the framework of the Shanghai Cooperation Organization. In a summit meeting held in June 2003 China,

Russia and other members of the SCO signed the SCO Charter and a formal document on the setting up of a regional anti-terrorism centre. The close cooperation between Russia and China has played a significant role in promoting multilateral cooperation within the framework of the SCO. Both China and Russia hope to maintain security and stability in Central Asia and prevent any change in the balance of power in the region resulting from the military presence of the United States. Both Russia and China hold that the present anti-terrorism campaigns in Afghanistan led by the US serves their own security interests. But Russia also demands that the US military actions in Central Asia should be transparent as far as possible and that there should be a time limit for its military presence. In this Russia is strongly supported by China.

A long term problem existing in Sino-Russian relations has been the fact that the development of economic and trade cooperation between the two countries has lagged behind that of their political cooperation. In particular cooperation in the fields of production and investment between the two countries is still very low. The leaders of the two countries have realized that without faster development of economic and trade cooperation between the two countries the strategic partnership would have no solid foundation. An attempt to correct this was made during the sixth regular meeting of the Prime Ministers of the two countries, which was held in St Petersburg on the eve of the September 11 incident. During the meeting, the Prime Ministers of the two countries discussed concrete proposals for cooperation, including construction of oil pipelines between China and Russia, aviation and aerospace, peaceful use of nuclear energy and joint development of new technologies. Since September 11, Sino-Russian cooperation in the field of military technology has continued to develop and a series of agreements on military technology has been signed between Russia and China. There has also been an attempt to expand cooperation in the fields of education, culture, health and sports.[90]

Another factor that leads to Sino-Russian partnership is their active involvement towards the creation of a multipolar world which is based on strong anti US undertones. Prior to the terrorist attacks on the US, China had become vociferous in its opposition to NATO expansion and Moscow had toughened her attitude to the US military presence on her southern borders and the US-Japan military alliance. During Russian Defence Minister Igor Sergeev's visit to China in October 1998, Moscow and Beijing stressed their common approach to three international issues: they categorically objected to NATO expansion in the east, denounced the use of force in Kosovo and disapproved of the US-Japan plans of establishing an anti-missile defence system. Russia and China have issued statements on multipolarization of the world that reflected their concern about the current international situation. In this connection a Chinese Foreign Ministry release stated:

> Faced with new challenges, all the countries should surmount the traditional concepts and go along with the tide of times, enhance exchanges and cooperation and strengthen their mutual coordination. They should actively boost world multipolarization and democratization of international relations and strive to establish a new international economic order adapted to the development levels and demands of various countries. They should reform the irrational international financial and trade system to safeguard the right to equal development of all countries, particularly the developing countries. The diversity of the development of civilizations of various countries should be respected. The various civilizations and the diverse roads to development should co-exist harmoniously, draw on others strong points to make up ones own weak ones in competition and comparison and make common progress through seeking common ground and shelving differences.[91]

However, while multipolarity remains a professed common goal there are differences in Sino-Russian perception about states that could form significant poles in this multipolar world. In December 1998, during his visit to India, the then Russian Foreign Minister Primakov advanced the idea of a triangular alliance of Russia, China and India. Russia's foreign policy shift and the failure of the envisaged pan-Atlantic political, economic and security integration diversified the power structure of the world. China's perception this structure remains ambivalent. The concluding chapter of the book takes up the discussion of this triangular relationship in some detail. What remains significant is that the consequent emergence of a multipolar structure makes up the premise to the shaping of Sino-Russian-US interaction in the Central Asian region.

NOTES AND REFERENCES

1. Su Ge, "On Sino-US-Russian Relations", *International Studies*, 7-9, 2002. (The article has been translated from the Chinese bi-monthly, *International Studies*, the Journal of the China Institute of International Studies)
2. Ge, "On Sino-US-Russian Relations".
3. Talgat Ismagambetov, "Some geopolitical peculiarities of Central Asia, past and present", in Sally N. Cummings (ed) *Oil, Transition and Security in Central Asia*, London and New York: Routledge-Curzon, 2003.
4. Yuri V. Tsyganov, "Russia and China: What is in the Pipeline?", in Gennady Chufrin (ed) *Russia and Asia:The Emerging Security Agenda*, New York: OUP, 1999.
5. Zhao Huasheng, "US Factor in Sino-Russian Relations", in *Contemporary World Configuration*, Shanghai: Shanghai Institute of International Studies, 2002.
6. Huasheng, "US Factor in Sino-Russian Relations".
7. Event Summary of a seminar on the CSIS Project *China's Emergence in Central Asia: Security Diplomatic and Economic Interests*, Forum One: "The Current State of China-Central Asia Diplomacy and Implications for US Foreign Policy", held on

Wednesday, February 5, 2003, www.csis.org/china/china_emergence.cfm

8. Eric Ringmar, "The Recognition Game: Soviet Russia Against the West", *Cooperation and Conflict*, Volume 37, No 2, June 2002.

9. James Goldgeier and Michael McFaul, "George W. Bush and Russia", *Current History*, October 2002.

10. Uzbekistan was considered a key state as far as basing rights for the US was concerned. The US Secretary of State Colin Powell, who was the key person negotiating with the CARs, pointed to this very clearly noting that the flight plan from Tajikistan into northern Afghanistan was treacherous and involved climbing over a tall mountain range. Uzbekistan was therefore the "enabling condition". Without it there could be no bombing in the north. Bombing in the south , where there was no significant opposition ground force, made no sense. Therefore though the Tajik President had agreed to all the US demands even before Uzbekistan, the emphasis remained on getting basing rights from Uzbekistan. Use of Uzbek bases was crucial for Combat Search and Rescue Operations without which there could be no aerial action. The most important Uzbek demand was that US interest be long standing. US Secretary of Defence Donald H. Rumsfeld assured President Karimov of the long standing nature of interest when in a meeting with the Uzbek President he noted that, "The interests of the United States is of a long standing relationship with this country." See Bob Woodward, *Bush At War*, London, Sydney, New York,Tokyo, Singapore, Toronto:Pocket Books, 2002, (pp 134, 148, 163, 172, 178, 181, 199) for details of the negotiations between the US and Uzbekistan and Tajikistan.

11. Cited from Goldgeier and McFaul, "George W. Bush and Russia."

12. Joel Hafvenstein, "Central Asia: Uzbekistan", *The NIS Observed: An Analytical Review*, Vol VIII, No 13, August 21, 2003.

13. Giorgi Kandelaki, "Uzbekistan Quits GUUAM", *Eursianet,* June 14, 2002 and "Uzbekistan Clarifies its Position on GUUAM", *Eurasianet*, June 26, 2002.

14. For details see Shahram Akbarzade, "US-Uzbek Partnership and

Democratic Reforms", *Nationalities Papers*, Vol 32, No 2, June 2004.

15. Charles Carlson, "Uzbekistan:Karimov Says Improved Relations With Russia Not at the Expense of US Ties", *Eurasia Insight*, September 9, 2003.

16. Igor Torbakov, "Uzbekistan Set to Diversify Its Security Opinions in Wake of Recent Militant Attacks", *Eurasia Insight*, April 22, 2004.

17. "United States Cuts off Aid to Uzbekistan", *Eurasia Insight*, July 21, 2004.

18 Olga Zakrzhevskaya, "Problemi Mezhdunarodnogo Terrorisma v Kontekste Tendentsii Obshemirobogo Razvitiya", Kazakhstan I Sivremenni Mir, No1 (2) 2002.

19. Conversation of the author with Professor Aziz Niyazi at the *Institut Vostokovedeniia*, Moscow, on November 26, 2003, where he emphasised that Tajikistan was not moving towards the US. In fact Tajikistan remained Russia's main ally in the Central Asian region and was aware of the destabilization that would follow if it came closer to the US.

20. Cited from *The NIS Observed: An Analytical Review*, Vol 9, No 16, October 15, 2004.

21. For details of the Central Asian position see Ata Khaitov, "Central Asian Responses to the Iraq Crisis: Hopes and Fears", *Russia and Eurasia Review*, Vol 2, Issue 5, March 4, 2003.

22. This was significant since from about the second half of President Yeltsin's term, particularly after the US attacks against Yugoslavia, relations between Russia and the United States had been in a state of sustained crisis. Serious differences between the two countries on a number of major issues far exceeded the common ground between them. Although the Bush administration had made some adjustments to its Russia policy from the middle of 2001, owing mainly to growing criticism at home and abroad to its tough stance towards Russia and to the EP-3 aircraft incident between the United States and China in April 2001, there had been no substantial improvement in Russian-US relations.

23. For details of this see inset on page 3 in Jessica T. Mathews, "September 11, One Year Later: A World of Change", *Carnegie Endowment for International Peace*, Special Edition 18, August 2002.
24. Cited from Ni Xiaoquan,"Sino-Russian relations Since the September 11 Incident", *Slavic Research Centre Occasional Paper No 91* on *The Sino-Russian Strategic Relationship? Current Views from the Border and Beijing*, Sapporo Slavic Research Centre, Hokkaido University, 2003.
25. For details of the improvement in Russo-US relations and what compelled it see, Xiaoquan,"Sino-Russian relations Since the September 11 Incident".
26. Svante E. Cornell, "America In Eurasia: One Year After," *Current History*, October 2002.
27. Cornell, "America In Eurasia: One Year After."
28. Cited from Woodward, *Bush At War,* p 118.
29. "Russia: Communist Leader Says NATO Forces In Central Asia A Threat", *RFE/RL Report*, 9 February, 2002.
30. *Nezavisimaya Gazeta*, October 9, 2001 cited in Shahram Akbarzadeh, "Keeping Central Asia Stable", *Third World Quarterly*, Vol 25, No 4, 2004.
31. Cited from Akbarzadeh, "Keeping Central Asia Stable".
32. Ibragim Alibekov and Sergei Blagov, "New Security Organization Could Help Expand Russia's Reach in Central Asia", *Eurasia Insight*, May 6, 2003.
33. Cited from Alibekov and Blagov, "New Security Organization Could Help Expand Russia's Reach in Central Asia".
34. Gregory Feifer,"2002 in Review: Putin's Foreign Policy Not seen as Harming Relations With the West", *RFE/RL Report*, 16 December 2002.
35. Ministry of Foreign Affairs of the Russian Federation, *Daily News Bulletin*, 28 September 2001 cited from Fotios Moustakis and Ella Ackerman, "Russo-Turkish Cooperation After September 11", *Central Asian Survey*, Vol 21, Number 4, December 2002.

36. Aerial Cohen, "Uncertainty Still Defines Russia's Role in Central Eurasia", *Eurasia Insight*, September 19, 2002.
37. Ahmed Rashid cited in Nikola Krastev,"Central Asia: "Taliban" Author Says Russia to Regain Influence in Unstable Region", *RFL/RE Report*, 22 March 2002.
38. Cited from Zamira Eshanova, "Central Asia: Diplomatic Visits Highlight US-Russian Competition", RFE/RL Report, 3 December, 2002.
39. *Slovo Kyrgyzstana*, 13 September 2001.
40. *Slovo Kyrgyzstana*, 27 September 2001.
41. Rafis Abazov,"Kyrgyzstan's Dilemmas", *Analysis of Current Events*, Volume 14, No 2, May 2002.
42. In fact on Februaray 26, 2004, *Nezavisimaya Gazeta*, suggested that Moscow is hoping to secure a permanent Russian military base in Tajikistan. Cited from Zafar Abdullayev, "Tajikistan, Russia Probe Military Partnership", *Eurasia Insight*, March 15, 2004.
43. Zafar Abdullayev, "Tajikistan, Russia Probe Military Partnership", *Eurasia Insight*, March 16, 2004.
44. Cited from Eshanova, "Central Asia: Diplomatic Visits Highlight US-Russian Competition."
45. Cited from Alibekov and Blagov, "New Security Organization Could Help Expand Russia's Reach in Central Asia".
46. Cited from Igor Torbakov, "Uzbekistan set to Diversify Its security Options in the Wake of Recent Militant Attacks", *Eurasia Insight*, April 22, 2004.
47. Taras Kuzio and Sergei Blagov, "GUUAM Makes a Comeback Bid with US Support", *Eurasia Insight*, July 7, 2003, Eurasianet.
48. Kuzio and Blagov, "GUUAM Makes a Comeback Bid with US Support".
49. Kandelaki, "Uzbekistan Quits GUUAM", and "Uzbekistan Clarifies its Position on GUUAM".

50. Kambiz Arman, "US Geopolitical Position Takes Hit in Tajikistan", *Euraisa Insight*, July 21, 2004.

51. Michael Lelyveld,"US/Russia: Officials Hail Energy Partnership", *RFE/RL Report*, 4 October 2002.

52. John Erickson, "Eurasian maneuvers", in Sally N. Cummings (ed) *Oil, Transition and Security in Central Asia*, London and New York: Routledge-Curzon, 2003.

53. For details of how this was attempted and the role of the oil companies see Gawdat Bahgat,"The New Geopolitics of Oil: The United States, Saudi Arabia and Russia", *Orbis*, Vol 47, No 3, Summer 2003.

54. For details of the debate see Igor Torbakov, "Policy Makers in Moscow debate the Limits of Russian Power in the Caucasus, Central Asia", *Eurasia Insight*, September 2, 2004.

55. Erickson, "Eurasian maneuvers".

56. For details see Michael Dillon, *Xinjiang, China's Muslim Far Northwest*, London and New York: RoutledgeCurzon, 2004.

57. David Finkelstein, "China's Emergence in Central Asia: Security, Diplomatic and Economic Interests", *CSIS Forum on the Current State of China-Central Asia Diplomacy and Implications for US Foreign Policy*, Wednesday, February 5, 2003.

58. For details see a report by Yu Bin, "United States-China Relations and Regional Security After September 11", *Issues and Insights*, No 2, April 2002.

59. Evan A. Feigenbaum, "The United States is Driving Russia and China Together Again", *International Herald Tribune*, December 28, 2000.

60. Cited from Dewardric L McNeal, "China's Relations with Central Asian States and Problems with Terrorism", *Congressional Research Service*, December 17, 2001.

61. McNeal, "China's Relations with Central Asian States and Problems with Terrorism".

62. Dan Ewing, "Changing Security Calculus", *Korea Herald*, January 21, 2002.

63. Phillip C. Saunders, "Can 9-11 Provide a Fresh Start for Sino-US Relations?" *Policy Forum Online*, Special Forum 33, October 31, 2001.

64. For details of China's interaction with the Central Asian states see the *Ministry of Foreign Affairs, China*, site online at english.peopledaily.com.cn/data/organs/state council.shtml.

65. Robert Sutter, "American-Chinese Relations After September 11", web article at www.cap.unimuenchen.de/transatlantic/topics/us_china.htm. See also Saunders, "Can 9/11 Provide a Fresh Start for Sino-US Relations?".

66. These views have been expressed by Michael Swain and Minxin Peo, "Rebalancing US-China Relations", Washington: *Carnegie Endowment Policy Brief*, February 13, 2002.

67. David Shambaugh, "From the White House, all Zigzags Lead to China", *Washington Post*, February 17, 2002 (internet version).

68. For a Chinese view of the Bush administration policy towards China see, Liu Jiang,"Sino-US Relations: Develop in Twists and Turns", a *Beijing Review* Cover Story available online at www.bjreview.com.cn/2002/200152(A).htm.

69. Among reviews of US domestic debate on China policy, see Kerry Dumbaugh, *China-US Relations*, Washington, The Library of Congress, Congressional Research Service, Issue Brief 98018.

70. Pan Zhongying, *Bush Visit and Sino-US Ties*, Honolulu:CSIS Pacific Forum, PACNET 8, February 8, 2002.

71. Frank Ching, "China Puts Growth Before Reunification," *Japan Times*, April 19, 2002 (internet version). For a detailed analysis of ways in which Sino-US relations can be improved and a more positive approach to the relationship see Chen Peiyao, "War Against Terrorism and the China-US Relations", a web article at

    www.apan-info.net/terrorism/terrorism_views.asp. It is significant that the author is the President of the Shanghai Institute of International Strategic Studies.

72. For a Chinese perspective of the details of the foundations of the relationship and the problems remaining within it see, Chen

Qimao, "Sino-Russian Relations After the Breakup of the Soviet Union", in Gennady Chufrin (ed) *Russia and Asia:The Emerging Security Agenda*, New York: OUP, 1999.

73. Iwashita Akihiro,"Opit Prigranichogo Sotrudnichestvo Rossii i KNR PZoslednye 10 Let", *Slavic Research Centre Occasional Paper No 91* on *The Sino-Russian Strategic Relationship? Current Views from the Border and Beijing*, Sapporo Slavic Research Centre, Hokkaido University, 2003.

74. For a detailed study of the development of Sino-Russian relations see Jyotsna Bakshi, *Russia-China Relations, Relevance for India*, Delhi: Shipra, 2004.

75. Evgeniy Bazhanov,"Russian Perspectives on China's Foreign Policy and Military Development", in Jonathan D Pollack (ed) *In China's Shadow: Regional Perspectives on Chinese Foreign Policy and Military Development*, RAND Publication, 1998.

76. Yevginy Primakov,"Rossiya Yishet Novoe Mesto v Mire", *Izvestia*, March 6, 1996.

77. Stephen Blank, "Which Way for Sino-Russian Relations?", *Orbis*, Summer 1998.

78. For Chinese writings that stress this position see "China- Russia Relations Remain Better than Russia-US Relations", *Peoples' Daily Online*, Thursday, November 28, 2002, english.people.com.cn/2002 11/28.

79. Alexander Lukin, *The Bear Watches the Dragon: Russia's Perceptions of China and the Evolution of Russian-Chinese Relations Since the Eighteenth Century*, New York:2003.

80. Akihiro Iwashita, *A 4000 Kilometer Journey Along the Sino-Russian Border*, Sapporo: Slavic Research Centre, Hokkaido University, 2004.

81. *Rossiskaya Gazeta*, October 5, 1996.

82. Bakshi, *Russia-China Relations*.

83. Bazhanov,"Russian Perspectives on China's Foreign Policy and Military Development".

84. Alexei D Voskressenski, "Current Concepts of Sino-Russian Relations and Frontier Problems in Russia and China", *Central Asian Survey*, Vol 13, No 3, 1994.

85. Witt Raczka, "Xinjiang and its Central Asian Borderlands", *Central Asian Survey*, Vol 17, No 3, 1998.

86. For a detailed study see Iwashita, *A 4000 Kilometer Journey Along the Sino-Russian Border.*

87. For details of the historical convergence of interests see Nabijan Tursun, "Sino-Russian Relations and the Uyghur Card", *Central Asia Monitor*, No 5-6, 2001.

88. Tursun, "Sino-Russian Relations and the Uyghur Card".

89. Xiaoquan,"Sino-Russian Relations Since the September 11 Incident".

90. For details see Xiaoquan,"Sino-Russian Relations Since the September 11 Incident".

91. "China's Views on the Current International Situation", *Ministry of the Foreign Affairs of the Peoples' Republic of China* 2000, www.fmprc.gov.cn.

Chapter 4

Regional Alignments in Central Asia

The Emergence of a "New" Dialogue?

That the "war against terrorism" would inevitably restructure regional alignments in Eurasia and reconfigure the international security environment was accepted as a forgone conclusion.[1] While the extent of the realignment remained elusive, a clear pointer to the fact, that a watershed was in sight, was accepted as evident. Certain statements made in the immediate post September 11 scenario were particularly noteworthy in this context. A representative example was a request by the NATO Secretary General, George Robertson, to the Central Asian states in the first week of October, 2001, asking them to balance their relationship with Russia with that of the West. This statement, which nearly went unnoticed in an eventful month that was projected to change the course of world politics, is significant for a number of reasons.

The first and most obvious, of course, is the irony of NATO sponsorship of Russia to its former constituent Republics, as the initial scramble, among the Central Asian states to associate with the "war", gained momentum. It was clear that NATO would prefer to deal with these states as aligned with Russia through the CIS (all the five Central Asian states, Kazakhstan, Kyrgyzstan, Turkmenistan, Uzbekistan and Tajikistan are part of the CIS) whereas statements emanating from the Central Asian region itself was not always clear on this. The second and more crucial significance was seen to lie in the recognition of the fact that an actual transition in terms of alignments and a real transformation of balance of power in Eurasia was likely, as events unfolded over the coming months. It also reflects, what was then the logical next step, in predicting a realignment of security arrangements in the region and the emergence of alternative global arrangements to deal with new challenges, a theme that became an abiding one in most writings on the "year after". Once again the Cold War type choice between two worlds was seen to be emerging as the accepted norm, in terms of security arrangements.[2]

This was noted as being particularly significant and projected as a reversal of the post Cold War scenario. With the end of the Cold War it was assumed that a more independent stance in terms of regional security forums was in sight since there remained no overarching global dynamic over regional initiatives. Writings on Asian Security Practice, for instance, noted:

> Local and regional dynamics are becoming more salient, and states appear to have greater latitude in shaping their immediate environments. Unlike the economic domain, where the Asian economies and their regional activities are becoming integrated into the global economy, the security domain seems to be witnessing the development of a much more independent regional system.[3]

In the post September 11 scenario, it was noted that this independent stance, at least as far as regional security arrangements were concerned, would change particularly in the region in the immediate neighbourhood of Afghanistan. Here, once again, it was noted that the "war against terrorism" would demonstrate the significance of global security alignments, particularly where the Central Asian region was concerned. In fact, analysts argued, that in the future all campaigns would be "a coalition of the willing" completely dominated by the US, and with contribution on a bilateral basis.[4]

In the Central Asian context, it was also argued that in the post 9/11 era Sino-Russian arrangements, for regional security, would no longer play any significant role in the efforts to deal with terrorism in the region. Analysts like Stephen Blank stressed:

> In the war against terrorism in Afghanistan and Central Asia,

> the Shanghai Cooperative Organization has played no role. This failure confirms its inutility as a security provider and adds to a long line of abortive attempts to reorganize Central Asia under Russian leadership or to form viable regional organizations for mutual cooperation. Thus the SCO illustrates the problems besetting the construction of viable regional organizations in Central Asia.[5]

Elaborated on this "failure", Blank noted that this was essentially one that resulted from Russian and Chinese efforts to make what was conceived as a confidence building measure into a collective security system and its subsequent projection as an Asian alternative to the system of alliances forged by the United States. Its failure was identified in promises to defend the states from terrorism, secessionism and separatism when neither Russia nor China could provide effective military support against terrorism and were unprepared and unable to invest heavily in security in the region. While Professor Blank's remarks are essentially addressed to the problem of the failure of the SCO in dealing with the threat of terrorism it reflects a common theme that stresses the failure of regional security initiatives against international terrorism in Central Asia. This is a theme that has become an abiding one in most writings on the "year after". It also reflects what is then the logical next step in predicting a realignment of security arrangements in the region and the emergence of alternative global arrangements to deal with new challenges.[6]

The emergence of these alternative arrangements is projected to effectively block the consolidation of what is identified as the "Sino-Russian condominium" over Central Asia that was underway until September 2001.[7] A Congressional Research Service note, for instance, clearly reflects this in observing:

> The US appears to have completely seized the initiative from the newly formed SCO regional grouping and has provided the SCO members with an unanticipated alternative for addressing the issue of regional terrorism.[8]

A number of reasons are put forward in favour of such arguments. The first is the new perception of threat from non-state actors. This is problematic since these non-state actors are beyond the control of international law and law enforcement agencies whose sanctions can only be enforced against states. It was assumed that dealing with perceptions of threat from other actors would remain within the internal jurisdiction of each state. However, the emergence of international terrorism with its ability to become a threat not just to the state from which it originated but also others is a new phenomenon that requires alternative means of control. The second is the increase in non traditional security threats, not just international terrorism but also drug smuggling, arms trafficking, international crime, international disputes caused by environmental deterioration and scramble for water and energy resources. The third is the threat posed by groups and states where modernization and globalization had not resulted in any substantial changes. It has been noted that the ability to deal with all three would depend on the success of international coalitions.[9]

Moving away from such arguments, that identified the post September scenario as a major watershed, this chapter argues that viable regional security alignments had maintained global linkages throughout the last decade. Post September 11 events merely highlighted arrangements that had already been in place. The chapter also argues for the recognition of a multiplicity of security arrangements dealing with multiple security issues as the norm rather than agreements under one global system. While older security arrangements remain in place, newer ones are being forged to deal with emerging security issues. This multiplicity of security arrangements is a reflection of the multilateralism that is now well entrenched in the policy of the Central Asian Republics as well as the Eurasian powers.

A confluence of factors, necessitated both by the compulsions of the regional powers as well as requirements of the new states resulted in such initiatives. Some of these, for instance, were necessitated by disputed borders and the presence of minorities across the borders of the states and the need to prevent secessionism by coming to some understanding about borders, like the Shanghai Cooperation Organization. Others, recognized that strategic borders of states extended well beyond the boundaries of individual nations and required global effort to guard, like the Collective Security Agreements of the CIS. Still others reflected the need for global linkages to meet new requirements in terms of not just internal security but also peacekeeping, management of crisis etc, like the Partnership for Peace. What was common to all of these was the presence of one or more global and/or regional power as part of the initiative. However, prior to an examination of these linkages, it would be interesting to briefly examine how regional initiatives became significant in the global scenario.

Regional initiatives, as a concept is hardly new. The 1960's witnessed a world-wide spate of such regionalist initiatives. Attempts to create common markets and free trade associations proliferated in the Middle East, Africa, the Pacific, Western Europe and the Americas. Most of these projects failed, and except in Western Europe and South East Asia, regionalist policies did not lead to major progress. Regionalism remained on the international agenda during the entire later period of the Cold War but with a much more limited scope. Regional rhetoric reappeared in the late 1980's in many parts of the world and this time, unlike in the previous period, it did not fail to be translated into political reality. Cohesive and effectively institutionalized regional experiences were now no longer confined to Western Europe.

A number of factors became significant here. The first was the legacy of borders determined in imperial times, that inevitably left large minorities in most states. The multiethnic profile of the nations meant the possibility of irredentism in all the states and a strong reason for alliances. With possibilities of global rivalries receding along with the security guarantees that reduced the possibility of internal instability the need to act in concert on particular issues increased. Common economic resources were another important reason for integrative tendencies. While Asian states have had a history of antagonistic relations, they also have a mutual interest in pursuing economic modernization, which requires stability. This mutual interest gave rise to multilateral forums, which attempted to limit the use of force, provided for sanctity of contracts and arranged for assignment and recognition of property rights.

Other factors that were seen to provided an impetus to regional forums were the end of the Cold War which had subordinated all regional arrangements; the need to deal with foreign security concerns at a regional rather than at a global level; outward oriented policies in the developing world; the rise of new trading blocs in the developed world; the decline of broad coalitions of third world countries, which were replaced by more viable regional coalitions and Western support for regional arrangements in the third world.[10] Among the above mentioned factors, it was assumed that the end of the Cold war significantly contributed to the regionalization of international politics. It was also assumed that security in Europe, Asia, Middle East or Africa could now be evaluated independently of developments in other regions. During the Cold War, Asian regional security was closely linked to and in many ways subordinated to the Soviet American confrontation and the associated Sino Soviet conflict. Attempts by Asian nations to escape the dynamics of Superpower competition, through movements and strategies such as nonalignment, neutrality and peace zones were only partially successful.

With the disintegration of the Soviet Union, when the Central Asian states emerged as independent republics, a similar examination of prospects of regional co-operation began.[11] Indeed one of the first, proposed by President Nazarbaev, envisaged the formation of a Eurasian Union. This was visualized as a multinational model that would aim at creating a unified state, through various stages of a confederation, and finally arriving at a union. While this failed to take off a number of other options were put forward.[12] It was generally pointed out that the Central Asian region has three options in terms of regional integration. The first is in terms of reinforcement of relationships with the CIS countries on a new economic and institutional basis, the second is the formation of a community of Central Asian states the third is in terms of integration with her immediate neighbouring states. However, with recent developments, a fourth in terms of alignment with the West and particularly one sponsored by the NATO through, the PfP now seems in sight.

This chapter is an attempt at understanding the extent to which regional forums in the Central Asian region actually reflect; what is generally identified as a reversal of trends in seeking Cold War type linkages with one global power in the post "war against terror" period. It begins with the recognition that the nature of this global linkage will be significantly different. In fact with changes in the perception of threats the nature of the security arrangements have changed with greater emphasis on the need for internal security and integrity. Also a multiplicity of arrangements seems to be in place with both bilateral and multilateral linkages being simultaneously maintained in various regional initiatives. This chapter begins with an examination of the extent to which Russian linkages will be transformed in the light of a new security environment, moves on to examine newer initiatives that engage both Russia and China in the region and then concludes with an examination of the extent to which NATO's influence will be effective in balancing traditional security arrangements in the region.

Treaty on Collective Security and "Indivisible" Security

The Alma Ata Declaration described the CIS as a community of independent and sovereign states. The agreement explicitly stated that the Commonwealth did not constitute a political union, federation or confederation. The overarching goal of the CIS was to maintain coordination of the CIS states policies by taking into account the individual features of the countries.[13] On March 20, 1992, the declaration of non-use of force and threat in interaction between member states of the CIS was signed in Kiev. The states resolved to settle disputes by peaceful means only. Thereafter, bilateral and multilateral agreements were signed, in 1995 in Almaty, in which the CIS states pledged to refrain from military, political, economic and other forms of pressure on each other. However, since these did not provide for situations of external threats, on 15 May 1992, during the fifth Summit Meeting of the CIS states in Tashkent, the Treaty on Collective Security (CST) was signed by Russia, Kazakhstan, Kyrgyzstan, Uzbekistan, Tajikistan and Armenia. This stipulated renunciation of entering into military unions, participation in groupings of states and also in actions directed against member states of the CST.

The signatory countries agreed that their security was indivisible. If one party to the agreement was subject to aggression, that would be regarded as aggression against all parties to the Treaty. Therefore, the other parties would immediately render the necessary assistance to the party, which was the object of aggression, including military assistance. The signatory countries also agreed to the principle of sharing responsibility for maintaining security, non interference in internal affairs, collective defence and making decisions on matters of principle with regard to safeguarding collective security through consultation. The agreement stipulated that some specific military bases and facilities of one member state could be stationed or deployed in other member states with the consent of the states concerned.[14] According to Leonid Bondarez, Senior Research Analyst of the International Institute of Strategic Studies of the Kyrgyz Republic, two strands of the security provision in the framework of the CST stand out.[15] The first is the formation of friendly relations and creation of crisis prevention mechanism within the CIS. The second is containment of possible external threats by united forces of the member states, which led to the creation of the military organization of the CIS. On July 6, 1992, the council of heads of CIS states decided to create the general command of the united armed forces of the CIS.

The signing of such a collective security agreement among the CIS states at the time was only natural. As far as the Central Asian states were concerned they were extremely weak in military and defence capability. It would take some time for them to establish their own somewhat comprehensive military forces. Signing such a collective security agreement with Russia certainly enhanced the security of these countries. In addition the Agreement also stipulated that the parties to the Agreement would not use force to settle disputes among themselves. This also reduced any possibility of Russia using force against the signatory countries. To Russia, on the other hand, the signing of such an agreement gave the existence of the CIS some substance. It also reduced political pressures to withdraw Russian troops from CIS states. At the same time it helped to secure Russia's special interest in Central Asia. However, the agreement was signed by only six of the CIS states and concluded without any clearly perceived external military threat. It has therefore been perceived, as basically a defensive mechanism to manage potential conflicts among the CIS states.[16] By 1998, Armenia, Belarus, Azerbaijan, Georgia, Kazakhstan, Kyrgyzstan, Tajikistan, Uzbekistan and Russia became signatories to this treaty. A joint anti-aircraft defence system was created as the first step towards implementation of the objectives of the CST. The main objective of this was to safeguard state air space and carry out joint anti-aircraft trainings. However, this remained the only practical result achieved during the first stage of creation of collective security system within the framework of the CIS. For the most part, interactions remained at the level of declarations.[17]

From the very beginning, differences also arose on the nature of collective defence. In May 1995, an agreement on protecting the external borders of the CIS was signed by seven states. However, Ukraine, Turkmenistan, Moldova, Azerbaijan and

Uzbekistan declined to sign. Earlier in February 1995, at a Joint meeting of the Council of Heads of Governments and Council of Heads of States, a proposal of joint defence of the CIS's external borders was seriously debated. However, Azerbaijan and Ukraine categorically opposed it. Many other CIS states noted that mutual cooperation on defence and borders was more acceptable than joint defence of the CIS external borders. In 1999 Azerbaijan, Georgia and Uzbekistan refused to sign the treaty.

Meanwhile, the signing of the Collective Security Treaty paved the way for the abolition of the Soviet era Turkestan Military District on 30 June 1992. However, even as the Soviet military was being disbanded, confrontation began to grow in Tajikistan. The creation of a collective peacekeeping force on the territory of Tajikistan was the first attempt at providing collective security. The force consisted of the 201 infantry division of the Russian Federation and subdivisions of forces of Kazakhstan, Kyrgyzstan and Uzbekistan. However, the largest part of the force came from Russia and subsequently intra regional factors led to the withdrawal of first the Uzbek and then Kyrgyz and Kazakh forces out of Tajikistan.[18] The conflict itself affected the nature of security arrangements in the region. Uzbekistan, as the country most affected by disorder in Tajikistan, sought to increasingly align itself in security relationships that gave it more flexibility than an alliance with Russia. In 1996 Uzbekistan announced its intention to join the Partnership for Peace. This was followed by Kazakhstan, Kyrgyzstan and Tajikistan.

A second effort to create a regional security system was implemented within the framework of the Central Asian Economic Cooperation Organization. In July 1994, an agreement on military technical cooperation was signed by Kazakhstan, Kyrgyzstan and Uzbekistan on the basis of which the Council of Defence Ministers was created. In 1997, a peacekeeping battalion, the Centrasbat '97, was created as a 500 strong battalion of Kazakh, Kyrgyz and Uzbek troops, under the aegis of the UN, for neutralization of possible causes of conflict and destabilization in the region.

After Tajikistan joined the organization, collaboration in the sphere of military cooperation was curtailed. In the year 2000, on the initiative of the Uzbek President, a decision for the elimination of military structure was made that led to the abolition of the council of ministers.[19]

Such developments meant that the prospects of the CIS providing for a foundation for the security in the region have not been rated highly.[20] This was partly because the CIS was formed in a period when Russia's priorities did not include a strongly integrated commonwealth.[21] Russia therefore failed to halt NATO's eastward expansion or to mobilize opposition to this project among the CIS members. With the exception of Belarus, in 1995 no member of the CIS accepted Russia's "counter block" rhetoric. The creation of a new security environment in Russia's western borders did not have any direct consequences for the security interests of the states in Central Asia or the Transcaucasus. Russia had apparently undermined the extent to which the CIS members would be able to dissociate their own security perspective from that of Russia. With the fading of the fears of a restoration of the USSR and in the light of the dangers of extremism, terrorism, drug trafficking and separatism, however, there appeared a new regional enthusiasm for strategic partnerships with Russia. However, with the exception of the Russian-Tajik partnership, these arrangements are mostly misnamed. They are tactical agreements that came into being as a result of the confluence of interests. When the interests change the alliances can be expected to shift.

It has also been noted that part of the failure of the security arrangements was due to the fact that CIS security was transformed into Russian hegemony over the areas where troops were stationed. This was hardly surprising given that Russia's engagement in Central Asia which was broadly based on its *Military Doctrine on Commonwealth of Independent States of November 1993*. The broad outline of this doctrine pushed forward the argument that (a) Russia as a great power has both regional and global responsibilities (b) the territory of the former Soviet Union is a geostrategic area in which Moscow has special interests (c) Russia has extra-territorial responsibilities when it comes to the well being of ethnic Russians, Russian citizens and Russian speaking communities throughout the CIS.[22]

As an example, critics point to Russia's 201 motorized infantry division, which has been stationed in Tajikistan since 1993 under a security arrangement, that included efforts to fight drugs and weapons smuggling across the Afghan border. Until recently the soldiers there worked under a CIS mandate, as part of the Commonwealth's peacekeeping troops. The mandate has since been lifted, but the troops remain as part of the bilateral agreement between Moscow and Dushanbe.[23] It was only in June 2004 that an agreement was signed between Russia and Tajikistan for gradual transfer of responsibility for border security to Tajikistan.[24]

Similarly Vladimir Romanenko, the Deputy Director of the CIS institute think tank notes that of the four hundred documents adopted by the CIS within a military cooperation framework, in practice only one, two or three really work. And these are the ones that have been signed on a bilateral basis.[25] Another factor weakening the collective security of the CIS, Romanenko adds, is that the agreements are often not collective. Tashkent, for instance abandoned the Collective Security Treaty in favour of drafting a bilateral military agreement with Russia to exchange weapons for natural gas. Georgia, Azerbaijan and Moldova have also dropped out of the treaty and Turkmenistan never signed it.

On the other hand, most observers tend to blame the CIS for something that it was clearly unable to accomplish, while failing to appreciate its very real contribution to the relative smoothness of the process of dismantling of the Soviet Union. The CIS, has and remains a form of transition from the unitary Soviet super state to national statehood. The most visible aspect of the CIS is the regular summit meeting of the leaders of the new states. The existence of this summit was instrumental in keeping the lines of communication open and preventing crisis. The CIS has to be commended for the remarkably civilized way in which the "divorce proceedings" among the Soviet successor states has been worked out.[26] As an institutional form given to a provisional arrangement with Moscow, the CIS may provide them with a political forum in which to discuss issues linked either to their internal sovereignty or to their external sovereignty.

As part of this there were plans by CIS member states Russia, Kyrgyzstan, Tajikistan and Kazakhstan to create a rapid action force to combat, what is perceived as the growing regional threat, of Islamic militant groups. Supporters of the plan called this a step towards an effective defence partnership. But some Russian analysts, looking at other joint military agreements by the CIS have doubted whether it will be effective. Alexie Malashenko, for instance, while doubting whether such joint action would be successful, adds that recent outbreaks of extremist violence in Central Asia casts future collaborative CIS efforts in a new light.[27]

However, a growing disillusionment in Russia about the strategic partnership agreements concluded over the past year has once again projected attention on security arrangements within the CIS. Iskander Khisamov, a regional analyst clearly states this in the journal *Ekspert* when he writes:

> There is no country, or even a group of countries or an international institution that can or would want to give Russia some guarantees that its security, territorial integrity or at least its economic interests will be respected. Thus no matter how weak or disintegrated the Commonwealth of Independent States might be, it remains Russia's main strategic priority.[28]

In keeping with this there have recently been moves by Russia to reassert her influence over the post Soviet space on the basis of the Collective Security Treaty. Analysts have noted that using anti-terrorism as a catch phrase, Russia is pushing to create a full fledged regional military bloc and a new regional security organization.[29] During 2001-2003 Moscow tried to characterize the CIS Collective Security Council (based on the CST) as an active regional organization. However, most of the work of this body tended to be declaratory. It has been argued that the fact that Russia was constrained by the need to share security responsibilities in Central Asia with western states and even China played a major part in this. It also influenced the capacity of a CIS Antiterrorism Centre located in Bishkek, which confined its task to exchange of information and analysis and become one of the several uncoordinated regional anti-terrorist structures in Central Asia.[30]

In May 2002 Russia agreed with Kazakhstan, Kyrgyzstan, Tajikistan, Belarus and Armenia to create a Collective Security Treaty Organization (CSTO). A year later it was launched on April 28, 2003 when the Presidents of Armenia, Belarus, Kazakhstan, Kyrgyzstan, Russia and Tajikistan met in Dushanbe and created a new military political organization, on the basis of the CIS Collective Security Treaty.[31] Its charter and legal status had been approved at an earlier meeting in Moldova in October 2002. The CSTO was launched to address new threats and challenges through a joint military command located in Moscow. The purpose of the CSTO is to guarantee "the security, territorial integrity and sovereignty of the member states". To this end it considers an act of aggression against any one state as an act of aggression against all members.

The member states agreed on military and military political mechanisms, resolved to form joint headquarters and a rapid deployment force and made a decision on coordinating political approaches. Three distinct regional collective security systems are now operating in the Caucasus, western CIS and Central Asia in Russia-Belarus, Russia-Armenia and Tajikistan-Kazakhstan-Kyrgyzstan. Kyrgyzstan has become the venue for the CSTO's military exercises. The Collective Security Forces are to be assembled there in case of need by the CSTO member states. The forces may be used to combat external aggression, to carry out anti-terrorist operations and to be involved in military maneuvers.

One of the most significant aspects of the Central Asian participation in the CSTO is the fact that it signals the recognition of Russia as a viable alternative in resolving regional security issues. It has been argued that as the dominant state in the CSTO, Russia is hoping to use it as a macro regional platform to support its standing, as a security manager for Central Asia, and to confirm recognition of the CSTO as a coequal security actor in the region with NATO.[32] While the organization seeks cooperation with the UN, OSCE, SCO and NATO there is also obvious recognition of the dominant Russian position in the organization. Central Asian analysts note that such actions denote that "the main efforts of the creation of the collective security system in Central Asia are concentrated within the framework of the CST".[33] With the aim of raising the effectiveness of the fight against terror, an anti-terrorist centre was created in Moscow in 2000. Along with this there was an attempt to exchange operative data systems of special agencies and creation of joint rapid action forces.

There are of course numerous factors that could hinder the viability of the organization, not the least of which is that the full implementation of its plans are yet to be realized and there is skepticism that it could end up remaining only on paper like a large number of other CIS integrative effort. The absence of Uzbekistan and Turkmenistan from the organization, the questionable financial viability of Russia, the multi-vector policy now followed by all the Central Asian states and disagreements among the member states about threat perceptions could also prove hard to resolve. Critics note that the main attraction of the CSTO framework for Kazakhstan, Kyrgyzstan and Tajikistan may simply be the Russian offer to sell military equipment bilaterally to its partner states at the prices and on the terms at which they are available to Russian armed forces.[34] However, what remains significant despite these drawbacks is the fact that the CSTO is an effort at addressing local, regional and international issues on a collective basis. What is also significant is that the creation of a rapid reaction force demonstrates Russian interest in developing sub CIS security groupings under Russian leadership and guidance. For Moscow the force also offers some hope that the Central Asian states may eventually agree to establish a "CIS regional command structure". However, the Central Asian states have not been very enthusiastic about the creation of a regionally defined but Russian dominated defence community.[35]

A NATO summit communiqué, in June 2004, emphasizing "special focus" on the Caucasus and Central Asia, led to a Russian reassertion of the role that the CIS could play in providing security in the region.[36] At a Press Conference in Moscow on July 1, 2004, Gleb Pavlovsky declared that only Russia could guarantee security in Central Asia and the Caucasus by stressing that "it is the CIS rather than NATO member nations that provide tangible guarantees of security on the border of this vast area".[37] This was echoed by Andrei Kokoshin, Chairman of the Russian Duma's CIS Affairs Committee, who pointed to the difficulties in Iraq as indicative of how ill equipped NATO member countries were for fighting terrorism, a key requirement in the Central Asian region today.[38] Russia emphasized this role by conducting a series of military exercises in Central Asia to underline assertions that regional concerns about terrorism are best solved within the CIS or SCO framework. As part of this, Russia concluded a strategic alliance agreement with Uzbekistan on June 17, 2004 and has tightened its ties with Tajikistan with a June 4, 2004 agreement on a land lease that would give Russia indefinite access to a military base outside the Tajik capital of Dushanbe. However, a recently concluded deal between Kazakhstan and a UK military firm to upgrade Kazakhstan's air defence systems could compromise its obligations under the CIS Treaty.

Post Beslan, Moscow once again emphasised the significance of the CIS as a forum committed to eradicating terrorism in Caucasus and Central Asia. In the CIS conference in September 2004, it became evident that the choice was clear; to either function as an effective organization or cease to exist as a geopolitical player. Since President Putin was chairing the CIS, a large part of the onus to propose a strategy capable of meeting the challenge fell on Moscow. In the course of the conference, the CIS leaders signed a statement that expressed solidarity with Russia in the fight against terrorism. This was particularly emphasised by Uzbek President Islam Karimov and Kyrgyz President Askar Akayev. President Karimov also proposed the creation of a CIS specific list of wanted terrorists and echoed Kremlin's calls for preemptive strike against terrorist training bases.[39] However, there was also disagreement between Georgian President Mikheil Saakashvili and President Putin about Moscow's involvement with South Ossetia and Abkhazia.

The Shanghai Agreement and "Confidence Building Measures"

The Shanghai Forum was formed to deal with the requirements of confidence building measures along the borders of the states. It has been noted that over the years, as the Shanghai 5 was transformed into the Shanghai 6, it developed as a multilateral cooperative mechanism.[40] The fields of cooperation have been expanded from security to various other aspects such as politics, foreign affairs, trade, economic sector and culture. As noted by a scholar from the Shanghai Institute of International Studies, the SCO strengthens mutual trust and cooperation among the five states, enables the five countries to strike in close coordination at various kinds of forces sabotaging peace and development in the region and to defend their own stability and development and initiates peaceful settlement of disputes and checks destabilizing factors.[41]

The Shanghai 5 also reflected commonality of Sino-Russian interests in the Central Asian region that has encouraged both to look beyond the many impediments of this relationship. The Chinese stake in the Shanghai 5 is dependent on the way it views Islam and treats its Muslim citizenry. Beijing's commitment in the Shanghai 5, to fight terrorism, is based on fears of Islamic secessionism in Xinjiang and its concern that it should not be branded as an anti-Muslim state before the other Central Asian states. The Russian initiative in the Shanghai 5 is seen as a direct outcome of its domestic political environment.[42] The collapse of the Soviet Union not only resulted in a "permanent arc of crisis along the northern and southern Caucasus" but has had wider ramifications. Although largely confined to the North Caucasus, the breakdown of law and order and the gradual loss of state authority and power are felt throughout Central Asia as well. As the principal successor state to the Soviet Union, Russia has claimed responsibility for containment of all intra regional conflicts. Moscow's current disposition towards the region includes its economic, security and great power interests. Also since Russia continues to follow its traditional interests in the Caucasian and Central Asian region she feels threatened by US incursions in the region.

As a formal multilateral forum, the Shanghai 5 owes its origin to the 26 April 1996 joint border agreement between China, Kazakhstan, Kyrgyzstan, Tajikistan and Russia. In the beginning, the aims and objectives of the grouping was rather vague. The document committed the leadership of the states to establish collectively a range of confidence building measures in the field of military cooperation along their common borders. Although there was no specific reference to it, the initiative was undertaken primarily to protect transborder trade among the states, which had increasingly come under attacks. As an appendage the agreement also entrusted the members to "stand against stirring up ethno-religious nationalism".[43]

Under the Shanghai Agreement the military forces of both sides stationed along the border areas promised not to attack each other. The agreement rules out conducting military exercises aimed against each other. It also specifies that limits will be imposed on the scale, scope and number of military exercises on both sides of the border areas. The concerned sides should inform each other of any major military activities taking place in any area within 100 kilometers of the border. It further stipulates that the concerned sides will invite each other to observe military exercises and will prevent any dangerous military activities. It also stipulates that friendly exchanges will be strengthened between the military forces and frontier guards of both sides.[44]

Since its inception, the organization has steadily increased its focus on the development of regional security situation and unrest in Kazakhstan, Kyrgyzstan and Tajikistan. In fact in recent years, the member nations have unanimously stated that non-traditional threats to their national interest and internal security could destabilize the existing ethno religious harmony within their borders and endanger their territorial sovereignty. Indeed the fear of secessionism is the main reason behind the Shanghai Forum's objective of regional cooperation in the military sphere. The initial Shanghai 5 agreement on strengthening confidence building measures, in 1996 brought a reduction of tension and initiated demilitarization along the borders.

After significant success in border delimitation and demilitarization, the Shanghai grouping shifted its focus to address the issue of militancy in the region.[45] At an August 1999 summit in Bishkek agreement was reached on practical measures in this direction though they were never implemented. In 2000 at the fifth summit meeting in Dushanbe two new initiatives were put forward. First, the Shanghai Five decided to establish an international organization for regional security and cooperation, which would be open to surrounding states and second Uzbekistan, attended this summit as an observer. The Shanghai organization declares itself to be a new model of regional cooperation which aims to produce good neighbourly relations, mutual trust, equality and common development and is neither allied with nor antagonistic to third parties. Its basic idea is to preserve the integrity of member states, which share common interests for combating "separatist" movements within their states and preventing outside interference. This also means that the concerned parties never support their own minorities in other member states. In this context Uzbekistan's position was very important for the Shanghai Five, since the future security and integrity of the member states could not be guaranteed without Uzbekistan's commitment to the partnership.[46]

At a meeting of the heads of state and government in Shanghai in June 2001, with Uzbekistan participating, the SCO declared its intention not only to create an "anti-terrorism" centre but also to make it the home of a joint (mainly Sino-Russian) rapid deployment force. This was also planned to function as a coordinating centre for the SCO and the CIS. After Uzbekistan joined the Shanghai 5 on June 14, 2001, the six countries declared that the Shanghai 5 mechanism would now be upgraded as the Shanghai Cooperation Organization, the first regional multilateral cooperative organization. Subsequently, the Shanghai Convention against terrorism, separatism, and extremism were signed by the six leaders on June 15, 2001. The establishment of the Anti-Terrorism Centre and the proposition of the CANFZ are important initiatives that will be taken in the near future.

While the Central Asian states have been unsuccessful in cooperating to achieve many common regional economic and political objectives, they found common cause in finding a solution to the Afghan crisis and the expanding array of sub national security threats. This has impelled them in the direction of relatively new forms of alliance. In 1993 China, Russia, Kazakhstan, Kyrgyzstan and Tajikistan commenced a diplomatic dialogue concerning their common borders. On 26 April 1996, the Presidents of the five Border States met in Shanghai to sign a package of fourteen agreements on border issues. The Shanghai Accord, constituted a breakthrough in establishing a framework for border normalization. More importantly the Shanghai Five or the Shanghai Forum evolved a region wide united front, to address the challenges to political normalization of the Central Asian region. Meeting in July 2000, the heads of the states of Russia, China, Kazakhstan, Kyrgyzstan and Tajikistan (with the Uzbek President as an observer) agreed to deepen interstate cooperation in diplomatic, commercial, military and technological and other areas with the purpose of reinforcing regional security and stability. The leaders pledged new cooperative initiatives in combating trafficking of drugs and weapons, in fighting terrorism, political extremism and separatism and in resolving disputes over transboundary resources such as water, energy and transport infrastructure.

A series of inter-governmental and inter departmental agreements in trade and economic spheres has been signed between the countries. These mainly pertain to trade and economic agreements, promotion and protection of investments and collaboration in the energy sphere. These provide a strong base for the growth of trade and economic collaboration between China and the Central Asian states within the framework of the SCO. However, a number of problems remain in trade and economic collaboration, among them difficulties in transportation across high mountainous regions, the fact that Chinese undertakings do not have a presence in Central Asia and that the market capacity in the region is limited and the lack of finance available for development.[47] Despite these there seems to be conviction on the Chinese side that the formation of the SCO has provided a new impetus to the development of economic cooperation between China and the Central Asian states. Sun Zhuangzhi, Director, Central Asian Department, Institute for East European, Russian and Central Asian Studies, Chinese Academy of Social Sciences, Beijing notes:

> With simplification of trade and investment mechanisms and the completion of a number of multilateral projects in the framework of the SCO, the problems of investment and transportation, which complicated the Chinese-Central Asian collaboration, were solved. China may facilitate the marketing of Central Asian resources and its products at the international level. Besides that, an all encompassing multilateral cooperation in the fields of politics, defence, culture and tourism may be beneficial for the development of trade and economic collaboration between China and the Central Asian states.[48]

In the immediate aftermath of September 11, reactions of the member states of SCO to the "war against terror" and their level of involvement varied. While Russia showed greater acceptability of the US presence in the region, China, faced with the possibility of the expansion of the NATO towards its western border was less enthusiastic. The reactions of the Central Asian states also varied. While all the states agreed to US presence in their territories, Uzbekistan's stance of close collaboration with the US military presence led to a passive attitude towards cooperation within the SCO. Uzbekistan did not participate in the Moscow meeting of the Defence/Military or the Astana meeting of heads of law enforcement agencies. However, Uzbekistan did sign the SCO charter and subsequently agreed to its regional anti-terrorist structure.

The presence of US troops in the Central Asian region has provoked China to take steps to counter the threats posed to its security. The Foreign Ministers of the SCO met in Beijing in January 2002, where, after analyzing the problems of regional security documents for fostering cooperation in the fields of maintaining regional security and stability and combating threats from terrorism, separatism and extremism were adopted. Peace and stability has been sought to be ensured through the motto "security through cooperation."

On May 28 and 29, 2003, heads of state of the member nations of the SCO met in Moscow to transform the SCO to a full fledged international organization. The Moscow summit has been judged as a major success particularly for China.[49] The summit has committed China, Russia and the Central Asian states to address regional issues ranging from terrorism to unfair trade practice in a practical format. At the Summit the leaders reached consensus on the institutionalization of the SCO and some major international issues. They agreed to launch a SCO Secretariat and a regional anti-terrorism centre no later than January 1, 2004. They also decided that the next summit would be held in Tashkent, Uzbekistan. As the organization revitalizes itself with a new flag and logo, several factors will become crucial for the long term viability of the organization. First, is the formation of the Bishkek counter terrorism centre. To be effective, it will have to ensure some coordination between the member states on issues of security. Secondly, the establishment of a permanent secretariat and a budget will be necessary to demonstrate the political and material commitment that member states are willing to provide. And thirdly, the SCO needs to prove that it can accomplish initial limited economic cooperation.

Speaking at the meeting the Chinese President Hu stressed that the SCO had gone through an extraordinary path and endured the test of time since its establishment two years ago. He added that the SCO's achievements had shown that the basic purpose and developing principles of the organization were correct and must be maintained and followed unswervingly. President Hu went on to point out that the international situation was currently undergoing deep changes, which present new tasks to the building of the SCO. He said that to press on with the construction of the SCO's standing bodies, deepening of cooperation in the economic and security fields and expanding the external exchanges of the organization is the central task of the SCO in the next stage of work.[50]

SCO Foreign Ministers held security talks once again in Tashkent, on September 5, 2003. Member states expressed the hope that the military maneuvers that were held in August 2003 which were named Cooperation 2003, would help to build the credibility of the SCO as a security alternative to the US military presence in the region.[51] The maneuvers were conducted in two stages. the first held on August 6, 2003, in eastern Kazakhstan, involved every member state except Uzbekistan, and was designed to improve the joint command and control structure and address other inter-operability issues. Such exercises are vital to enhance the SCO's capabilities, in part because China's military establishment has little experience in coordinating operations with the armed forces of other nations. The exercise also included a mock operation to free passengers from a hijacked commercial airliner. The second stage, held later in China, involved an operation to uproot separatist fighters who, under a hypothetical scenario, had infiltrated the region.

There remains a debate on whether the SCO would be able to develop itself as a counterweight to US military presence in Central Asia. Some analysts like Roy Allison have noted that the probability of this kind of struggle should not be overstated.[52] First, since September 11 the Central Asian states have expected and received much more practical assistance in countering regional security threats from new bilateral security programmes, particularly from the United States rather than the SCO. Second Russia views the CSTO, rather than the SCO, as the natural counterweight to the new US strategic presence and Moscow's engagement in the SCO which may be determined by a wish to constrain the growth of Chinese influence in Central Asia as much as by a wish to develop a structure for regional balancing against the United States.[53] However, Allison goes on to point out that these factors should not belie the significant role played by the SCO in enabling Chinese security concerns to be aired in a regional framework.

US actions against Iraq were another testing issue as far as the SCO was concerned. Though both Russia and China criticized US unilateralism in Iraq they followed different approaches to how to tackle the Iraq issue.[54] However, the SCO was almost silent as far as the war on Iraq was concerned and could not issue any official statement.[55] The SCO declaration of May 29, 2003 in Moscow contains only one paragraph on Iraqi reconstruction and has nothing to suggest an anti American orientation except a statement calling for a "democratic world order".

Central Asian analysts have generally commented favourably on the achievements of the SCO.[56] However, there is also the recognition that the process is far from complete.

> The potential abilities of the organization have not been fully exhausted. Upto this day, the main goal of the organization was the problem of security in the region. However, the leaders of the six states have pointed out the necessity of intensifying the development of the programme of economic cooperation. This sphere of activity has a very promising future. A combined market of the SCO states will be the largest in the world.[57]

NATO and "Global" Security Initiatives

Traditionally, Russian tendency has been to see American engagement in the Central Asian region as a zero-sum game, whereby any gains for the US automatically meant a loss for Russia. This meant that considerable efforts were spent in blocking or limiting American political, economic and military involvement in Central Asia. Russian foreign and security policy elites expressed a continuing fear that American involvement in the region, particularly in the development of energy resources was simply opening a wedge of what would ultimately become American military presence. American corporations may lead the process, but Pentagon would quickly follow.[58]

On the other hand, Russia realized that her own focus of security concerns has changed with greater attention on controlling the flows of weapons, drugs, refugees and radicalism and terrorism. Russian elites increasingly concerned about the dangers of nuclear proliferation and of biological and chemical weapons in the hands of terrorists, welcomed American efforts to remove nuclear warheads from the three successor states that possessed them, Ukraine, Belarus and Kazakhstan and acquiesced in American efforts to remove stocks of fissile materials from Kazakhstan. More recently, the threat of biological terrorism has become an area of increasing concern. The US is also involved in ways to neutralize this material in the region. There is thus clearly a trade off between costs and benefits. While there is disquiet about prospects of a major American presence in the region, it has also been argued that American reinforcement of the stability of the Central Asian countries and of Russia's southern borders could be of considerable benefit at a time when Russia alone is not capable of managing the new threats in the region.

In the post 9/11 context there has been considerable rethinking on NATO's relationship with Russia. Under the NATO-Russia Founding Act on Mutual Relations, Cooperation and Security, there has been a pledge to intensify cooperation to fight terrorism. It has been argued that it will take effort to transform past hostilities, prevailing suspicion and skepticism as well as surpass disagreements over topical issues such as Russia's policy in dealing with the Chechen issue. However, NATO-Russia rapprochement will signal a major transformation in the sphere of international security.[59] Official statements from both sides have reflected this; though whether it would signal anything beyond an increased level of cooperation to deal with new security challenges remains to be seen. What this rethinking would entail for the Central Asian states requires reexamination. While the enlargement of the NATO, in the Central Asian region, had been viewed very negatively in Russia, to begin with, over time it was accepted as inevitable.

The development of American relations with the Central Asian states began in the post 1991 period, when the Clinton administration moved to create diplomatic, political and economic ties with countries, as part of the effort to view the States as potential members of the new community of democratic and market oriented economies. The US also committed itself to promoting and protecting the security and sovereignty of these new states. Under the leadership of Defence Secretary William Perry, the Partnership for Peace (PfP) programme was inaugurated, as both a way of handling the delicate issue of NATO enlargement but also as a way to develop broader ties with the Central Asian states. This programme laid the framework for a growing network of cooperative, political and military ties, with Uzbekistan in particular, which was to play an unexpected role in facilitating joint efforts after September 11.

The significant instrument for further expansion of the US role in the region was through the PfP. The Ministerial Meeting of the North Atlantic Cooperation Council (NACC), in Brussels in January 1994, launched a programme to transform relationship between the NATO and participating countries.[60] This new programme was aimed to go beyond dialogue and cooperation and forge a real partnership, which would be called Partnership for Peace. NACC and other CSCE countries, able and willing to contribute to the programme, were invited to join. It was pointed out that the PfP, which would operate under the authority of the North Atlantic Council, would forge new security relationships between the North Atlantic Alliance and its Partners for Peace. The Partnership was expected to expand and intensify political and military cooperation through out Europe, increase stability, diminish threats to peace and build strengthened relationships by promoting the spirit of practical cooperation and commitment to democratic principles that underpin the Alliance.

It was agreed that NATO would consult any active participant in the Partnership if that partner perceived a direct threat to its territorial integrity, political independence or security. At a pace and scope determined by the capacity and the desire of the individual participating states concrete steps towards transparency in defence budgeting, promoting democratic control of defence ministries, joint planning, joint military exercises and creating an ability to operate with NATO forces in such fields as peacekeeping, search and rescue and humanitarian operations and others would be agreed on. To promote closer military cooperation and inter-operatability within the Partnership framework, it was proposed that peacekeeping field exercises be held beginning in 1994.

2001 marked the first decade of partnership of the NATO and PfP. The North Atlantic Cooperation Council first met in December 1991. It was established to help break down east-west divisions and build up mutual trust in the wake of the end of the Cold war by bringing together NATO Allies with former Warsaw Pact countries in a forum for security dialogue and cooperation. Three years later the Partnership for Peace was launched to enable Partner countries to develop individual programmes of practical cooperation with NATO as a complement to the opportunities for multilateral political dialogue afforded by the NACC.[61] The Euro-Atlantic Partnership Council was created in 1997 to replace the NACC and build its achievements.

Over the past decade strategies built around partnership and cooperation rather than political confrontation and military competition have dramatically altered the Euro Atlantic Security environment. NATO and partner countries consult regularly on security issues, their forces interact frequently and conduct joint exercises and their soldiers are deployed alongside each other, in NATO led peace support operations in the Balkans.

Aimed at promoting transparency and generating mutual confidence, the Euro Atlantic Partnership Council (EAPC) brought together 27 Partners and 19 Allies for regular consultation on issues encompassing all aspects of security and all regions of the Euro Atlantic area. Meetings take place regularly at the level of ambassadors, foreign and defence ministers and chiefs of defence. A two year EAPC Action Plan provides for long term consultations and cooperation on a range of political and security related matters, including regional issues, arms control, peacekeeping, defence and economic issues, civil emergency planning and scientific and environmental issues. In the wake of the terrorist attacks on the US in September 2001 increased attention is to be given to combat international terrorism. EAPC and ad hoc working groups focus on other areas of particular interests, such as regional cooperation in south eastern Europe and the Caucasus or global humanitarian 'mine action' and preventing the spread of small arms and weapons.

While the EAPC is a multilateral forum, it also serves as the political framework for the PfP, a major programme of the bilateral cooperation between NATO and individual Partner countries. The basic aims of the PfP are to promote transparency in national defence planning, military budgeting and the democratic control of national armed forces, as well as to develop the capacity for joint action between forces from partner countries and those of NATO member countries, for example in peacekeeping or disaster response operations. Enshrined in the PfP Framework Document is a commitment by the Allies to consult bilaterally with any Partner country that perceives a direct threat to its territorial integrity, political independence or security.

Individual Partnership programmes were drawn between NATO and Partner countries from an extensive menu of activities — the PfP work programme — according to each country's specific interests and needs. The biennial Programme contains more than two thousand activities ranging from large military exercises to defence related cooperation in fields, such as crisis management, peacekeeping, civil emergency planning, air traffic management and armaments cooperation.[62] Georgia, Azerbaijan and Uzbekistan agreed to enter into Individual Partnership Action Plans with NATO, at the Istanbul summit, in June 2004.

In the post 9/11 years Central Asia has significantly figured at NATO summits. In the June 28-29 2004 NATO summit at Istanbul member states expressed a desire to "put special focus on engaging with our partners in the strategically important regions of the Caucasus and Central Asia". In a communiqué issued at the conclusion of the summit NATO emphasized that it will seek to increase its profile, in what was described as "strategically important regions of the Caucasus and Central Asia".[63] As part of this, NATO has agreed on improving liaison arrangements, including the assignment of two liaison officers as well as special representatives for the two regions from within the international staff. At the same time, however, an attempt was made to reassure Russia by stressing that these efforts to transform the alliance should not be perceived as a threat by any country or organization.[64]

Among Central Asian analysts there is still a debate on the kind of military presence that the NATO is planning for the region. Anar Khamzayeva, Expert at the Centre for Foreign Policy and Analysis, Almaty, questions whether the Central Asian states stand to gain from their strategic cooperation with the West. However, she concludes that, though, providing energy security to the US will be a major focus of NATO, its engagement in the region will "contribute to substantial progress in dealing with internal and external stability and security challenges in the region of Central Asia".[65] There is general agreement that a major requirement for this is long term presence to allow the Central Asian states to deal with the spillover of possible tensions in their states from Afghanistan, that could result from their engagement in the anti-terrorist campaign. The benefits from this participation are not ignored.

> For the Central Asian states, ... participation in the EAPC and the PfP presented them an opportunity to integrate into the global security structures, to engage in practical military-political cooperation and regular consultations with the alliance on a wide variety of matters in the fields of peacekeeping, arms control and disarmament, defence planning, scientific cooperation and defence related environmental issues. This should be seen as a foundation for further intensive collaboration of western military personnel with their counterparts in the region, for increase in technical support and joint exercises.[66]

Similarly, Bakhtiyor Irishmatov, Senior Research Fellow at the Institute of Strategic and Regional Studies, Tashkent, notes:

> A key area of NATO-Central Asian cooperation is civil defence to minimize the damage from terrorist attacks. From Uzbekistan's point of view, this will require extensive cooperation and consultations with NATO institutions for planning and policy making, establishing special areas of cooperation, increased interaction with NATO member

countries for optimal utilization of training resources and cooperation in the area of urban planning as civil defence.[67]

Another initiative that appears to have made a comeback in the recent years is the GUUAM. The GUAM was founded in October 1997, through agreements between Georgia, Ukraine, Azerbaijan and Moldova with the initial purpose of exploring options for defence cooperation between Ukraine and the states south of Caucasus. Between 1999 and 2002 Uzbekistan joined as a member of the group, which was then designated as GUUAM. The GUUAM was expected to provided a tentative consultative channel on security issues between south Caucasus and Central Asia. Uzbekistan's suspension of its membership in April 2002 reflected both a desire to focus on bilateral approaches to security and a failure of the group to develop any substantive security policy agreement that supported Uzbekistan's priorities.[68] In principle, the GUUAM had an ambitious regionalist security agenda. It aimed to establish the conceptual foundations and strategies for cooperative security; to develop new approaches capable of conclusively resolving conflicts in the GUUAM region; to outline the main directions and forms of military-technical cooperation within GUUAM framework; and to work to strengthen GUUAM's partnership with NATO. However, there was little joint activity on these issues and maintaining defence cooperation among disparate states became difficult. Military-technical cooperation among the member states of the group began to be conducted on a bilateral rather than a multilateral level.[69]

It has been noted that the catalyst for the reemergence of the organization from near oblivion was the United States.[70] Since September 11, GUUAM's potential for security cooperation has been reinvigorated, assisted by American interests in cooperation over issues of border security, the security of transport corridors and terrorism. GUUAM-US cooperation began to accelerate in December 2002, with a programme to develop trade and improve border and customs control to combat organized crime and narcotics trafficking.

At a meeting held on July 3-4, 2003 at the Ukrainian resort of Yalta, members agreed to focus on developing trade and enhancing anti-terrorist cooperation. They also issued a joint statement with the United States on the need to take steps against international terrorism and weapons of mass destruction as well as to intensify the battle against organized international criminal activity. Leaders of the group agreed to set up a regional law enforcement centre to combat terrorism and organized crime. The US pledged aid to assist in anti-terrorist operations. Three GUUAM-US initiatives were launched at the Yalta meeting. The first will deal with training mobile anti-terrorist units to guard pipelines and combat terrorism. In addition, Washington expressed its willingness to increase the number of Special Forces based in Georgia to assist the training of border forces. The two sides will additionally develop a centre to facilitate information exchanges, designed to counter terrorism, organized crime and drug trafficking. The third project will be the creation of a GUUAM Parliamentary Assembly.

Moscow tends to view the GUUAM as a devise for the projection of US and NATO influence among the CIS states. Russian officials have stated explicitly that "Russia will continue to counter any attempts to bring a military component into GUUAM's activities".[71] While disparate objectives and capabilities have hampered GUUAM activites, it has enabled limited functional multilateral cooperation between some of its members in other fields, such as energy policy and some coordination on defence issues. For Russia it has raised the specter of growing geopolitical pluralism within the CIS.

Non-traditional Threats to Security and Central Asian Initiatives

The role of regional initiatives on a Central Asian level, as primary providers of security, has not been rated very high. It has been observed that such initiatives would be unable to convey hard defence guarantees, create joint military units, negotiate arms reductions or enforce the end of overt conflicts. On the other hand the ability of overseas security structures located far from the territory to provide effective regional security in the region has also met with criticism from regional experts who have noted their lack of efficiency in providing security.[72]

The impact of Central Asian regional initiatives on security however, has been more oblique and subtle. It begins with their existential significance as groups of states that recognize themselves as sharing some elements of community and can define their national identity as complementary rather than adversial to their neighbours. Regular meetings and the creation of personal ties encourage *esprit de corps* and may help to defuse crisis. Non traditional security issues like environment, defence against pollution, water management, drug smuggling, organized crime, migration and refugees provide more useful areas for regional discourse. In addition there have been attempts at economic cooperation with an understanding that economic development is conducive to the security of the region.[73]

In addition, Kazakhstan, Uzbekistan and Kyrgyzstan took a decision to form a Joint Council of Defence Ministers at the Interstate Council meeting in December 1995. The concept of cohesion in defence matters meant joint exercises, mutual supplies, maintenance of arms and equipment or their upgradation and procurement of advanced arms. A blueprint for coordinating defence efforts was also prepared and circulated.[74] Similarly, the recently formed Central Asian Battalion composed of forces from Kazakhstan, Kyrgyzstan and Uzbekistan, for increasing and coordinating local peace keeping endeavours is another example in this direction. There have also been moves to set up regimes for controlling organized crime, drug trafficking, terrorism and illegal migration and supporting environmental protection. There have, for instance, been a series of Central Asian summits on water management and the Aral Sea crisis leading to an agreement by which each state pledged 0.3 per cent of its GNP to an environmental fund supporting the resolution.

In December 2001 another regional association, the Central Asian Cooperation (CAC) was created.[75] It was born after a number of bilateral and multilateral meetings in Tashkent on December 27-28, 2001 between Uzbek President Karimov, Kazakh President Nursultan Nazarbaev, Kyrgyz President Askar Akayev and Tajik President Imomali Rakhmanov. The new organization replaces the Central Asian Economic Commonwealth. President Karimov declared that the CAC would have as its purview issues of military policy, economy, and humanitarian cooperation. The four founding members also agreed to create joint electricity, gas, transportation and irrigation networks.

The Tashkent Declaration, adopted by the participants on the occasion, proclaims an increase in political, economic and humanitarian cooperation, joint fight against international terrorism, drug smuggling and religious and political extremism. In the negotiations, preceding the quadrilateral, agreements were signed on trade, border delineation, security and law enforcement. To boost trade Uzbekistan promised to loosen restrictions and open its borders to Tajik transit trade. Dushanbe is also hoping to receive more oil and gas in exchange for the hydroelectric power that it generates. There were also promises of reduced tariffs on goods imported by Uzbekistan from Tajikistan and talks about cutting the price of Uzbek natural gas flowing into Tajikistan.

It is generally accepted that the purpose for any regional organization is two fold. The acceleration of economic development and the reinforcement of regional stability. Evaluated on these two criteria, it may well be said that regional initiatives in the Central Asian region has, till date, not proved to be very successful. It is undeniable that compared to the more successful of regional efforts, a great deal remains to be achieved. However, before any evaluation of these efforts it is crucial to keep in mind that ten years is insufficient to judge the failure or success of any such regional endeavour. Also in a number of indirect ways both development and stability have been contributed to by the regional processes. Representative of this are the numerous agreements that have been made regarding environmental degradation. This is a case which in the Central Asian region could lead to regional instability and also affect economic development.

Some analysts have argued that the fact that environmental degradation can lead to serious conflict is doubtful and that it is difficult to identify specific links between environmental problems and major threats to security.[76] Skeptics include those who are concerned with more "traditional" issues like territorial disputes and balance of power as threatening to regional security. In the Central Asian region, for instance, problems associated with "nation building" in the background of artificially drawn borders and the existence of numerous ethnic groups, within each of the states, have been identified by analysts as the focus of future flashpoints. What is largely ignored in the course of such analysis is that environmental problems are rapidly reaching a stage where they will threaten regional security. Threats to stability posed by disputes over pollution, food, water and energy resources bring to the forefront questions about the extent to which environmental issues shape the security agenda.

This is particularly so since the ecological crisis in the Central Asian region overlays and aggravates a structural, economic and social crisis. Central Asia is a developing region, characterized by a high share in agricultural production, low industrialization, mass unemployment and a high population growth. With the standard of living considerably below the Soviet average it was mainly dependent on the subsidies from the centre. The disintegration of the Soviet Union meant the beginning of a new process of nation building in the region and the redefinition of political and cultural identities. It also saw the emergence of a new international water basin, the Aral, with all consequent consequences for the political, ethnic and economic relations between the states. The entire political geography changed and once shared natural resources, that were controlled by central directions, became the "national wealth" of the newly independent states. Rivers became national borders and the division into up and down stream riparians became politically relevant.

While it is accepted that environmental issues are unlikely to be the primary cause of conflict, it is also argued that they play a complex role in shaping relations among states. And the success of regional initiatives in the Central Asian region cannot be denied. Speaking to the Carnegie Endowment for International Peace, Dr Kadir Gulomov, Minister of Defence in Uzbekistan noted that security has many aspects. Efforts to promote regional cooperation through the use of water and energy resources is an important way to reduce tensions in the area.[77]

A very significant achievement in terms of ensuring security in the region is the Conference on Interaction and Confidence Building in Asia. The CICA vision for security in Asia elaborates on multilateral approaches towards promoting peace and security and visualizes itself as the forum for dialogue, consultation and adoption of decisions and measures on the basis of consensus on security issues in Asia. The CICA identifies certain elements, as challenges to security and seeks to find ways to eliminate them. In this context it resolves to support efforts for the elimination of weapons of mass destruction, to ensure the establishment of nuclear free zones, to curb excessive accumulation of conventional armaments, condemn terrorism, not to render any assistance to separatist movements in other states, reject the use of religion as a pretext for terrorists and separatists, emphasize the significance of curbing the movement of illicit drugs and corruption. In the context of achieving these objectives the CICA will take necessary steps for the elaboration and implementation of measures aimed at enhancing cooperation and creating an atmosphere of peace, confidence and friendship. All states are encouraged to resolve their disputes peacefully through negotiations in accordance with the principles enshrined in the UN Charter and International law. After 2001, major emphasis in the CICA has been given to broad non-traditional security threats. At the summit meeting held in Kazakhstan in June 2002, there was a call for action against a range of such threats and for the elaboration of confidence building measures. The dialogues in the CICA show that that the central Asian states view themselves as part of macroregions extending to their east and south, a view encouraged by the prevailing discourse on transnational terrorism.

The last decade has witnessed a major change in the nature of security and this has been accompanied by a broader academic debate on the boundaries of security. While the dominance of the military in perceptions of security remains, it is now recognized that there are other problems, like environmental degradation, which may not pose an immediate security threat to the state, but nonetheless are major potential threats that require resolution. Generally these lend themselves to resolution through novel forms of collaboration and cooperation thereby bringing into focus varied initiatives that have evolved to deal with them.

Security, whether narrowly or broadly defined, may be guaranteed both by regional institutions and by issue, specific global ones. It needs to be emphasized that the two systems need not exist in isolation. President Karimov, had emphasized this in his address to the 48th Session of the UN General Assembly where he had clearly noted that regional security can be viewed solely in concert with global security.[78] The relation between the two only appears problematic when their roles are projected as contradictory. However, with the recognition that poverty, marginalization and lack of development are security concerns that are as significant as the threat from the proliferation of arms, the complimentary nature of the roles of these various initiatives assume significance.

NOTES AND REFERENCES

1. See for instance Gail Lapidus "Central Asia in Russian and American Foreign Policy After September 11, 2001", Presentation

from *Central Asia and Russia: Responses to the War on Terrorism,* a panel discussion held at the University of California, Berkeley on October 29, 2001 and Svante E.Cornell, "Introduction," *Nordic Newsletter of Asian Studies, No 3,* 2002.

2. See for instance, A Menteshashvili, "Security and Foreign Policy in the Central Asian and the Caucasian Republics," www.nato.int/acad/fellow97-99/menteshashvili.pdf, where she notes, "In geopolitical aspect Washington considers Uzbekistan as a serious counterweight to Russian influence in Central Asia."

3. Muthiah Alagappa, *Asian Security Practice: Material and Ideational Influences*, Stanford: Stanford University Press, 1998, p 4.

4. See for instance Anatol Lieven, "The End of NATO", *Prospect*, December 2001, cited from Anar Khamzayeva, "Novaya Strategiya NATO? Ee Posledstviya Dliya Tsentralnoi Azii", *Kazakstan i Sovremennie Mir*, No 1 (2) 2002.

5. Stephen Blank, "The Shanghai Cooperative Organization: A Post Mortem," *Nordic Newsletter of Asian Studies*, No 3, 2002.

6. For writings that stress on the inevitability of change in geopolitical alignments around Central Asia and the image of the region as "liberated" from the Russo-Chinese condominium institutionalized in the SCO, see Cornell," Introduction".

7. Robert Cutler, "Redrawing the Architecture of Central Asian Security," *Central Asia Caucasus Analyst*, February 27, 2002.

8. Dewardric L. McNeal, "China's Relation with Central Asian States and Problems with Terrorism," *CRS Report for Congress*, December 17, 2001.

9. For details of this argument see Yu Xintian, "September 11 Incidents and Change in Security Concept," *Shanghai Institute for International Studies*, Vol 9, No 2, May 2002.

10. Bruno Coppieters "Conclusions: The Failure of Regionalism in Eurasia and the Western Ascendancy over Russia's Near Abroad", in Bruno Coppieters, Alexei Zverev and Dmitri Trenin (eds) *Commonwealth and Independence in Post Soviet Russia*, London and Portland: Frank Cass, 1998.

11. See for instance Paul Kubicek, "Regionalism, Nationalism and Realpolitik in Central Asia", *Europe-Asia Studies*, Vol 49, No 4, 1997.

12. For a detailed analysis of the nature of Central Asian regional security initiatives see Anita Sengupta, *Region, Regionalization, Regionalism: The "Myth" of Tsentralnaya Aziia Revisited*, unpublished paper presented at a seminar on "Central Asia: Ten Years of Independence", organized by the Maulana Abul Kalam Azad Institute of Asian Studies and the Central Asian Studies Division, Jawaharlal Nehru University, at the IIC, New Delhi, on 21-22 November 2001.

13. Gregory Gleason "Inter-State Cooperation in Central Asia from the CIS to the Shanghai Forum", *Europe-Asia Studies*, Vol 53, No 7, 2001.

14. *Nezavisimasti*, 6 July, 1994, cited in Guangcheng Xing, "Security issues in China's Relations with Central Asian States", in Yongjin Zhang and Rouben Azizian, *Ethnic Challenges beyond Borders: Chinese and Russian Perspectives of the Central Asian Conundrum*, Oxford: Macmillian in association with St Antony's College Oxford,

15. Leonid Bondarez, "Formirovaniye Systemi Collectivnoi Bezopasnosti v Tsentralnoi Azii — osobennosti, itogi, perspectivi", *Kazakhstan i Sovremennie Mir*, No 2(5), 2003.

16. Bondarez,"Formirovaniye Systemi Collectivnoi Bezopasnosti v Tsentralnoi Azii — osobennosti, itogi, perspectivi".

17. Bondarez,"Formirovaniye Systemi Collectivnoi Bezopasnosti v Tsentralnoi Azii — osobennosti, itogi, perspectivi".

18. Bondarez, "Formirovaniye Systemi Collectivnoi Bezopasnosti v Tsentralnoi Azii — osobennosti, itogi, perspectivi".

19. Bondarez, "Formirovaniye Systemi Collectivnoi Bezopasnosti v Tsentralnoi Azii — osobennosti, itogi, perspectivi".

20. Bruno Coppieters "Conclusions.

21. For details see Anita Sengupta "What is Central Asia to Russia? The Heartland Debates and Russia's Central Asian Policy", in

Professor Shams-Ud-Din (ed) *India and Russia Towards Strategic Partnership*, New Delhi: Lancers, 2001

22. Michael R. Lucas, "Russia and Peacekeeping in the former USSR" *Aussenpolitik*, Vol 46, No 2, 1995, cited in Amalendu Misra, "Shanghai Five and the Emerging Alliance in Central Asia: The Closed Society and its Enemies", *Central Asian Survey*, Vol 20, No 3, 2001.
23. Sophie Lambroschini "Central Asia: CIS Force Not Best Way to Combat Islamic Threat Say Analysts," *Radio Free Europe-Radio Liberty*, May 23, 2001.
24. Kambiz Arman, "US Geopilitical Position Takes Hit in Tajikistan", *Eurasia Insight*, July 21, 2004.
25. Cited from Arman, "US Geopilitical Position Takes Hit in Tajikistan".
26. Dmitri Trenin,"Introduction" in Coppieters, Zverev and Trenin (eds) *Commonwealth and Independence in Post Soviet Russia.*
27. Cited from Lambroschini, "Central Asia: CIS Force Not best way to Combat Islamic Threat".
28. Cited from Igor Torbakov, "Russia Moves to Reassert Influence In Central Asia, Caucasus," *Eurasia Insight*, December 18, 2002.
29. Torbakov, "Russia Moves to Reassert Influence in Central Asia, Caucasus."
30. Roy Allison, "Regionalism, regional structures and security management in Central Asia", *International Affairs*, Vol 80, No 3, May 2004.
31. For details see S. Adnan Ali Shah, "Collective Security Treaty Organization (OKDB): Prospects and Challenges", in P. Mykhtarova (ed) *Problemi Regionalnoi Vezopasnosti, Politicheskogo i Ekonomichiskogo Razvitiya Tsentralnaaziatskogo Regiona v Kontekske Interesov Kazakhstana*, Almaty: TOO, 2003.
32. Allison, "Regionalism, regional structures and security management in Central Asia".
33. Bondarez, "Formirovaniye Systemi Collectivnoi Bezopasnosti v Tsentralnoi Azii — osobennosti, itogi, perspectivi".

34. Allison, "Regionalism, regional structures and security management in Central Asia".

35. Allison, "Regionalism, regional structures and security management in Central Asia".

36. In this context it is important to keep in mind that in the post 9/11 scenario, there had been marked improvement in Russia-NATO relations. At various forums the idea of "NATO at 20" was floated indicating the 19 regular NATO members plus Russia. It was stressed that Russia would not become a full-fledged member of the group and would not have veto rights, but there would be greater consultation, coordination and cooperation between the two. The most important development in this regard was the formal establishment of the NATO-Russia Council in Rome in May 2002.

37. Cited from Sergei Blagov, "In Central Asia, Russia Pushes Back Against NATO Influence", *Eurasia Insight*, July 21, 2004.

38. Cited from Blagov, "In Central Asia, Russia Pushes Back Against NATO Influence".

39. Cited from Igor Torbakov, "Wanted: A New CIS Policy For Russia", *Eurasianet*, September 30, 2004.

40. Pan Guang, "China-Central Asia-Russia Relations and the Role of the SCO in the War Against Terrorism," *SIIA Journal*, Vol 9, No 2, May 2002.

41. Guang, "China-Central Asia Russia Relations."

42. Misra, "Shanghai Five and the Emerging Alliance in Central Asia: The Closed Society and its Enemies."

43. *Beijing Review*, 13-19 May, pp 6-8, cited in Misra, "Shanghai Five: The Emerging Alliance".

44. *Xinhua News Agency*, 26 April, 1996.

45. For details see Cutler, "Redrawing the Architecture of Central Asian Security."

46. The debate over Uzbekistan's entry into the Shanghai Five has been detailed in Akihiro Iwashita, "The Shanghai Cooperation Organization and Its Implications for Eurasian Security: A new

Dimension of "Partnership" After the Post Cold War Period", in S Tabata and A. Iwashita (eds) *Slavic Eurasia's Integration into the World Economy and Community*, (forthcoming) Sapporo: Slavic Research Centre, 2004.

47. Sun Zhuangzhi, "Economic Collaboration in Central Asian region and the SCO", in K. Santhanam and Ramakant Dwivedi (eds) *India and Central Asia: Advancing the Common Interest*, New Delhi: Anamaya Publishers, 2004

48. Zhuangzhi, "Economic Collaboration in Central Asian region and the SCO".

49. Matthew Oresman,"The Moscow Summit: Tempered Hope for the SCO", *Central Asia-Caucasus Analyst*, Wednesday, June 4, 2003.

50. "Third SCO Summit Meeting Held in Moscow", *Ministry of Foreign Affairs of the Peoples' Republic of China*, 2000, www.fmprc.gov.cn.

51. Roger N. McDermott," Shanghai Cooperation Organization Takes Significant Steps Towards Viability", *Eurasia Insight*, September 9, 2003.

52. Allison, "Regionalism, regional structures and security management in Central Asia".

53. Similar views were expressed by Andrei Valentinivich Grozin, Director of the Department of Central Asia and Kazakhstan, in the course of a conversation with the author at the *Institut Diasporii i Integratsii* (*Institut Stan SNG*) Moscow, on November 27, 2003. He noted that Russia and the Central Asian states would welcome India into the SCO as a counterweight to China and that there was apprehension that the growth of Chinese influence within the SCO would affect the organization negatively.

54. For details see Iwashita, "The Shanghai Cooperation Organization and Its Implications for Eurasian Security".

55. It has been suggested that Uzbekistan's resistance stopped all actions by the SCO against US actions in Iraq. For details see Iwashita, "The Shanghai Cooperation Organization and Its Implications for Eurasian Security".

56. Bondarez, "Formirovaniye Systemi Collectivnoi Bezopasnosti v Tsentralnoi Azii — osobennosti, itogi, perspectivi".

    However, there remains opinion to the contrary. In the course of a conversation with the author, on November 26, 2003 at the *Institut Vostokovedennia* in Moscow, Professor Shaken Nadirov, an ethnic Kazakh associated with the *Institut Vostokovedeniia*, pointed out that the SCO was a Chinese creation, aimed at dealing with separatism in Xinjiang. As such it has nothing to do with the Kazakh people.

57. Assylbek Tauasarov, "SHOS Priobretaet Realnie Ochertaniya", *Kazakhstan i Sovremennie Mir*, No 2(5), 2003.

58. Gail Lapidus "Central Asia in Russian and American Foreign Policy After September 11, 2001", Presentation from *Central Asia and Russia: Responses to the War on Terrorism,* a panel discussion held at the University of California, Berkeley on October 29, 2001.

59. Khamzayeva, "Novaya Strategiya NATO? Ee Posledstviya Dliya Tsentralnoi Azii".

60. For details see *Press Communique M-1(94)2*, Issued by the Heads of the States and Governments participating in the Meeting of the North Atlantic Council, NATO Headquarters, Brussels, 10-11 June 1994.

61. For details see "Partnership and Cooperation", *NATO Fact Sheets* available online.

62. The matters included within the ambit of the Partnership (for details see *Partnership Work Programme* for 2000-2001, NATO Partnership for Peace Documents) include:
    1. Air Defence Related Matters
    2. Airspace Management/Control
    3. Consultation, Command and Control, including Communications and Information Systems, Navigation and Identification systems, Inter-operatability Aspects, Procedures and Terminology.
    4. Civil Emergency Planning
    5. Crisis management
    6. Democratic Control of Defence Forces and Defence

Structures
7. Defence Planning, Budgeting and Resource management
8. Planning, Organization and Management of national Defence Procurement Programmes and International Cooperation in Armaments Field
9. Defence Policy and Strategy
10. Planning Organization and Management of National defence Research and Technology
11. Military Geography
12. Language Training
13. Consumer Logistics
14. Medical Services
15. Meteorological Support for NATO/Partner Forces
16. Military Infrastructure
17. Political and Defence Efforts
18. Conceptual, Planning and Operational Aspects of Peacekeeping
19. Operational, Material and Administrative Aspects of Peacekeeping
19. Operational, Material and Administrative Aspects of Standardization
20. Military Exercises and related Training Activities
21. Military Education, Training and Doctrine

63. Mevlut Katik, "NATO Embraces Central Asia and the Caucasus st the Istanbul Summit", *Eurasia Insight*, July 21, 2004.

64. Katik, "NATO Embraces Central Asia and the Caucasus".

65. Khamzayeva, "Novaya Strategiya NATO? Ee Posledstviya Dliya Tsentralnoi Azii".

66. Osman Yavuzalp, "On the Front Line", *NATO Review*, Vol 49, No 4, Winter 2001.

67. Bakhtiyor Irishmatov, "Role of NATO in Post-Soviet Territory and its Role in Combating Terrorism", in K. Santhanam and Ramakant Divedi (eds) *India and Central Asia: Advancing the Common Interest*, New Delhi:Anamaya Publishers, 2004.

68. Allison, "Regionalism; regional structures and security management in Central Asia".

69. Allison, "Regionalism, regional structures and security management in Central Asia".

70. Taras Kuzio and Sergei Blagov, "GUUAM Makes a Comeback Bid US Support", *Eurasia Insight*, July 7, 2003.

71. Russian First Deputy Foreign Minister V Trubnikov, "Tenth anniversary of the Commonwealth of Independent States", *International Affairs* (Moscow) 2002, cited from Allison, "Regionalism, regional structures and security management in Central Asia".

72. See for instance Mashan Meiirzhan, a member of the Institute for Development of Kazakhstan, "Regional Security as a System Factor in Central Asian Integration," in Jasjit Singh (ed) *Peace and Security in Central Asia*, New Delhi:IDSA, September 2000.

73. Meiirzhan, elaborates on the role of the Central Asian Economic Union in this regard in his article," Regional Security as a System Factor in Central Asian Integration."

74. *Kazakhstanskaya Pravda*, December 16, 1995, cited in Tabassum Firdous, *Central Asia Security and Strategic Imperatives*, Delhi: Kalpaz Publications, 2002.

75. Ariel Cohen, "Central Asians Launch Another Regional Association", *Central Asia-Caucasus Analyst*, January 16, 2002.

76. Daniel Deudney," The Case Against Linking Environmental Degradation and National Security", *Millennium: Journal of International Studies*, Vol 19, No 1, 1990.

77. Cited from *Carnegie Endowment for International Peace, Meeting Report*, Vol 2, No 8, November 3, 2000, www.ceip.org/files/events/gulomov.asp?EventID==218

78. Islam A Karimov, *Address by H.E. Islom Karimov President of the Republic of Uzbekistan at the 48th Session of the United Nations*, Tashkent:Uzbekiston, 1993.

Epilogue

The debate on multilateralism, defined in the broadest sense, as international cooperation among more than two states in the international arena, has reemerged in the light of a pervading unilateralist impulse, emanating from the Bush administration in recent years.[1] While a debate on the reform of the United Nations had been an ongoing process, prior to recent US actions, multilateral approach towards regional issues, particularly security issues, with emphasis on confidence building, preventive diplomacy and conflict resolution, was being increasingly accepted as significant to the maintenance of regional security and promotion of regional development. Multilateral confidence building measures reflected the belief that through regularized dialogue and consultation existing and potential conflicts could be effectively managed without the necessity of recourse to coercion. It was pointed out that multilateralism is distinctive, not merely because it coordinates national policies in groups of three or more states, which is something that other organizational forms also do, but additionally because it does so on the basis of certain principles of ordering relations among states.[2]

Questions about the viability of multilateralism was revived in the background of US actions in Iraq, that bypassed the United Nations as the principle global multilateral forum. Collective security as a distinct multilateral approach towards global security was the centrepiece of the United Nations Charter. The lack of institutionalized sanction against states, that deliberately defied the principle, however, proved to be its major impediment. However, the United Nations was not the only multilateral forum under review. An emphasis on bilateral arrangements with the

US also brought into question the viability of regional multilateral forums, particularly in the immediate neighbourhood of Afghanistan. The debate that followed the US actions, however, was less about strategic choices but more a matter of disagreement about the very meaning and purpose of multilateralism.[3] The debate has since moved in numerous directions.[4] While most of it has been a critique of a process, that is still largely defined by states according to convenience, a significant part of the debate also focuses on it as an ideal to be aspired for in a global system that is now being identified as unipolar.[5]

As against this unipolar and unilateralist tendency, multilateral options are being advocated by a significant part of the global community.[6] In recent times, Russia and China have advocated global multilateralism and have emphasized the necessity of strengthening the role of the United Nations.[7] They have also sought multilateral solutions to conflicts in their immediate neighbourhood. They share similar views with regard to opposing unilateralist actions by a US led NATO extending beyond Europe into Central and South Asia. The extent to which such common concerns can lead to the development of multilateral co-operation in particular regions remains to be seen, particularly in the light of fact that multilateralism is often variously defined by them and commitment to multilateral options have varied particularly in cases which are identified as significant in terms of national interest. For instance, analysts have noted that while China's thinking on multilateralism and regional security cooperation has evolved over the last decade, it is yet to demonstrate that it accepts the principles of multilateralism unequivocally. It is pointed out that China follows *conditional multilateralism*, which is characterized, by a low degree of institutionalization of the multilateral forum.[8]

However, there are certain areas where there is broad agreement on the requirement of multilateral action. For instance, there have been attempts to explore multilateral options in terms of security and confidence building in the Central Asian region by Russia and China. The Central Asian states are part of the Commonwealth of Independent States (CIS) and as such most of them are signatories to the Collective Security Treaty (CST). In addition they are also part of the Shanghai Cooperation Organization (SCO), which includes Russia and China. Russia and China, along with a number of other Asian states, are part of the Conference on Confidence Building and Interaction in Asia (CICA), a Central Asian initiative at confidence building in the region.

The most common comment about regional security arrangements, in the post 9/11 scenario was, that, given the US presence in the region, multilateral processes initiated by Russia and China would take a back seat. A significant part of strategic writing, emanating from western scholarship, brought into question their role in the post 9/11 scenario, and assumed that Sino-Russian arrangements for multilateral regional security would no longer play any significant role in the efforts to deal with terrorism in the region.[9] In fact, it was suggested that regional multilateral forums would no longer be significant and once again most security agreements would be bilateral. It was also argued that to the limited extent that multilateral options would be considered as viable, transregional institutions would tend to be favoured at the expense of regional collectivities.[10]

In the light of such statements a number of issues assume significance. The first and foremost is the question of the viability of multilateralism in the region and the extent to which the states themselves are willing to be part of multilateral process. A second issue is the attitude of Russia and China towards multilateralism in general and about the status of their role in multilateral processes in the Central Asian region. A third is a debate on the role that India, as part of Russia-China-India axis, can play in the multilateral process in Central Asia.

Most writings on transformations in strategic structures in the Central Asian region stressed on the undermining of multilateral security structures. The transition back to the bilateral, in terms of security arrangements, was in fact predicted as the most significant aspect of the transition. The emphasis on the eclipse of multilateralism, was based on the facts that there are significant cleavages within the region, that the experience of the CIS has been less than successful, that current regimes lay more emphasis on regime security rather than regional security and that given the facts the emphasis was on building states and nations, efforts would be towards building national security structures rather than regional security structures.

Moving away from arguments that identify the post September 11 scenario as a major watershed, this study has been an attempt at arguing that viable regional security structures had maintained global linkages throughout the last decade. Post September 11 events merely highlighted arrangements that had already been in place. It has also been argued that the recognition of a multiplicity of security arrangements dealing with multiple security issues, as the norm rather than agreements under one global system, is a necessity in the region. While older security arrangements remain in place, newer ones are being forged to deal with emerging security issues. This is not just a reflection of the presence of Russia, China and the United States as parts of various security structures that exist in the region but also a professed policy, that the states themselves follow. This becomes crucial in any understanding of transitions that the Central Asian security structure has undergone, in the recent past, and in examining questions that the "war against terror" has thrown up in the region.

Speaking at a Conference in Tashkent Farhod Fozilovich Tolipov, Assistant Professor at the University of World Economy and Diplomacy, Tashkent, raises a number of new political and legal questions that the "war against terror" seems to have thrown up, particularly for states, like Uzbekistan, whose territories are being utilized for the conduct of the war. He emphasizes:

> The states involved in anti-terrorist campaigns of the future will always be faced with an option connected with a particular perception of the possible consequences of these campaigns for these states themselves in a much wider framework than the fight against terrorism itself.[11]

There is thus, the necessity of a correlation of the national interests of the state, stable long term world order and the war against terror. This, he notes, will be difficult to achieve in the light of ontological problems regarding the definition of terror. Similarly, he raises the issue of "military intervention beyond national borders in the fight against terrorism" and the requirement of legitimation of this intervention. He raises several questions in this connection. First, can all states, threatened by terrorism, work according to this formula, or is it valid for only some states? Secondly, how will military intervention beyond national borders be legitimated? Third, how and who will decide that in each case it is actually the fight against terrorism, since it has no universally accepted definition?[12]

Tolipov argues that Central Asia should be considered as an independent "security system".[13] As such participation of the Central Asian states in a single anti-terrorist coalition should be supplemented by their independent cooperation in this sphere. He then raises a more significant question of whether the Central Asian states benefit if their recent exclusive dependence on Russia is replaced by inclusive "pluralistic dependence on several centres of power". And also which formula of regional security would be acceptable, not only to external powers but also to the Central Asian states themselves.

In the light of these perceptions it is not surprising that what seems to be emerging in the region is a somewhat different scenario. Rather than bilateralism or multilateralism, the Central Asian states opted for what was termed as a *multivector* policy where choices were kept open for both bilateral and multilateral agreements on particular issues according to specific security perceptions of individual states. Options for bilateral agreements were kept open with all the major powers, Russia, China and the United States.

There are interesting examples of the Central Asian states participating in different interstate organizations and in plans involving states outside the region, simultaneously. For example, with the exception of Turkmenistan, the Central Asian states are participants of both the SCO and various NATO programmes. Kyrgyzstan joined the World Trade Organization in 1998, although this contradicted with the principles and interests of the customs union of various post Soviet states and of the Eurasian Economic Community, headed by Russia, which was set up on the basis of the customs union and in October 2000 and of which Kyrgyzstan is also a member. Kazakstan has been involved both with the Tengiz-Novorossiisk and the Baku-Ceyhan oil pipeline projects, the main lobbyists for which are respectively, the Russian Federation and the USA. Talgat Ismagambetov, notes that this allows the Central Asian states to maneuver between the interests of the three world powers and where possible to extract for themselves certain short term advantages without solving any problems related to the entire area of their national security.[14] On the other hand, since 9/11 attempts by regional powers to reinforce multilateralism has been seen to be on the increase.

While the significance of the international coalition in dealing with issues of regional security was the dominant focus of literature on the region, in the year following the events of September 11, certain other changes also became evident. Increasingly there was a movement by the Central Asian states to accommodate both the US and Russia within their security arrangement. This meant that while bilateral arrangements with the US remained in place there was no attempt to move away from multilateral arrangements within the CIS or the SCO either, at least as far as some of the states were concerned. Agreements with multiple states and participation in multiple organizations are the common norm in the region today. Strategic writings from Kazakhstan, for instance, clearly indicate that this is the preferred *multivector* policy that the state pursues. Concluding the study on the post September 11 scenario in Central Asia it is pointed out:

> The multivector approach of foreign policy of RK has once again confirmed its expediency in complex conditions of international anti-terrorist campaign. It is necessary to pay attention to the following aspect of the foreign policy of RK in this period: inspite of the fact that Kazakhstan promoted active cooperation on the bilateral level, the importance of the regional factor and multilateral level of cooperation has greatly increased in our policy, for the last year.[15]

Such statements call for a reevaluation of the significance of multilateral regional forums, particularly in the light of statements that predicted their demise, in dealing with problems of regional security. They also call for a more detailed analysis of evolving multilateral processes in the region like the Shanghai process.

In 1996, Russia announced the establishment of a strategic cooperation partnership with China. The rationale for evolving such a mechanism of cooperation was based on a number of factors. First, both sides recognized the dividends of a strategic partnership and Beijing has been consistent in nurturing it with good results. The Moscow-Beijing bipartisan consensus was in favour of evolving a multilateral strategy to combat threats to regional security. This was the outcome of a strong and increasingly stable bilateral entente between the two states.[16] Second, as part of a growing convergence of interests, Moscow and Beijing have pledged not to interfere in each other's domestic affairs. China has defended Russia's use of military force in the Caucasus and Moscow now defends Beijing's policy towards Taiwan, Tibet and Xinjiang. To craft issues of national interest around regional security appears to be the Sino-Russian agenda. Third, and most important, the two share a resentment against a unipolar system dominated by the United States. Anxiety about the expansion of US military and economic intervention in Central Asia and the inevitable clash of interests has helped in forging a Sino-Russian entente in the Central Asian region through the creation of the Shanghai mechanism.

This alliance, projected as "constructive strategic partnership" was essentially a counterweight to the American power and aimed at restoring multipolarity to the international system.[17] The Shanghai Forum has been identified as a new type of constructive diplomacy, which would provide Russia and China with a forum to keep in check their nascent rivalry in the region and to coordinate positions on major regional and international issues. Prior to the terrorist attacks on the US, China had become vociferous in its opposition to NATO expansion and Moscow had toughened her attitude to the US military presence on her southern borders and the US-Japan military alliance. During Russian Defence Minister Igor Sergeev's visit to China in October 1998, Moscow and Beijing stressed their common approach to three international issues: they categorically objected to NATO expansion in the east, denounced the use of force in Kosovo and disapproved of the US-Japan plans of establishing an anti-missile defence system.

It was under these circumstances that in 1997, Russia and China issued a statement on multi-polarization of the world that reflected their concern about the current international situation.

In this context, this description of the Chinese concept of multipolarization by the Ministry of Foreign Affairs, China is important:

> Currently, while complex and deep changes are taking place in the international situation, the trend towards world multipolarization has not changed. There are nearly 200 countries with a population of more than 6 billion in the world. A myriad of differences exists between these countries in ethnic traditions, religions and cultures, economic levels

> and political systems. It is hardly possible to image how to unify them with one model and one value or to "lead" them by one country. The basic norms governing international relations on equality of sovereignty and non interference in each other's international affairs between the member states as stipulated in the Charter of the United Nations are absolutely not outdated. The history and culture, social systems and development models of various countries should be respected. The multipolarization process may be zigzag, protracted and full of struggles, but this is a historical trend independent of human will. It is in conformity with the common aspirations and interests of the majority of countries and conducive to world peace and security.
>
> Our efforts to promote the development of the world towards multipolarization are not targeted at any particular country nor are they aimed at re-staging the old play of contention for hegemony in history. Rather, these efforts are made to boost the democratization of international relations which help the various forces in the world, on the basis of equality and mutual benefit, enhance coordination and dialogue, refrain from confrontation and preserve peace, stability and development jointly.[18]

This constructive strategic partnership had various facets. It not only addressed the issue of multipolarization and democratization of international relations but also reflected the need for a reform of the global order. However, the search for a greater political space within this emerging order was also of equal significance. Andrei Nikolaev, Chairman of the Russian State Duma Defence Committee, elaborates on this when he writes:

> The existing structures designed to regulate international relations within the framework of international law cannot deal with the rapidly growing new international security problems. This explanation justifies discussions of the crisis

of the United nations, its Security Council and other organizations including the NATO.

> ...we are witnessing the aggravation of competition in the struggle for a new redivision of the world and establishment of a new international order. Unlike in the past, when the world was redivided as a result of world wars and socio political revolutions, today the redivision of the world is proceeding at the will of one superpower and its closest allies. This has cast a new light on the issue of military might,as the guarantor of security of one state or a group of states. Such attempts to redivide the world, whatever reasons may be used to justify them, mean that the military organization, the current state and development prospects and the existence of weapons for deterring aggression are becoming the top priority for many states.[19]

The question that begs an answer is whether there can be a common strategic framework within which these issues may be addressed; given the fact that interests and perspectives of divergent states need to be taken into account. The Asian region is now poised for long term economic success. The extent to which this success is realized hinges on stability and a relatively calm security environment. Here, the most significant issue that remains unresolved is that of the shape of the future power balance. Responding to the new security environment is the new requirement and whether multilateral processes supported by Russia and China succeed, remains to be seen.

The process of the formation of the SCO was deeply connected with the creation of the "strategic partnership" between Russia and China. The signing of the Shanghai Agreement in 1996 came just after a declaration of Sino-Russian "strategic partnership" in Moscow. In the Russian foreign policy context the idea of a "partnership" had first been used vis a vis NATO as the "partnership for peace" in 1994. This phrase, proposed by the Clinton administration, was meant to denote a "peaceful buffer" between Russia and the NATO.[20] As Russian foreign policy shifted in the mid 1990's President Yeltsin first talked about a "constructive partnership" and then a "strategic partnership" with Zhang Zemin, in 1996. The two parties declared their partnership as non-union and non-bloc.[21]

The SCO, whose core is based on Russo-Chinese partnership, turned into a multilateral partnership coping with a new threat in the SCO border areas. In 1996 Russian diplomacy had appealed for this "strategic partnership" as a model, which in the 21st century could overcome the historic antagonism between countries with a long, shared border and suggested its desire for the enlargement of the partnership between China and India which share a long border.[22] China, however was more cautious about the use of the term "partnership" and expansion of Shanghai organization.

Chinese strategic writings identified the constructive strategic partnership between China, Russia and the Central Asian Republics as a stabilizing multilateral institution that will help define stability and cooperation in the region.[23] The effectiveness of the SCO in dealing with a number of issues and particularly border problems has also been noted as significant in recent Central Asian strategic writings.[24] In common with their Chinese counterparts these also point out that the continuing significance of the mechanism would depend on the relationship between Russia and China, as the two main axis of the organization. While there has been cooperation within the SCO, the Chinese policy of developing the western regions and Russian policy of strengthening the collective security mechanism, underscores the fact that there are continuing attempts at consolidating their respective positions within the region. There is also a clear recognition that today this is dependent on a number of factors, the most significant of which is the development of Russo-American and Sino-American relations.

It is undeniable that today the Central Asian region forms a significant part of the interaction between Russia, China and the United States. This became more particularly so in the aftermath of September 11 with the recognition of the significance of the region in any "war against terror". As American presence increased and the US was offered basing rights by the Central Asian states, an entirely new set of geopolitical relations was seen to be emerging where traditional areas of interest were projected to have been transformed. Along with this was the realization that the United States has developed important stakes in the region and its periphery, which would demand, continued American presence. The region is now a significant part of the strategic concerns, that lies at the core of the US's interests.[25] Among them are the search for energy resources that can help reduce American dependence on West Asia, the campaign to fight terrorism and extremism globally, the importance of creating markets for goods and services globally and the need to prevent the dominance of potential rivals, China and Russia, in a region of strategic significance to the US.

Yet, it is equally significant that the US perception of the region has moved beyond that of the region as an arena for a new great game. Strobe Talbot, Former American Deputy Secretary of State, reflected this sentiment when he pointed out "...we want all responsible players in the Caucasus and Central Asia to be winners".[26] The US focus is therefore to construct cooperative instruments in the region. In order to do so it will seek to secure Russian support and Chinese acquiescence. There is clear recognition that this is a pragmatic necessity. A confrontationist US policy will require material and manpower commitment that the US will find difficult to commit in the region. There is also recognition within Russia and China that the US presence is a reality, which cannot be ignored.

It is this realization that has led to the search for new partnerships. In fact, in the wake of the "war against terror" a number of non-traditional partnerships emerged. America and Russia became new partners in the fight against terrorism. While

India has not been not at the forefront of the military campaign in Afghanistan, there is recognition of the convergence of interests on the issue of terrorism in the South-Central Asian region and this has led, as some analysts point out to the "rebirth" of military cooperation and discussions on a "new strategic framework" between the United States and India.[27]

One such proposed alliance is a triangular strategic partnership between Russia-China and India. This proposed partnership has not just been aimed against the eastward expansion of Western alliances but also as a means of counterbalancing the influence of neighbouring countries in the region. Whether this relationship will emerge as significant still remains to be seen. The idea of a strategic triangle has been present in a general way in much of Russian policy thinking for a number of years.[28] In fact, the Declaration on the Further Development and Intensification of Cooperation between the Republic of India and the Russian Federation issued on June 30, 1994 clearly stated: "Both the sides reiterate their deep interests in promoting peace and stability in the areas between the border of the Republic of India and the Russian Federation".[29] Central Asia and Afghanistan had therefore figured as areas of common concern to Russia and India.

However, this axis has received little attention from the Chinese side. Commenting on this triangular alliance, a Chinese scholar from the China Centre for Contemporary Affairs, Beijing, notes that the many unresolved issues in Sino-Indian relationship would act as impediment to this. In fact he goes on to point out that the prospects of Sino-Russian and Russo-Indian relationship is much better than a Sino-Indian one.[30] In addition he points out that India, Russia and China all attach importance to their relationship with the United States. In fact, even President Putin, while on visits to Beijing and New Delhi, in December 2002, stressed that while he backed the idea of a triangular alliance, at the same time maintaining relations with Washington remained significant.[31] A trilateral relationship based only on feelings of anti American unilateralism would therefore not be in accordance with the national interest of any of the states. Zhao Yuyun also goes on to point out that while Russia attaches significance to this triangular relationship both India and China seem to be more cautious. What is of significance is to "promote world multilateralism, prevent unilateralism, improve bilateral relations among the three and strengthen international co-operation of anti terrorism".[32] It has also been argued that the axis is implausible since India and China are competing economies.[33] In fact, it has been argued that the very application of the term *axis* or *triangular axis* may have been relevant in the context of the Cold War, but in the present situation it may be more useful to talk of coalitions, and that too for specific purposes.[34] Russian analysts saw in China's refusal in forming an axis or bloc a pragmatic recognition that this could adversely affect Western investments in China.[35]

Despite this there are certain indications of a renewed interest in the axis. For instance, there is a growing arms sale relationship between Russia and China and Russia and India. Russia and China have discussed the possibility of developing a joint missile defence system and have cooperated with each other on international and regional matters. Russia and India also recently held their first joint naval exercises. Similarly, economic and trade cooperation between Russia and China has made headway.[36] There are a number of other converging interests that could add substance to the axis talks. All three protested against the Iraq war and what they viewed as a rejection of the rules of the international game. In fact, in the present context the possibility of a formal or informal strategic unity between the three appears most likely. They still back the primacy of the United Nations Security Council, in solving crisis and support the principle of non-intervention in the internal affairs of the state.

Apart from shared concerns of US domination the three have other common interests and mutually reinforcing needs. All three are wary of militant groups and want stability in central Eurasia.

For Russia, Central Asia is a critical southern perimeter and home to a large ethnic Russian population. For China, Central Asia is a region bordering the critical Xinjiang Autonomous areas. For India, developments in the Central Asian region are critical for her own security. There have also been attempts to address bilateral issues that have bedeviled relations between the countries. While Russia and China have fixed their borders, there have been attempts at solving border disputes between India and China through confidence building measures.[37] However, while there is motivation to cooperate on strategic, security and economic issues the idea of the axis is still to evolve into clear cut strategy. Han Hua, a South Asian expert at the Beijing University clearly points to this when he notes that the triangle is an idea so far still in the second track, it has not been translated into anything formal.[38]

In India a "track two diplomacy" has focused on arranging meetings between representatives of the three states.[39] A general literature has also begun to evolve on the subject though it has been noted that this deals with general issues, setting out to measure the potential for cooperation though avoiding focus on any one area of possible triangular relationship. Studies have noted:

> Neither trilateral trading links nor the significance of overlap of the military production establishment or even charting out feasible paths of cooperation has been explored to any extent. Nor has there been a careful study of crucial times when positions coincide/diverge as in the case of the run up to the Iraq crisis of 2003. Either leading actors treat the notion as far fetched, merely a gambit to be played upon to contain the expansion of US authority. Or it is acknowledged that there are still relationships in the making.[40]

However, it has been noted that changed global politics, and particularly the recent upgradation of the status of Pakistan to a non NATO ally by the US, should facilitate closer linkages between China and India and further strategic cooperation within the triangular framework.[41] Another area of confluence of interests relates to ballistic missile defence where any US attempt to deploy theater missile defence in Pakistan would affect both Chinese interests and India. However, it is also pointed out that the extent to which this happens would depend on how far China redefines it military relationship with Pakistan. Also the Sino-Indian boundary issue will continue to bedevil the triangular cooperation.[42] It has also been argued that the possibility of the emergence of this strategic triangle remains low given the present structure of international politics where the US has more comprehensive ties with Russia, China and India than any two of them have between themselves.[43]

The emergence of a formal strategic India-Russia-China triangle thus does not appear to be on the agenda in the immediate future, given the numerous other issues that would first have to be resolved on the bilateral level. There is recognition of this within Moscow as well and as a result attempts at improvement of Sino-Indian relations have been positively reported in the Moscow Press.[44] The inclusion of India within multilateral forums, like the SCO remains, to be seen though the advantages of her inclusion are clear in certain circles within Russian strategic thinking.[45] While China does not seem keen on the idea, some analysts even within China have stressed the necessity of inclusion of both India and Pakistan within the forum.[46] Moreover, India and Central Asia do share common concerns and India is a part of CICA, a confidence building measure in Asia that has been initiated by the Kazakh President Nursultan Nazarbayev.

While a India-Russia-China axis is yet to emerge, there is realization that a common multilateral approach is the only viable option in terms of looking towards solutions in a number of areas. For instance, all three states have significant stakes in the working of multilateral institutions in the Central Asian region. How far they remain significant parts of the process, is yet to be seen. What is important is that there now seems to be recognition about the need for a multiplicity of institutions dealing with multiple security issues that involve more than two states, particularly in regions where the possibility of conflict is high.

From the Indian point of view the last decade of the 20th century presented a major strategic challenge as far the Central Asian region was concerned. With the collapse of the former USSR and subsequent Russian retreat from the region, the regional balance was altered and India's favoured position in a region, that was identified by its strategic thinkers as "India's extended strategic neighbourhood", was reduced.[47] The emergence of a number of regional players and the potential for local conflicts also significantly changed the strategic environment for India. Along with this was the fact that much of the Central Asian borders are fluid having been demarcated out of political considerations rather than any ethnic contiguity. The possibilities of demographic changes and the proliferation of non-state actors was also a distinct possibility. The fact that Afghanistan and parts of the Central Asian region were emerging, as significant opium producers, also made India vulnerable to opium trade. The consequent proliferation of small arms is also a destabilizing factor. As far as India is concerned Afghanistan, terrorism, illicit drug trade and extremism have been identified as significant areas where there could be collaboration. [48]

The Indian and Central Asian positions merge on a number of these issues of common concern. The people of the region have an ancient tradition of close and friendly relations, which resulted in the development of cultural and economic cooperation. This relation strengthened further due to common heritage and commitment to ideals of tolerance, democracy, secularism and the desire for peace. Another issue of common concern is terrorism and here too the position of the two countries is similar. The Central Asian states strongly condemned the terrorist attack on the Indian Parliament, on December 13, 2001.

In this connection Central Asian initiatives to collectively deal with security issues has been noted as significant by India. The progress of the Conference on Interaction and Confidence

Building Measures in Asia was noted with satisfaction. The CICA vision for security in Asia elaborates on multilateral approaches towards promoting peace and security and visualizes itself as the forum for dialogue, consultation and adoption of decisions and measures on the basis of consensus on security issues in Asia. CICA identifies certain elements as challenges to security and seeks to find ways to eliminate them. In this context it resolves to support efforts for the elimination of weapons of mass destruction, to ensure the establishment of nuclear free zones, to curb excessive accumulation of conventional armaments, condemn terrorism, not to render any assistance to separatist movements in other states, reject the use of religion as a pretext for terrorists and separatists, emphasize the significance of curbing the movement of illicit drugs and corruption. In the context of achieving these objectives the CICA will take necessary steps for the elaboration and implementation of measures aimed at enhancing cooperation and creating an atmosphere of peace, confidence and friendship. All states are encouraged to resolve their disputes peacefully through negotiations in accordance with the principles enshrined in the UN Charter and International law.[49]

India also noted the progress being made by the SCO as a regional organization. Central Asian states, particularly Kazakhstan, expressed the belief that considering India's geographical proximity in the neighbourhood and its active participation on regional and global matters of cooperation, India's membership of the SCO would add to the organization.[50] India and the Central Asian states also agreed upon the expediency of expanding the Security Council of the UN to make it more representative and efficient. In fact there is also enthusiasm about the Russia-China-India triangle among Central Asian scholars.[51] The President of Kazakhstan, noting the role being played by India in world affairs, supported India as an appropriate candidate as a permanent member of a restructured UN Security Council. President Nazarbaev's support for the inclusion of India as a permanent member of the UN Security Council and the SCO is significant, since both the countries are fighting cross border terrorism and insurgency. In the Indian case it is Pakistan sponsored terrorism in Kashmir and in the Kazakh case it is the threat of the Islamic Movement of Uzbekistan. However, some analysts have also warned that the inclusion of India would involve the SCO into the larger foreign policy zone of competition involving other South Asian states.[52]

While the Indian inclusion into the SCO and the Indo Kazakh Joint Working Group on counter terrorism could be the precursor for a common approach to counter terrorism in the region, given the Chinese position on the matter of expansion of the SCO to include India, or any other state for that matter, does not seem to be the immediate agenda.[53] However, India has joined the SCO as an observer and Iran and other countries like Pakistan have expressed their interest to be a part of it. Russia and China agree, in substance, that the first candidate for the expansion should be Mongolia and Mongolia has joined the SCO working committee as an observer. Given that, the SCO projects itself as an attempt at creating a multilateral "peaceful buffer" in the Eurasian world expansion of the membership and cooperation with other states seems inevitable. The apprehension against expansion is that the more the SCO expands, as a macroregional structure, the less likely it is to have an operational role in security policy or to correspond with the common concerns out of which a Central Asian security identity might emerge.[54]

Despite these limitations analysts have noted that the multilateralism, that the SCO epitomizes, remains significant.[55] Concluding his speech at the plenary Session of the Council of Ministers of Foreign Affairs of the SCO, Kasymzhomart Tokayev, the State Secretary-Minister of Foreign Affairs of Kazakhstan emphasizes this by noting:

> The Shanghai Cooperation Organization can and should by means of joint efforts (emerge as) an efficient instrument of ensuring stability and security in the region; an instrument of the creation of efficient mechanisms of trade, economic, cultural and humanitarian cooperation.[56]

Rather than the development of a new round of geopolitical rivalry in the immediate aftermath of the entry of US forces in the region, the dynamics of major powers' strategic interaction in the Central Asian region has moved towards collaboration. An assessment of their behaviour demonstrates a remarkable degree of shared strategic interests that have sustained their collaboration in the region. This does not imply that Russian, Chinese and American decision makers do not wish to increase their influence over the region. Russian officials are eager to stop further decline of their influence in the region. Chinese policy makers have an expanding array of interests in the region that demands an expanded presence. Both Russian and Chinese officials wish to limit the US role in the region and advocate a multipolar strategy. On their part American policy makers have expressed a preference for "stability" and "development" in the region which can only be served by their continued and enhanced presence.

However, for all three the most pressing security problems are not in Central Asia and are not ones that can only be achieved at the expense of the other. On the contrary they require collaboration from the other powers. For Russia, the war in Chechnya remains the most significant. China is most concerned about the Uighur separatist movement. Russian and Chinese officials claim that both the Chechen and Uighur movements have transnational links with the Taliban and *Al-Qaeda*. The United States has classified both the Taliban and the *Al-Qaeda* as terrorist organizations and recognize them a chief security threats but at the same time has shifted its priorities to the Persian Gulf.

In the light of such developments the observation of the Viennese philosopher, Ludwig Wittgenstein, in 1929, seems particularly relevant. He noted:

> When we think of the world's future, we always mean the destination it will reach if it keeps going in the direction we can see it going now; it does not occur to us that its path is not a straight line, but a curve, constantly changing direction.[57]

NOTES AND REFERENCES

1. See for instance Stephen Schlesinger, "The United States and the World: Is a Return to Multilateralism Possible?", in C. Uday Bhaskar and others (ed.) *United Nations: Multilateralism and International Security*, Delhi, Shipra Publications, 2005.

2. John Gerard Ruggie (ed) *Multilateralism Matters, The Theory and Praxis of an Institutional Form*, New York: Columbia University Press, 1993.

3. For a detailed analysis of the various visions about multilateralism see Joachim Krause, "Multilateralism: Behind European Views", *The Washington Quarterly*, Vol 27, No 2, Spring 2004.

4. John Van Oudenaren, "What is Multilateral", *Policy Review 117* and "Unipolar Versus Unilateral", *Policy Review, No 124.*

5. This idea is represented in this quote from a Chinese scholar Huang Zhengji who notes, "multipolarity just refers to the multiple forces in the international community that are possessed of certain strengths and are representative of certain interests" see Hung Zhengji,"The Irresistible Multipolarity Trend of the World", *International Strategic Studies*, No 4, 1997.

6. In the Central Asian region the emergence of "new" threats has led to calls for reform of the UN and creation of effective multilateral forums to curb terrorism. See for instance this speech by the State Secretary-Minister of Foreign Affairs of the Republic of Kazakhstan, "Vestupleniye Kasymzhomarta Tokayeva na Transaziatskom Parlamentskom Forume PA OSCE "vorba protiv terrorizma: ucpekhi, noviye ugrozi", *Kazakhstan i Sovremennie Mir*, No 2 (5), 2003, where he clearly notes that "there is no alternative to global multilateral cooperation of nations".

7. In recent times Russia has stressed the significance of multilateralism. See for instance *Speech by Minister of Foreign Affairs of the Russian Federation Igor Ivanov at the Joint Session of Federation Council and State Duma Foreign Affairs Committees*, February 12, 2004 where points to "assertion of multilateralism in international relations, the strengthening of the role of the UN and International law", Russian Ministry of Foreign

Affairs, http://www.russianembassy.org. Similarly the Ministry of Foreign Affairs, China elaborating on foreign policy clearly points to the necessity of multilateral options, www.fmprc.gov.cn/eng

8. For a detailed analysis of this conditional multilateralism see Jing-dong Yuan, *Asia-Pacific Security: China's Conditional Multilateralism and Great Power Entente*, Strategic Studies Institute Publication, Carlisle, Pennsylvania, 2000.

9. For writings that stress on the inevitability of change in geopolitical alignments around Central Asia and the image of the region as "liberated" from the Russo-Chinese condominium institutionalized in the SCO, see Svante E. Cornell," Introduction," *Nordic Newsletter of Asian Studies*, No 3, 2002. See also Stephen Blank," The Shanghai Cooperative Organization: A Post Mortem," *Nordic Newsletter of Asian Studies*, No 3, 2002.

10. See for instance, S Neil MacFarlane, "The United States and Regionalism in Central Asia", *International Affairs*, Vol 80, No 3, May 2004, who argues that the US has actively promoted the establishment of the NATO's PfP, rather than seeking to establish a free standing regional security structures, and similarly in the economic sphere, has promoted accession to the WTO far more consistently than any regional trading structures.

11. Farkhod Fozilovich Tolipov, "Regional Security in Central Asia in the Context of the Fight Against Terrorism", in K. Santhanam and Ramakant Dwivedi (eds) *India and Central Asia: Advancing the Common Interest*, New Delhi: Anamaya Publishers, 2004.

12. Tolipov, "Regional Security in Central Asia in the Context of the Fight Against Terrorism".

13. A security system, as defined by Barry Buzan, is a group of states whose security interests bind them sufficiently closely so that their national security cannot be realistically considered separate from each other.

14. Talgat Ismagambetov, "Some geopolitical peculiarities of Central Asia, past and present", in Sally N. Cummings (ed) *Oil, Transition and Security in Central Asia*, London and New York: Routledge-Curzon, 2003.

15. M. Ashimbaev et all eds, *New Challenges and New Geopolitics in Central Asia After September 11*, Almaty: Kazakhstan Institute for Strategic Studies, 2003.

16. Stephen Blank, "Which Way for Sino-Russian Relations?", *Orbis*, Summer 1998.

17. For Chinese writings that stress this position see "China- Russia Relations Remain Better than Russia-US Relations", *Peoples' Daily Online*, Thursday, November 28, 2002, english.people.com.cn/2002 11/28.

18. See website of the Ministry of Foreign Affairs, China www.fmprc.gov.cn/eng

19. Andrei Nikilaev,"Lessons from Iraq", *The Statesman*, Thursday, 10 April, 2003.

20. This however did not work since the US changed its cautious policy towards the NATO and Poland, the Czech Republic and Hungary became a part of it. For details see V Zhurkin, "Russia and the Enlargement of NATO", in T Hayashi (ed) *The Emerging New Regional Order in Central and Eastern Europe*, Sapporo: Slavic Research Centre, 1997.

21. See the text of the Russo-Chinese Joint Declaration in *Sbornik: Rossiisko-Kitaiskikh Dogovorov*, 1999 cited from Akihiro Iwashita, "The Shanghai Cooperation Organization and Its Implications for Eurasian Security: A New Dimension of "Partnership" After the Post Cold War Period", in S Tabata and A. Iwashita (eds) *Slavic Eurasia's Integration into the World Economy and Community*, (forthcoming) Sapporo: Slavic Research Centre, 2004.

22. *Krasnaia Zvezda*, April 30, 1996, cited from Iwashita, "The Shanghai Cooperation Organization and Its Implications for Eurasian Security".

23. Pan Guang, "China-Central Asia-Russia Relations and the Role of the SCO in the War Against Terrorism", *SIIS Journal*, Vol 9, No 2, May 2002.

24. Ashimbaev et all eds, *New Challenges and New Geopolitics in Central Asia After September 11*.

25. For details see Amitabh Mattoo, "United States of America and

Central Asia: Beginning of the Great Game", in Nirmala Joshi (ed) *Central Asia The Great Game Replayed, An Indian Perspective*, Delhi: New Century Publications, 2003.

26. Strobe Talbott, "A Farewell to Flashman: American Policy in the Caucasus and Central Asia," Speech at the Central Asia Institute, School of Advanced International Studies, The John Hopkins University, July 21, 1997.

27. Zhang Guihong,"US Security Policy Towards South Asia After September 11 and Its Implications for China: A Chinese Perspective", *Strategic Analysis*, Vol 27, No 2, April-June 2003.

28. The idea of a strategic co-operation with China and India has been present in Russian foreign policy thinking for a long time. E.M Primakov put forward this idea in Delhi in December 1998, as part of a search for partners to create a greater space for Russian maneuver. The idea it was also present in Andrei Kozerev's "new approach" to Asia. For a detailed analysis see Hari Vasudevan, "Russia-India-China Cooperation. The Shaping of a Notion in Russian Foreign Policy", in Mahavir Singh (ed.) *Building a New Asia,* Delhi, Shipra Publications, 2005. On the eve of his visit to India in October 2000, President Putin mentioned the idea and this was repeated by Igor Ivanov, the Russian Foreign Minister in November 2001.

29. Cited from Jyotsna Bakshi,"Sino-Russian Strategic Partnership in Central Asia: Implications for India", *Strategic Analysis*, Vol XXV, No 2, May 2001.

30. Zhou Yuyun, "Strategic Triangle of China, India, Russia: Ideality and Reality", in Singh (ed.) *Building a New Asia.*

31. See Robert Marquand, "Putin Pushes Strategic Triangle with China, India", *Christian Science Monitor*, December 6, 2002.

32. Yuyun, "Strategic Triangle of China, India, Russia".

33. Sergei Blagov, "Russia-China-India: An Axis of Denials", *Asia Times Online*, July 3, 2003.

34. See Subhash Kapila, "Russia-China-India Triangle Strategically Inadvisable", *South Asia Analysis Group*, Paper No 408. Kapila goes on to point out to reasons why the triangular relationship is inadvisable for India.

35. Commersant, *Daily Review*, December 24 1998, cited from Jyotsna Bakshi, *Russia-China Relations, Relevance for India*, Delhi: Shipra, 2004.

36. Julie M. Rahm, "Russia,China,India: A New Strategic Triangle for a New Cold War?", *Parameters*, Winter 2001-02.

37. For a detailed discussion see Rahm, "Russia,China,India: A New Strategic Triangle for a New Cold War?".

38. Cited from Marquand, "Putin Pushes Strategic Triangle with China, India".

39. Among Indian authors writing on the Russia-China-India axis see Devendra Kaushik, "The New Geopolitics of Central Asia: Russia, China, India", *Contemporary Central Asia*, Vol 3, No 2, August 1999 and "The Eurasian Perspective of an Emerging Asian Security Structure: A New Vista for India-China Strategic Cooperation", in Mahavir Singh (ed) *Asia Annual 2003*, Delhi: Shipra Publications, 2003.

40. Vasudevan, "Russia-India-China Cooperation. The Shaping of a Notion in Russian Foreign Policy".

41. R.R. Subramanian, "Russia-China-India: Strategic Cooperation in a Pan Asian Order", in Singh (ed.) *Building a New Asia.*

42. Subramanian, "Russia-China-India: Strategic Cooperation in a Pan Asian Order."

43. See Harsh V. Pant, "The Moscow-Beijing-Delhi Strategic Triangle: An Idea Whose Time May Never Come", *Security Dialogue*, Vol 35 (3), 2004.

44. Cited from Bakshi,"Sino-Russian Strategic Partnership in Central Asia: Implications for India".

45. Sergei Lounev, "Russia-China-India Prospects of a Joint Fight Against Terrorism", in Omprakash Misra and Sucheta Ghosh (ed) *Terrorism and Low Intensity Conflict in South Asian Region*, New Delhi: Manak, 2003.

46. Guihong, "US Security Policy Towards South Asia After September 11 and Its Implications for China: A Chinese Perspective".

47. Julie A MacDonald and S Enders Wimbush, "India's Energy Security", *Strategic Analysis*, Vol 23, No 5, August 1999.

48. Irina Komissina, "India: Cooperation with the Central Asian Countries in Regional Security", *Central Asia and the Caucasus*, No 6(24), 2003.

49. For a detailed analysis of CICA see Murat Laumulin, *The Security, Foreign Policy, and International Relationship of Kazakhstan After Independence, 1991-2001*, Almaty: Kazakhstan Institute of Strategic Studies and Freidrich Ebert Shiftung, 2002 and Ashimbaev et all eds, *New Challenges and New Geopolitics in Central Asia After September 11.*

50. See for instance Atul Aneja, "India Asked to Join Central Asian grouping", *The Hindu*, February 13, 2002.

51. Conversation of the author with Professor Shanken Nadirov at the *Institut Vostokovedeniia* in Moscow, where he noted that Primakov's idea was "sincere and perceptive".

52. Cited from Ibragim Alibekov, "India set to Expand Presence in Central Asia", *Eurasianet, Business and Economics*, April 7, 2004.

53. See "Commentary: Russia-China-India, A New Geometry", *Pravda Online*, December 2, 2002.

54. Roy Allison, "Regionalism, regional structures and security management in Central Asia", *International Affairs*, Vol 80, No 3, May 2004.

55. Iwashita, "The Shanghai Cooperation Organization and Its Implications for Eurasian Security".

56. Cited from "Vistupleniye Kasymzhomarta Tokayeva na Plenarnom Zasedanii Soveta Ministpov Inostrannix Del Shanxhaiskoi Organizatsii Sotrudnichestvo", *Kazakhstan i Sovremennie Mir*, No 2(5), 2003.

57. Ludwig Wittgenstein, *Culture and Value*, Chicago: University of Chicago Press, 1980.

Select Bibliography

Abazov Rafis, "Kyrgyzstan's Dilemmas", *Analysis of Current Events*, Volume 14, No 2, May 2002.

Abdullayev Zafar, "Tajikistan, Russia Probe Military Partnership", *Eurasia Insight*, March 15, 2004, http://www. eurasianet.org.

Akbarzadeh Shahram, "Keeping Central Asia Stable", *Third World Quarterly*, Vol 25, No 4, 2004.

Akbarzade Shahram, "US-Uzbek Partnership and Democratic Reforms", *Nationalities Papers*, Vol 32, No 2, June 2004.

Akimbekov Sultan, *Afganskii Uzel I Problemi Bezopasnosti Tsentralnoi Azii*, Almaty, 2003.

Alagappa Muthiah, *Asian Security Practice: Material and Ideational Influences*, Stanford: Stanford University Press, 1998.

Alibekov Ibragim and Sergei Blagov, "New Security Organization Could Help Expand Russia's Reach in Central Asia", *Eurasia Insight*, May 6, 2003, http://www. eurasianet.org.

Alibekov Ibragim, "India Set to Expand Presence in Central Asia", *Eurasianet, Business and Economics*, April 7, 2004 , http://www. eurasianet.org.

Alimov Kadir Z., "The Rediscovery of Uzbek History and its Foreign Policy Implications", in Fredrick Starr (ed) *The Legacy of History in Russia and the New States of Eurasia*, New York: M.E. Sharpe, 1994.

Allison Roy, "Regionalism, regional structures and security management in Central Asia", *International Affairs*, Vol 80, No 3, May 2004.

Allison Roy and Lena Johnson (eds) *Central Asian Security: The New International Context*, Washington: Brookings Institute Press, 2001.

Allison Roy and Christopher Bluth (eds) *Security Dilemma in Russia and Eurasia*, London: RIIA, 1998.

Ameri Nasser Saghafi, "The Fundamentals of the Russian Outlooks and Strategies", *Amu Darya, Iranian Journal of Central Asian Studies*, Vol 4 No 5, Spring/Summer 2000.

Anderson John, *The International Politics of Central Asia*, Manchester and New York: Manchester University Press, 1997.

Aneja Atul, "India asked to Join Central Asian grouping", *The Hindu*, February 13, 2002.

Arman Kambiz, "US Geopilitical Position Takes Hit in Tajikistan", *Eurasia Insight*, July 21, 2004, http://www. eurasianet.org.

Ashimbaev M. "Security in Central Asia: Do the Risks of Destabilization Remain?", *Central Asia's Affairs*, No 1, 2003.

Ashimbaev M. et all eds, *New Challenges and New Geopolitics in Central Asia After September 11*, Almaty: Kazakhstan Institute for Strategic Studies, 2003.

Ashimbaev M., "Conceptual Problems and Threats to Security in the Caspian-Central Asian Region", *Central Asia's Affairs*, No 2, 2003.

Auezov Murat Mukhtarovich, "India, Russia and China in the Emerging Dynamics of Central Asia", in K. Santhanam and Ramakant Dwivedi (eds) *India and Central Asia: Advancing the Common Interest*, New Delhi:Anamaya Publishers, 2004.

Bahgat Gawdat, "The New Geopolitics of Oil: The United States, Saudi Arabia and Russia", *Orbis*, Vol 47, No 3, Summer 2003.

Bakshi Jyotsna, *Russia-China Relations, Relevance for India*, Delhi: Shipra, 2004.

Bakshi Jyotsna, "Sino-Russian Strategic Partnership in Central Asia: Implications for India", *Strategic Analysis*, Vol XXV, No 2, May 2001.

Barthold V.V., *Turkestan Down to the Mongol Invasion*, (reprint) London: Lowe and Brydone, 1968.

Bazhanov Evgeniy, "Russian Perspectives on China's Foreign Policy and Military Development", in Jonathan D Pollack (ed) *In China's Shadow: Regional Perspectives on Chinese Foreign Policy and Military Development*, RAND Publication, 1998.

Behar Busra Ersanli, "Rediscovering Multidimensionality: Turkey's Quest for Partnership with the Turkic Republics", *Private VIEW,* Winter, 1997.

Ben-Adam Justin, "China", in David Westerlund and Ingvar Svanberg (eds) *Islam Outside the Arab World*, London:Curzon Press, 1999.

Bhaskar C Uday, Santhanam K and others (ed.), United Nations: Multiculturalism and International Security, Delhi: Shipra, 2005.

Bin Yu, "United States-China Relations and Regional Security After September 11", *Issues and Insights*, No 2, April 2002.

Blagov Sergei, "In Central Asia, Russia Pushes Back Against NATO Influence", *Eurasia Insight*, July 21, 2004, http://www. eurasianet.org.

Blagov Sergei, "Russia-China-India: An Axis of Denials", *Asia Times Online*, July 3, 2003.

Blank Stephen, "The Shanghai Cooperative Organization: A Post Mortem," *Nordic Newsletter of Asian Studies*, No 3, 2002.

Blank Stephen, "Which Way for Sino-Russian Relations?", *Orbis*, Summer 1998.

Bondarez Leonid, "Formirovaniye Systemi Collectivnoi Bezopasnosti v Tsentralnoi Azii — osobennosti, itogi, perspectivi", *Kazakhstan i Sovremennie Mir*, No 2(5), 2003.

Brauer, Birgit "Central Asia Readjusting to Life in Putin's Orbit", *Central Asia and Caucasus Analyst*, March 29, 2000.

Calabrese John, "China's Policy Towards Central Asia: Renewal and Accommodation", *Eurasian Studies*, No 16, Autumn-Winter 1999

Carlson Charles, "Uzbekistan:Karimov Says Improved Relations With Russia Not at the Expense of US Ties", *Eurasia Insight*, September 9, 2003 http://www. eurasianet.org. .

Carnegie Endowment for International Peace, Meeting Report, Vol 2, No 8, November 3, 2000, www.ceip.org/files/events/gulomov.asp.

Chang Felix K., "China's Central Asian Power and Problems", *Orbis*, Vol 41, No 3, Summer 1997.

Ching Frank, "China Puts Growth Before Reunification," *Japan Times*, April 19, 2002 (internet version).

Chokaev Mustafa, "Turkestan and the Soviet Regime", *Journal of Royal Central Asian Society*, Vol 28, 1931.

Choudhary L.K., "Islamic Militancy and Terrorism in Xinjiang: China's Anxiety and Concerns", *India Quarterly*, Vol LVIII, No 2, April-June 2002.

Chufrin Gennady (ed) *Russia and Asia:The Emerging Security Agenda*, New York: OUP, 1999

Cohen Ariel, "Central Asians Launch Another Regional Association", *Central Asia-Caucasus Analyst*, January 16, 2002.

Cohen Ariel, "Uncertainty Still Defines Russia's Role in Central Eurasia", *Eurasia Insight*, September 19, 2002, http:/ www.eurasianet.org.

Coppieters Bruno, Alexei Zverev and Dimitri Trenin (eds) *Commonwealth and Independence in Post Soviet Eurasia*, London: Portland; Frank Cass, 1998.

Coppieters Bruno, "Conclusions: The Failure of Regionalism in Eurasia and the Western Ascendancy over Russia's Near Abroad", in Bruno Coppieters, Alexei Zverev and Dmitri Trenin (eds) *Commonwealth and Independence in Post Soviet Russia*, London and Portland: Frank Cass, 1998.

Cornell Svante E, "Introduction," *Nordic Newsletter of Asian Studies*, No 3, 2002.

Cornell Svante E., "America In Eurasia: One Year After," *Current History*, October 2002.

Craig Harris Lillian, "Xinjiang, Central Asia and the Implications for China's Policy in the Islamic World", *The China Quarterly*, No 133, March 1993.

Cummings Sally N (ed) *Oil, Transition and Security in Central Asia*, London and New York: Routledge-Curzon, 2003.

Cutler Robert M, "Redrawing the Architecture of Central Asian Security," *Central Asia Caucasus Analyst*, February 27, 2002.

Cutler Robert M., "Russia Slouches Towards Central Asia," *Central Asia and Caucasus Analyst*, April 12, 2000.

Deudney Daniel, "The Case Against Linking Environmental Degradation and National Security", *Millennium: Journal of International Studies*, Vol 19, No 1, 1990.

Dillon Michael, *Xinjiang — China's Muslim Far Northeast*, London and New York: Routledge Curzon, 2004.

Dorian James P, Brett Wigdortz and Dru Gladney, "Central Asia and Xinjiang, China:Emerging Energy, Economic and Ethnic Problems", *Central Asian Survey*, Vol 16, No 4, 1997.

Drew W.J., "Sinkiang:The Land and the People", *Central Asian Review*, Vol XVI, No 3, 1968.

Drobizhyeva Leokadia, "Russian Ethnic Attitudes in Changing Political Situations," *Economic and Political Weekly*, Special Number, December 18, 1995.

Dumbaugh Kerry, *China-US Relations*, Washington, The Library of Congress, Congressional Research Service, Issue Brief 98018.

Dunlop John, "Russians Confronting a Loss of Empire— 1987-1991", *Political Science Quarterly*, Vol 108 (4) Winter 1993-94.

Erickson John, "Eurasian Maneuvers", in Sally N. Cummings (ed) *Oil, Transition and Security in Central Asia*, London and New York: Routledge-Curzon, 2003.

Eshanova Zamira, "Central Asia: Diplomatic Visits Highlight US-Russian Competition," *RFE/RL Report*, 3 December, 2002, www.rferl.org

Evans P.B., H.K. Jacobson and R.D. Putnam (eds) *Double Edged Diplomacy*, Berkeley: University of California Press, 1993.

Feifer Gregory, "2002 in Review: Putin's Foreign Policy Not Seen as Harming Relations With the West", *RFE/RL Report*, 16 December 2002, www.rferl.org

Feigenbaum Evan A., "The United States is Driving Russia and China Together Again", *International Herald Tribune*, December 28, 2000.

Finkelstein David, "China's Emergence in Central Asia: Security, Diplomatic and Economic Interests", *CSIS Forum on the Current State of China-Central Asia Diplomacy and Implications for US Foreign Policy*, Wednesday, February 5, 2003.

Firdous Tabassum, *Central Asia Security and Strategic Imperatives*, Delhi: Kalpaz Publications, 2002.

Fishlock Trevour, *Out of Red Darkness, Reports from the Collapsing Soviet Empire*, London: John Murray, 1992.

Forsythe Rosemarie, "The Politics of Oil in the Caucasus and Central Asia", *Adelphi Papers* No 300, London:Oxford University Press, 1996.

Freedman Robert O. "Russia and Central Asia Under Yeltsin", *Central Asia Monitor*, No 4, 1996.

Galyamova Virina, "Vozrozhdayushiesya Gigant i Kitaiskaya Ugroza v Istorichiskoi Retrospektive", *Kazakhstan i Sovremennie Mir*, Vol 1, No 2, 2002.

Ge Su, "On Sino-US-Russian Relations", *International Studies*, 7-9, 2002. Gennady Chufrin (ed) *Russia and Asia:The Emerging Security Agenda*, New York: OUP, 1999.

Gladney Dru C, "The Ethnogenesis of the Uighur", *Contemporary Central Asia*, Vol 9, No 1, 1990.

Gleason Gregory "Inter-State Cooperation in Central Asia from the CIS to the Shanghai Forum", *Europe-Asia Studies*, Vol 53, No 7, 2001.

Gokalp Zia, *The Principles of Turkism*, Leiden: E.J. Brill, 1992.

Goldgeier J. and Michael McFaul, "George W. Bush and Russia", *Current History*, October 2002.

Goldstein J and R.O. Keohane, *Ideas and Foreign Policy*, New York: Cornell University Press, 1993.

Gretsky Sergei, *Russia's Policy Towards Central Asia*, Washington D.C.: Carnegie Moscow Centre, 1997.

Guang Pan, "China-Central Asia-Russia Relations and the Role of the SCO in the War Against Terrorism," *SIIA Journal*, Vol 9, No 2, May 2002.

Guihong Zhang, "US Security Policy Towards South Asia After September 11 and Its Implications for China: A Chinese Perspective", *Strategic Analysis*, Vol 27, No 2, April-June 2003.

Hafvenstein Joel, "Central Asia: Uzbekistan", *The NIS Observed: An Analytical Review*, Vol VIII, No 13, August 21, 2003.

Hanks Reuel, "The Islamic Factor in Nationalism and Nation Building in Uzbekistan- Causative Agent or Inhibitor?", *Nationalities Papers*, Vol 22 (2), 1994.

Hauner Milan, *What is Asia To Us? Russia's Asian Heartland Yesterday and Today*, Boston: Unwin Hyman, 1990.

Huasheng Zhao, "US Factor in Sino-Russian Relations", in *Contemporary World Configuration*, Shanghai: Shanghai Institute of International Studies, 2002.

Hymen Antony, "Turkestan and Pan Turkism Revisited", *Central Asian Survey*, Vol 16, No 3, 1997.

International Monetary Fund Direction of Trade Statistics Handbook, August 1998.

Irishmatov Bakhtiyor, "Role of NATO in Post-Soviet Territory and its Role in Combating Terrorism", in K. Santhanam and Ramakant Dwivedi (eds) *India and Central Asia: Advancing the Common Interest*, New Delhi: Anamaya Publishers, 2004.

Islamov Bakhtior A, "Post Soviet Central Asia and the Commonwealth of Independent States", in Beatrice Manz (ed) *Central Asia in Historical Perspective*, Westview Press: Boulder, 1994.

Iwasaki, Ichiro, "The Initial Phase of Transition of Russo Central Asian Economic Relations- An Institutional Approach", *Islamic Area Studies Working Paper Series*, No 11, Islamic Area Studies Project, Tokyo, Japan.

Iwashita Akihiro, "The Shanghai Cooperation Organization and Its Implications for Eurasian Security: A New Dimension of "Partnership" After the Post Cold War Period", in S Tabata and A. Iwashita (eds) *Slavic Eurasia's Integration into the World Economy and Community*, (forthcoming) Sapporo: Slavic Research Centre, 2004.

Iwashita Akihiro, *A 4000-Kilometer Journey Along the Sino-Russian Border*, Sapporo: Slavic Research Centre, Hokkaido University, 2004.

Iwashita Akihiro, "Opit Prigranichogo Sotrudnichestvo Rossii i KNR PZoslednye 10 Let", *Slavic Research Centre Occasional Paper No 91* on *The Sino-Russian Strategic Relationship? Current Views from the Border and Beijing*, Sapporo Slavic Research Centre, Hokkaido University, 2003.

J. Rosenau, *International Politics and Foreign Policy*, New York: Free Press, 1969.

Jackson Nicole J., *Russian Foreign Policy and the CIS: Theories, debates and actions*, London and New York: Routledge, 2003.

Jiali Ma, "Central Asia: Geostrategic Situation and Big Powers' Policy", *Contemporary Central Asia*, Vol 3, No 1, April 1999.

Jiang Liu, "Sino-US Relations: Develop in Twists and Turns", a *Beijing Review* Cover Story available online at www.bjreview.com.cn/2002/200152(A).htm.

Jingjie Li, "Pillars of the Sino Russian Partnership", *Orbis*, Vol 44, No 4, Fall 2000.

Johnson Lena, "Russia and Central Asia: Post 11 September, 2001", *Central Asia and the Caucasus*, No 1 (19) 2003.

Johnson Lena, *Keeping the Peace in the CIS: The Evolution of Russian Policy*, Discussion Paper 81. London: RIIA, 1999.

Johnson Lena, *Russia and Asia, A New Web of Relations*, London: RIIA, 1998.

Jon Rudelson Justin, "The Uighurs in the Future of Central Asia", *Nationalities Papers*, Vol 22, No 2, 1994.

Joshi Nirmala (ed) *Central Asia The Great Game Replayed, An Indian Perspective*, Delhi: New Century Publications, 2003.

Kairgeldina Dariya, "Mezhdunarodnoi Konferentsii SEAP: Vezovi Regionalnoi Bezopasnosti v Tsentralnoi Azii", *Kazakhstan I Sovremennie Mir,* No2 (5), 2003.

Kaliyeva Raikhan, "Role i Mesto Rossii vo Vneshnie Politike Kazakhstana", *Kazakhstan I Sovremennie Mir,* No2 (5), 2003.

Kandelaki Giorgi, "Uzbekistan Quits GUUAM", June 14, 2002 *Eurasianet*, http://www. eurasianet.org.

Kandelaki Giorgi, "Uzbekistan Clarifies its Position on GUUAM", June 26, 2002 *Eurasianet*, http://www. eurasianet.org.

Kapila Subhash, "Russia-China-India Triangle Strategically Inadvisable", *South Asia Analysis Group*, Paper No 408.

Karimov Islam. A., *Uzbekistan on the Threshold of the Twenty-First Century, Threats to Security, Conditions of Stability and Guarantees of Progress*, Tashkent: Uzbekiston, 1997.

Karimov Islam A.," Yedinstvo Proshlovo i Budushyevo" in Islam A. Karimov *Turkestan Nash Obshei Dom*, Tashkent: "Uzbekiston", 1995.

Karimov Islam A., *Address by H.E. Islom Karimov President of the Republic of Uzbekistan at the 48th Session of the United Nations*, Tashkent:Uzbekiston, 1993.

Karimov Islam A., *Uzbekistan— The Road of Independence and Progress*, New Delhi, 1993.

Kasenov Oumirserik, "Central Asia: National, regional and Global Aspects of Security", in Roy Allison and Christopher Bluth (eds) *Security Dilemma in Russia and Eurasia*, London: RIIA, 1998.

Katik Mevlut, "NATO Embraces Central Asia and the Caucasus st the Istanbul Summit", *Eurasia Insight*, July 21, 2004, http://www.eurasianet.org.

Kaushik Devendra, "The Eurasian Perspective of an Emerging Asian Security Structure: A New Vista for India-China Strategic Cooperation", in Mahavir Singh (ed) *Asia Annual 2003*, Delhi: Shipra Publications, 2003.

Kaushik Devendra, "The New Geopolitics of Central Asia: Russia, China, India", *Contemporary Central Asia*, Vol 3, No 2, August 1999.

Kazakhstan Risks Review, No 6 (12) 2003.

Kazykhaanov Ye, "New Challenges to Security in Central Asia: A Multilateral Approach", *Central Asia's Affairs*, No 1, 2003.

Khaitov Ata, "Central Asian Responses to the Iraq Crisis: Hopes and Fears", *Russia and Eurasia Review*, Vol 2, Issue 5, March 4, 2003.

Khamzayeva Anar, "Novaya Strategiya NATO? Ee Posledstviya Dliya Tsentralnoi Azii", *Kazakstan i Sovremennie Mir*, No 1 (2) 2002.

Komissina Irina, "India: Cooperation with the Central Asian Countries in Regional Security", *Central Asia and the Caucasus*, No 6(24), 2003.

Koolaie Elaheh, "Russia and Central Asia: Opportunities and Shortcomings in the Utilization of Regional Resources", *Amu Darya, Iranian Journal of Central Asian Studies*, Vol 4 No 5, Spring/Summer 2000.

Kortunov Andrei and Andrei Shoumikhin, "Russia and Central Asia: Evolution of Mutual Perceptions, Policies and Interdependence", in Yongjin Zang and Rouben Azizan (eds) *Ethnic Challenges Beyond Borders, Chinese and Russian Perspectives of the Central Asian Conundrum*, London: Macmilian in association with St Antony's College, Oxford, 1998.

Kozhikov Adil, "Transformatsiya Politiki Rossii v Tsentralnoi Azii, Analiz tekyshikh Tendentsii", *Kazakhstan I Sovremennie Mir*, No 1, 2001.

Krahmann Elke, "Conceptualizing Security Governance", *Cooperation and Conflict*, Vol 38(1), 2003.

Krastev Nikola,"Central Asia: "Taliban" Author Says Russia to Regain Influence in Unstable Region", *RFE/RL Report*, 22 March 2002, www.rferl.org

Krause Joachim, "Multilateralism: Behind European Views", *The*

Washington Quarterly, Vol 27, No 2,

Krivonogov Victor, "Kazakhstansko-Kitaiskie Togovo, Ekonomicheskie i Nayuchno-Tekhnicheskiye Otnosheniya" *Kazakhstan i Sovremennie Mir*, No1(4), 2003.

Kubicek Paul, "Regionalism, Nationalism and Realpolitik in Central Asia", *Europe-Asia Studies*, Vol 49, No 4, 1997.

Kulchik Yuiry, Andrey Fadin and Victor Sergeev, *Central Asia After the Empire*, London and Chicago: Pluto Press, 1996.

Kuzio Taras and Sergei Blagov, "GUUAM Makes a Comeback Bid US Support", *Eurasia Insight* July 7, 2003, Eurasianet, http://www.eurasianet.org.

Lachowski Z., "Pursuing Military Stability in Central Asia: European Perspective", *Central Asia's Affairs*, No 2, 2003.

Lambroschini Sophie "Central Asia: CIS Force Not Best Way to Combat Islamic Threat Say Analysts," *Radio Free Europe-Radio Liberty*, May 23, 2001.

Lambroschini Sophie, "Central Asia: Russia Sanctioning Anti-Islamic Crackdown" *RFE/RL Report*, Moscow, 2 August, 2000, www.rferl.org

Lapidus Gail, "Central Asia in Russian and American Foreign Policy After September 11, 2001", Presentation from *Central Asia and Russia: Responses to the War on Terrorism,* a panel discussion held at the University of California, Berkeley on October 29, 2001.

Lattimore Owen, *The Inner Asian Frontiers of China*, (reprint) Hong Kong: Oxford University Press, 1988.

Laumulin Murat, *The Security, Foreign Policy, and International Relationship of Kazakhstan, After Independence, 1991-2001*, Almaty: Kazakhstan Institute of Strategic Studies and Freidrich Ebert Shiftung, 2002.

Laumulin M, "Kazakhstan in the System of Multilateral Regional Systems of Security", *Central Asia's Affairs*, No 2, 2003.

Laumulin M., "Current Strategies and International Relations in Central Asia", *Central Asia's Affairs*, No 1, 2003.

Lelyveld Michael,"US/Russia: Officials Hail Energy Partnership", *RFE/RL Report*, 4 October 2002, www.rferl.org

Light M. and A.J.R. Groom (eds) *International Relations: A Handbook of Current Theory*, London: Frances Pinter, 1994.

Liu Qingjian, "Sino-Central Asian Trade and Economic Relations: Progress, Problems and Prospects", in Yongjin Zang and Rouben Azizan (eds) *Ethnic Challenges Beyond Borders, Chinese and*

Russian Perspectives of the Central Asian Conundrum, London: Macmilian in association with St Antony's College, Oxford, 1998.

Lounev Sergei, "Russia-China-India Prospects of a Joint Fight Against Terrorism", in Omprakash Misra and Sucheta Ghosh (ed) *Terrorism and Low Intensity Conflict in South Asian Region*, New Delhi: Manak, 2003.

Lucas Michael R., "Russia and Peacekeeping in the former USSR" *Aussenpolitik*, Vol 46, No 2, 1995.

MacDonald Julie A and S Enders Wimbush, "India's Energy Security", *Strategic Analysis*, Vol 23, No 5, August 1999.

MacFarlane S Neil, "The United States and Regionalism in Central Asia", *International Affairs*, Vol 80, No 3, May 2004.

Makarenko Tamara, "Russian Language in Kyrgyzstan: Balancing the Security with Economics", *Central Asia and Caucasus Analyst*, May 10, 2000.

Malashenko Alexie, "Turning Away from Russia: New Directions for Central Asia", in Bruno Coppieters, Alexei Zverev and Dimitri Trenin (eds) *Commonwealth and Independence in Post Soviet Eurasia*, London: Portland; Frank Cass, 1998.

Malik Dr J. Mohan, "China, Central Asia, India and Pakistan Now Come Face to Face with Vigorous Separatism", *Defence and Foreign Affairs Strategic Policy*, 30 September, 1993.

Mandelbaum Michael (ed) *Central Asia and the World*, New York: Council on Foreign Relations Press, 1994.

Manz Beatrice (ed) *Central Asia in Historical Perspective*, Westview Press: Boulder, 1994.

Marquand Robert, "Putin Pushes Strategic Triangle with China, India", *Christian Science Monitor*, December 6, 2002.

Mathews Jessica T. "September 11, One Year Later: A World of Change", *Carnegie Endowment for International Peace*, Special Edition 18, August 2002.

Mattoo Amitabh, "United States of America and Central Asia: Beginning of the Great Game", in Nirmala Joshi (ed) *Central Asia The Great Game Replayed, An Indian Perspective*, Delhi: New Century Publications, 2003.

McDermott Roger N., "Shanghai Cooperation Organization Takes Significant Steps Towards Viability", *Eurasia Insight*, September 9, 2003, http://www.eurasianet.org

McNeal Dewardric L, "China's Relations with Central Asian States and Problems with Terrorism", *Congressional Research Service*, December 17, 2001.

Meiirzhan Mashan, "Regional Security As A System Factor in Central Asian Integration," in Jasjit Singh (ed) *Peace and Security in Central Asia*, New Delhi:IDSA, September 2000.

Melet Yasmin, "China's Political and Economic relations with Kazakhstan and Kyrgyzstan", *Central Asian Survey* Vol 17, No 2, 1998.

Misra Amalendu, "Shanghai Five and the Emerging Alliance in Central Asia: The Closed Society and its Enemies", *Central Asian Survey*, Vol 20, No 3, 2001.

Misra Omprakash and Sucheta Ghosh (ed) *Terrorism and Low Intensity Conflict in South Asian Region*, New Delhi: Manak, 2003.

Moustakis Fotios and Ella Ackerman, "Russo-Turkish Cooperation After September 11", *Central Asian Survey*, Vol 21, Number 4, December 2002.

Munroe Ross H, "Central Asia and China", in Michael Mandelbaum (ed) *Central Asia and the World*, New York: Council on Foreign Relations Press, 1994.

Mykhtarova P. (ed) *Problemi Regionalnoi Vezopasnosti, Politicheskogo i Ekonomichiskogo Razvitiya Tsentralnaaziatskogo Regiona v Kontekske Interesov Kazakhstana*, Almaty: TOO, 2003.

Naby Eden, "Uighur Elites in Xinjiang", *Central Asian Survey*, Vol 5, No 3/4 1986.

Naumkin Vitaly (ed) *Central Asia and Transcaucasus: Ethnicity and Conflict*, Westport, CT: Greenwood Publishing Group, 1994.

Naumkin Vitaly V., "The Emerging Geopolitical Balance in Central Asia: A Russian View" in Gennady Chufrin (ed) *Russia and Asia:The Emerging Security Agenda*, New York: OUP, 1999.

Niazi H, "Security and Stability in Central Asia: Iran's View", *Central Asia's Affairs*, No 2, 2003.

Nikilaev Andrei, "Lessons from Iraq", *The Statesman*, Thursday, 10 April, 2003.

Olcott Martha Brill, "How New is the New Russia? Demographic Upheavals in Central Asia", *Orbis*, Fall 1996.

Oleg Limanov, "China's Policy Towards Central Asia in the Post Soviet Era", in P Stobdan (ed) *Building A Common Future: Indian and Uzbek Perspectives on Security and Economic Issues*, New Delhi: Knowledge World in association with IDSA, 1999.

Olimov Mouzaffar, "The Policy of Russia in Central Asia: A Perspective from Tajikistan", in Gennady Chufrin (ed) *Russia and Asia:The Emerging Security Agenda*, New York: OUP, 1999.

Omidvarnia Mohammad-Javed, "Sino-Russian Relations on the Verge of the 21st Century", *Amu Darya, Iranian Journal of Central Asian Studies*, Vol 4 No 5, Spring/Summer 2000.

Oresman Matthew, "The Moscow Summit: Tempered Hope for the SCO", *Central Asia-Caucasus Analyst*, Wednesday, June 4, 2003.

Oudenaren John Van, "What is Multilateral", *Policy Review No 117* and "Unipolar Versus Unilateral", *Policy Review, No 124*.

Palat Madhavan, "Eurasianism as an Ideology for Russia's Future", *Economic and Political Weekly*, Special Number, December 18, 1993.

Pant Harsh V. "The Moscow-Beijing-Delhi Strategic Triangle: An Idea Whose Time May Never Come", *Security Dialogue*, Vol 35 (3), 2004.

Peisheng Yao, "Desyatiletiye Kitaisko-Kazakhstanskikh Otnoshenie:Itogi I Perspektivi", *Kazakhstan I Sovremennie Mir*, No 1 Vol 2, 2002.

Podberezsky Igor V., "Between Europe and Asia: The Search for Russia's Civilizational Identity" in Gennady Chufrin (ed) *Russia and Asia:The Emerging Security Agenda*, New York: OUP, 1999.

Pollack Jonathan D (ed) *In China's Shadow: Regional Perspectives on Chinese Foreign Policy and Military Development*, RAND Publication, 1998.

Press Communique M-1(94)2, Issued by the Heads of State and Government participating in the Meeting of the North Atlantic Council, NATO Headquarters, Brussels, 10-11 June 1994.

Primakov Yevginy, "Rossiya Yishet Novoe Mesto v Mire", *Izvestia*, March 6, 1996.

Primbetov Serik, "Tsentralnoaziatskiye Ugrozi I Vizovi", *Kazakhstan I Sovremennie Mir*, No 1 Vol 2, 2002.

Privetstvennoye Picmo Presidenta RK N.A. Nazarbayeva Uchastnikam Mezhdunarodnoi Konferentsii SEAP "Vezovi Regionalnoi Bezopasnosti v Tsentralnoi Azii", *Kazakhstan I Sovremennie Mir,* No2 (5), 2003.

Problemi Bezopasnosti v Azii, Moscow: Rossiskaya Akademiya Nayuk Institut Vostokovedenia, 2001.

Qimao Chen, "Sino-Russian Relations After the Breakup of the Soviet Union", in Gennady Chufrin (ed) *Russia and Asia:The Emerging Security Agenda*, New York: OUP, 1999.

Qing-Li Yuan, "Population Changes in the Xinjiang Uighur Autonomous Region (1949-1984)", *Central Asian Survey*, Vol 9 No 1, 1990.

Raczka Witt, "Xinjiang and its Central Asian Borderlands", *Central Asian Survey*, Vol 17, No 3, 1998.

Rahm Julie M., "Russia ,China, India: A New Strategic Triangle for a New Cold War?", *Parameters*, Winter 2001-02.

Ringmar Eric, "The Recognition Game: Soviet Russia Against the West", *Cooperation and Conflict*, Volume 37, No 2, June 2002.

Rudelson Jon Justin, "Uighur Historiography and Uighur Ethnic Identity Change", in Ingvar Svanberg (ed) *Ethnicity, Minorities and Cultural Encounters*, Uppsala: Centre For Multiethnic Research, 1991.

Ruggie John Gerard (ed), *Multilateralism Matters, The Theory and Praxis of an Institutional Form*, New York: Columbia University Press, 1993.

Rumer Boris (ed), *Central Asia in Transition: Dilemmas of Political and Economic Development*, New York and London: M.E. Sharpe, 1996.

Rywkin Michael, "Cadre Competition in Uzbekistan, Ethnic Aspects," *Central Asian Survey*, Vol 5, No 3/4, 1986.

Santhanam K and Ramakant Dwivedi (eds), *India and Central Asia: Advancing the Common Interest*, New Delhi:Anamaya Publishers, 2004.

Sarkisyanz Manue l, "Russian Conquest in Central Asia: Transformation and Acculturation", in Wayne S. Vucinich (ed) *Russia and Asia - Essays on the Influence of Russia on the Asian People*, Hoover Institute Press, 1972.

Saunders Phillip C., "Can 9-11 Provide a Fresh Start for Sino-US Relations?" *Policy Forum Online*, Special Forum 33, October 31, 2001.

Schlesinger Stephen, "The United States and the World: Is a Return to Multilateralism Possible?" in C Uday Bhaskar and others (ed) *United Nations: Multilateralism and International Security*, Delhi Shipra Publications, 2005.

Selebyerstova S., "Deti Russkikh Starozhelov v Uzbekistane" *Vostok*, No 2, 1994.

Sengupta Anita, *Frontiers into Borders: The Transformation of Identities in Central Asia* (published for Maulana Abul Kalam Azad Institute of Asian Studies) Delhi and London: Hope India Publications and Greenwich Millennium Press Ltd, 2002.

Shah, S. Adnan Ali, "Collective Security Treaty Organization (OKDB): Prospects and Challenges", in P. Mykhtarova (ed) *Problemi Regionalnoi Vezopasnosti, Politicheskogo i Ekonomichiskogo Razvitiya Tsentralnaaziatskogo Regiona v Kontekske Interesov Kazakhstana*, Almaty: TOO, 2003.

Shambaugh David, "From the White House, all Zigzags Lead to China", *Washington Post*, February 17, 2002 (internet version).

Shaoqin Zhao, "Nation May Import 50 million tonnes of crude Oil in 2000", *China Daily*, July 3, 2000.

Shirazi Habibollah Abolhassan, "Russian and American National Interests in Central Asia", *Amu Darya, Iranian Journal of Central Asian Studies*, Vol 4 No 5, Spring/Summer 2000.

Singh Jasjit (ed), *Peace and Security in Central Asia*, New Delhi:IDSA, September 2000.

Singh Mahavir (ed), *Asia Annual 2003*, Delhi: Shipra Publications, 2003.

Singh Mahavir (ed), *Building A New Asia*, Delhi: Shipra Publications, 2005.

SovslyeV.V., O.A. Pidayeva and A.I. Markova, *Uzbekistan—Nezavisimi Kronika Sovetii*, Tashkent: Uzbekiston, 1993.

Starr Frederick S, "Making Eurasia Stable", *Foreign Affairs*, January/February Vol 75 No 1, 1996.

Starr Fredrick (ed), *The Legacy of History in Russia and the New States of Eurasia*, New York: M.E. Sharpe, 1994.

Stavridis S. and C. Hill (eds), *Domestic Sources of Foreign Policy*, London: Berg Publishers, 1996.

Stobdan P. (ed), *Building A Common Future: Indian and Uzbek Perspectives on Security and Economic Issues*, New Delhi: Knowledge World in association with IDSA, 1999.

Subramanian R.R, "Russia-China-India: Strategic Cooperation in a Pan Asian Order", in Mahavir Singh (ed.) *Building a New Asia:* Delhi, Shipra Publications, 2005.

Sutter Robert, "American-Chinese Relations After September 11", web article at www.cap.unimuenchen.de/transatlantic/topics/us_china.htm.1.

Svanberg Ingvar (ed), *Ethnicity, Minorities and Cultural Encounters*, Uppsala: Centre For Multiethnic Research, 1991.

Swain Michael and Minxin Peo, "Rebalancing US-China Relations", Washington: *Carnegie Endowment Policy Brief*, February 13, 2002.

Syroezhkin K.L., *Mife I Realnost Ethnicheskogo Separatizma v Kitai I Bezopasnost Tsentralnoi Azii*, Almaty: Institut Vostokovedeniya, 2003

Tabata S and A. Iwashita (eds) *Slavic Eurasia's Integration into the World Economy and Community*, (forthcoming) Sapporo: Slavic Research Centre, 2004.

Talbott Strobe, "A Farewell to Flashman: American Policy in the Caucasus and Central Asia," Speech at the Central Asia Institute, School of Advanced International Studies, The John Hopkins University, July 21, 1997.

Tang Shiping, "Economic Integration in Central Asia: The Russian and Chinese Relationships", *Asian Survey*, Vol XL, No 2, April 2000.

Tauasarov Assylbek, "SHOS Priobretaet Realnie Ochertaniya", *Kazakhstan i Sovremennie Mir*, No 2(5), 2003.

Tauuuasarov Assylbek, "SHOS Priobretaet Realnie Ochertaniya", *Kazakhstan I Sovremennie Mir,* No2 (5), 2003.

Tokhtakhodjaeva Marfua and Elmira Turgumbekova, *The Daughters of Amazons: Voices from Central Asia,* Lahore: Shirkat Gah Womens' Research Centre, 1996.

Tolipov Farkhod Fozilovich, "Regional Security in Central Asia in the Context of the Fight Against Terrorism", in K. Santhanam and Ramakant Dwivedi (eds) *India and Central Asia: Advancing the Common Interest*, New Delhi: Anamaya Publishers, 2004.

Torbakov Igor, "Russia Moves to reassert Influence In Central Asia, Caucasus," *Eurasia Insight*, December 18, 2002, http://www. eurasianet.org.

Torbakov Igor, "Uzbekistan Set to Diversify Its Security Opinions in Wake of Recent Militant Attacks", *Eurasia Insight*, April 22, 2004, http://www. eurasianet.org.

Torbakov Igor, "Wanted: A New CIS Policy For Russia", *Eurasianet*, September 30, 2004, http://www. eurasianet.org.

Torbakov Igor, "Policy Makers in Moscow debate the Limits of Russian Power in the Caucasus, Central Asia", *Eurasia Insight*, September 2, 2004, http://www. eurasianet.org.

Trenin Dmitri, "Introduction" in Bruno Coppieters, Alexei Zverev and Dmitri Trenin (eds) *Commonwealth and Independence in Post Soviet Russia*, London and Portland: Frank Cass, 1998

Trubnikov V, "Tenth Anniversary of the Commonwealth of Independent States", *International Affairs* (Moscow) 2002

Tsentralnaya Aziia v Systeme Globalnik Otnoshenii, Sbornik Materialov Conferentsii, Almaty: KISI and CSCE, 2002.

Tsmagambetov Talgat, "Some geopolitical peculiarities of Central Asia, past and present", in Sally N. Cummings (ed) *Oil, Transition and Security in Central Asia*, London and New York: Routledge-Curzon, 2003.

Tsyganov Yuri V., "Russia and China: What is in the Pipeline?", in Gennady Chufrin (ed) *Russia and Asia:The Emerging Security Agenda*, New York: OUP, 1999.

Tursun Nabijan, "Sino-Russian Relations and the Uyghur Card", *Central Asia Monitor*, No 5-6, 2001.

Valkenier Elizabeth Kridl, "Russian Policies in Central Asia : Change or Continuity," *SAIS Review*, Vol 14, (2) Summer-Fall 1994.

Vasudevan Hari, "Russia-India-China Cooperation. The Shaping of a Notion in Russian Foreign Policy", in Mahavir Singh (ed.) *Building a New Asia:* Delhi, Shipra Publications, 2005.

Voskressenski Alexei D, "Current Concepts of Sino-Russian Relations and Frontier Problems in Russia and China", *Central Asian Survey*, Vol 13, No 3, 1994.

Vucinich Wayne S. (ed), *Russia and Asia - Essays on the Influence of Russia on the Asian People*, Hoover Institute Press, 1972.

Waltz K, *Theory of International Politics*, London: Addision-Wesley, 1979.

Wei Cui-Yi, "Ancient Chinese Historical Records About Central Asia", *Central Asian Survey*, Vol 5, No 2, 1986.

Weihman Ted, "China Making Diplomatic Push in Central Asia", *Eurasianet*, June 9, 2003, http://www.eurasianet.org.

Wheeler Geoffrey, *The Modern History of Soviet Central Asia*, London: Weidenfeld and Nicolson, 1964.

Woodward Bob, *Bush At War*, London, Sydney, New York, Tokyo, Singapore, Toronto:Pocket Books, 2002

Xaiohua Dai, "China-Kazakhstan Trade and Economic Cooperation Promising", *Beijing Review*, Vol 41, No 20, May 18-24, 1998.

Xiang Lanxin, "China's Eurasian Experiment", *Survival*, Vol 46, No 2, Summer 2004.

Xiaoquan Ni, "Sino-Russian Relations Since the September 11 Incident", *Slavic Research Centre Occasional Paper No 91* on *The Sino-Russian Strategic Relationship? Current Views from the Border and Beijing*, Sapporo Slavic Research Centre, Hokkaido University, 2003.

Xing Guangcheng, "Security Issues in China's Relations with Central Asian States" in Yongjin Zang and Rouben Azizan (eds) *Ethnic Challenges Beyond Borders, Chinese and Russian Perspectives of the Central Asian Conundrum*, London: Macmilian in association with St Antony's College, Oxford, 1998.

Xintian Yu, "September 11 Incident and Change in Security Concept," *Shanghai Institute for International Studies*, Vol 9, No 2, May 2002.

Yahuda Michael, "China's Search for a Global Role", *Current History*, September 1999.

Yavuzalp Osman, "On the Front Line", *NATO Review*, Vol 49, No 4, Winter 2001.

Yuan Jing-dong, *Asia-Pacific Security: China's Conditional Multilateralism and Great Power Entente*, Strategic Studies Institute Publication, Carlisle, Pennsylvania, 2000.

Yuyun Zhou, "Strategic Triangle of China, India, Russia: Ideality and Reality", in Mahavir Singh (ed.) *Building a New Asia:* Delhi, Shipra Publications, 2005.

Zagorski Andrei, "Regional Structures of Security Policy Within the CIS", in Roy Allison and Christopher Bluth (eds) *Security Dilemma in Russia and Eurasia*, London: RIIA, 1998.

Zakrzhevskaya Olga, "Problemi Mezhdynarodnogo Terrorizma v Kontexte Tendensssssstii obshemirobogo Razvitiya", *Kazakhstan I Sovremennie Mir*, No 1(2), 2002.

Zang Yongjin and Rouben Azizan (eds), *Ethnic Challenges Beyond Borders, Chinese and Russian Perspectives of the Central Asian Conundrum*, London: Macmilian in association with St Antony's College, Oxford, 1998.

Zatulin K.F et all , *Natsionalnaya Bezopasnosti Kazakhstana, Problemi I Perspekti*, Moscow: Institut Stran SNG, 1998.

Zhengji Hung, "The Irresistible Multipolarity Trend of the World", *International Strategic Studies*, No 4, 1997.

Zhongying Pan, *Bush Visit and Sino-US Ties*, Honolulu:CSIS Pacific Forum, PACNET 8, February 8, 2002.

Zhuangzhi Sun, "Economic Collaboration in Central Asian region and the SCO", in K. Santhanam and Ramakant Dwivedi (eds) *India and Central Asia: Advancing the Common Interest*, New Delhi: Anamaya Publishers, 2004

Zhuangzhi Sun, "US Strategy in Central Asia", *Beijing Review*, Vol 43, No 26, June 26, 2000.

Zhurkin V, "Russia and the Enlargement of NATO", in T Hayashi (ed) *The Emerging New Regional Order in Central and Eastern Europe*, Sapporo: Slavic Research Centre, 1997.

Zviagelskaya Irina D, "Russia's Policy Options in Central Asia", in Gennady Chufrin (ed) *Russia and Asia:The Emerging Security Agenda*, New York: OUP, 1999.

Zvyagelskaia Irina D, "Central Asia and the Caucasus: New Geopolitics", in Vitaly Naumkin (ed) *Central Asia and Transcaucasus: Ethnicity and Conflict*, Westport, CT: Greenwood Publishing Group, 1994.

Index

U

V

W

X

Y

Z